LOST AND FOUND

JAMEY GLASNOVIC

ADRIFT IN THE
CANADIAN ROCKIES

LOST AND
FOUND

RMB

Rocky Mountain Books
www.rmbooks.com

Library and Archives Canada Cataloguing in Publication

Glasnovic Jamey, 1968-, author
    Lost and found : adrift in the Canadian Rockies / Jamey Glasnovic.

Issued in print and electronic formats.
ISBN 978-1-77160-051-4 (pbk.).—ISBN 978-1-77160-052-1 (html).—
ISBN 978-1-77160-053-8 (pdf)

    1. Glasnovic Jamey, 1968-. 2. Mountain life. 3. Canadian Rocky Mountain Parks World Heritage Site (Alta. and B.C.)—Biography. 4. Rocky Mountains, Canadian (B.C. and Alta.)—Biography. I. Title.

FC219.G493 2014   971.1   C2014-904020-2
                                   C2014-904021-0

Cover photo: *Canmore by night* © ginevre
Maps: Jocey Asnong
Printed in Canada

Rocky Mountain Books acknowledges the financial support for its publishing program from the Government of Canada through the Canada Book Fund (CBF) and the Canada Council for the Arts, and from the province of British Columbia through the British Columbia Arts Council and the Book Publishing Tax Credit.

 Canadian Heritage   Patrimoine canadien   Canada Council for the Arts   Conseil des Arts du Canada

BRITISH COLUMBIA ARTS COUNCIL
Supported by the Province of British Columbia

This book was produced using FSC®-certified, acid-free paper, processed chlorine free and printed with vegetable-based inks.

To my mother –
without her early guidance and inspiring
efforts in life, I would be much less.

CONTENTS

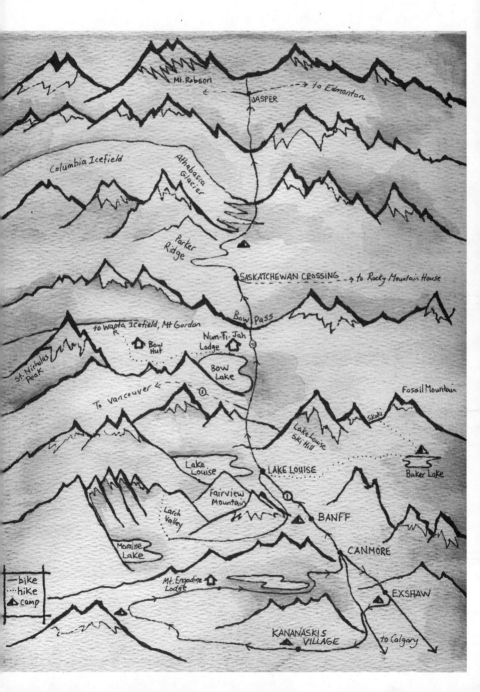

PART ONE

THE ROAD AHEAD

1.

THE ICEFIELDS PARKWAY

Sun's up, mm hm, looks okay, the world survives until another day.
And I'm thinking about eternity, some kind of ecstasy got a hold
on me.

—Bruce Cockburn

It's official: I'm an idiot.

At least that's how I feel as snow continues to fall in an increasingly energetic fashion and the temperature drops at a rate even a seasoned meteorologist would find alarming. I've been thinking about the consequences of this turn of events for about 15 minutes now and can come up with no other conclusion than that I'm an idiot. The worst part of it all is not the cold, or the wind, or the even the snow, but the realization that my discomfort as a result of all three is entirely self-inflicted. There is no one to blame for the predicament I find myself in and no great conspiracy to pin my growing anguish on. I chose this and must now suffer the consequences. I can only hope the weather's downward spiral doesn't end up killing me.

Surviving a snowstorm is not an unusual accomplishment in Canada; millions of people do it every winter by simply staying inside. But getting caught in an October blizzard, miles from the nearest anywhere, while struggling up the side of a mountain on a bicycle – well, that's a different story. There is a measure of responsibility to it. Sure, this wind-driven squall has come out of nowhere, but it is autumn in the higher elevations of the Rocky Mountains, a place where bad weather can be expected in any month of the year. It even snowed a little bit yesterday, and the day before that, and still I act surprised by this unpleasant development.

All around me, the mountains are nothing more than an ocean of white and shades of pale grey, and even though it is not yet three o'clock, the remaining daylight suddenly has a murky, menacing quality to it. Shadows and ghost images in every direction hint of the incredible scenery the storm is obscuring, but there are no solid reference points beyond the dark, sloppy asphalt beneath my wheels. With the availability of campsites on the road ahead far from certain, a single thought keeps pushing to the front of my consciousness: Why am I doing this again?

As I churn uphill at a pace that will never be mistaken for impressive, that line of inquiry simply begs another: Why can't I be like a normal person, content in my idyllic little mountain town, with a solid relationship, steady employment and favourite pub already sorted out? After all, who consciously abandons – no, actively escapes – what many often refer to as a "paradise on earth," in order to subject himself to these harsh conditions? A question worthy of consideration on a deserted roadway, over a couple hundred laboured pedal strokes, and as big fluffy flakes work their way under the back of my collar, the only answer I can come up with is: an imbecile, that's who.

Things could be worse, I suppose. The gusting wind could be blowing downhill into my face, forcing me to push my bike uphill at a walk. A flat tire would also be a disaster right now, for sure; frozen hands desperately trying to manipulate small tools as sudden inactivity encourages a drop in core body temperature and flash-freezes sweat and melted snow to my skin. So, in light of the precarious state of affairs on the back side of Parker Ridge, just above the Big Bend on a stretch of road appropriately named the Icefields Parkway, I have no choice but to carry on while pondering the mechanics of perception and, it must be said, my entire decision-making process. It is, after all, fully within my power to be splayed out on a familiar couch with a cold beer and a bag of chips, with nothing more challenging than three periods of televised hockey to worry about. But no, I'm determined to be out in the world, with all that that entails, and this is the reward for imagining there's more to life than to eat, sleep, work, repeat: a whiteout on a bike. As I may have mentioned already, I'm *not too bright*.

In my defence, pedalling up Sunwapta Pass on the Icefields Parkway in Jasper National Park seemed like a good idea from the comfort of my home a few months ago. And indeed, it was comfort that helped drive me out in the first place (or more precisely, an overabundance of false comfort) – but in alternating my hands up under the front of my warmest cross-country ski top to keep them from freezing while I grind up a climb that is going to take at least another hour to complete, it's impossible to avoid putting any and all motivations under the microscope. I believe they call it soul-searching, and in this preoccupied state I've failed to notice a vehicle – the only one I've seen in the last ten minutes – coming up quickly from behind.

"Hey! You're the mmmaaaannnnnnnn!"

At least I think that's what the young man in the passenger seat of a new Jeep Wrangler just shouted as the vehicle sped along somewhat recklessly, his arm thrust out the window in the universal "thumbs up" salute. With the wind blowing all over the place in the tight valley, and the

Doppler effect dragging the words along the side of the mountain, it's hard to tell for sure, but for morale's sake I choose to take the shout-out as a compliment: a simple gesture meant to convey respect for the effort. Or perhaps it was an expression of sympathy and relief at not actually being me. Maybe he was just making fun of my predicament. Regardless of the true intent, it could be said that in addition to making foolish decisions that lead to unpleasant encounters with the weather, it's also possible I'm "the man," which admittedly is a boost to my sagging spirit and tired legs.

Re-energized by the improbable cheering section, I have no choice but to push on, with the hope of reaching the top of the pass, and the Columbia Icefield campground just beyond it, before dark – and of course to survive the night with my more distant extremities intact. Winter is not quite in full swing, but it is clearly getting ready to slam the door on the season for hikers, cyclists, dreamers and lost souls alike.

PART TWO

CLOSE TO HOME

2.

TROUBLE IN PARADISE

And I can't decide over right or wrong,
You left the feeling that I just do not belong.

—Beth Orton

In April 2008, six months before my battle with the weather gods on Sunwapta Pass, I was inconsolable and most certainly was not "the man." I'd been living in Canmore for close to four years and would have described it to the uninitiated as a charming, prosperous and obscenely picturesque community situated along Alberta's mountainous western edge. From the balcony of my rented two-storey condo, I had an uninterrupted view of the mountains that started down the valley to the left, at the famous and oft-photographed Three Sisters, swept along the face of Mount Lawrence Grassi and Ha Ling Peak, hit a midpoint at Whiteman's Gap, continued along the 12-kilometre eastern face of the Mount Rundle massif and ended at the imposing bulk of Cascade Mountain, off in the distance to the right.

The entire vista is part of the Front Ranges of the Rocky Mountains, and the section visible from my balcony is a small piece in the continuous chain of mountains that form the backbone of North America, from Mexico in the south all the way up to the Yukon Territory in the north. My personal bit of scenery sits about dead centre of those two extremes and is nothing short of world class. While true summer often passes too quickly in the Rockies – especially compared to the long, sweltering summers of my youth back in eastern Canada – fall is generally mild, and winter's chill is tempered with plenty of sunshine and more skiing opportunities than one person could take advantage of in a single lifetime. In fact, the Rockies are becoming an increasingly popular adventurer destination for outdoor sports enthusiasts year-round. Rock and ice climbing abound, and cross-country and backcountry ski trails shift seamlessly into hiking and mountain biking routes with every change of season.

My introduction to the Bow Valley Corridor, however, came nearly two decades ago, while I was riding a road bike, and I admit I never even gave Canmore more than a passing glance. I was headed out to the Pacific Coast from Calgary and in my haste to knock off miles didn't even stop on my way through to Banff. At that time, I was obsessed with long-distance bike touring, even though it wasn't the preferred, or trendy, way to travel in North America. Wherever regular people went by airplane or by car, the cool kids rode motorbikes, and a small percentage of fanatics, eccentrics and nerds pedalled. But I was infatuated with the mountain West, and in my mind the Canadian Rockies were a sanctuary of wonder and a revelation of nature that should be experienced at ground level – or as the legendary alpinist Reinhold Messner has said, by fair means. In my idealized mindset, planes were for people in a rush, and cars demonstrated a lack of imagination. RVs just made me nauseous.

At any rate, my heart was in the right place for a proper sweat- and grime-stained adventure, and my body was willing; I just wasn't aware enough to take the time to appreciate what I was experiencing. Back in the mid-'90s,

I covered the 275 kilometres from Calgary to Golden in three days in a desperate effort to get from here to there, and the Rocky Mountains turned out to be little more than a blur of peaks and valleys and trees. But they left an indelible impression, and in the years that followed I returned again and again and again to hike and ski and paddle and climb. I developed a deep appreciation for the beauty of this place; a genuine respect for the challenges presented by the landscape now shapes my worldview. I continue to champion my adopted hometown as one without equal and conveniently ignore nagging doubts about this place. I try to smile and be friendly at least some of the time, while quietly pretending that living in paradise isn't slowly killing me.

One of the reasons I've been brainwashed into thinking my home is nothing short of paradise is that people tell me so just about every other day. When my parents come on their yearly visit, they can't help but mention it once every 25 minutes. If I take a walk downtown in the summertime, I inevitably overhear waddling folks with funny accents and odd clothes – who have been known to stop abruptly in the middle of the street with compact cameras in hand – mumbling something to that effect. And whenever I go on vacation, the ride back to town in the airport shuttle is filled with fresh, energetic people who can hardly believe such a well-kept secret exists in North America, less than an hour and a half from an international airport. In fact, it's not unusual for cameras and camera phones to leap out of pockets and purses while we're travelling at 100 kilometres an hour along the highway, 60 or 70 kilometres from where the mountains actually begin. Such is the power of this place.

Often I am exhausted from my own travels and can

only manage faint amusement at the naked wonder of my fellow shuttle passengers, but must also concede what they are saying is true: Canmore is located in a truly breathtaking part of the world. With stunning snow-capped mountains, glacier-fed rivers and streams and a vast forest blanketing the lower slopes in a sea of green, there is no denying that the Bow Valley is picture-postcard perfect. In recent promotional material, the Banff Lake Louise Tourism Bureau has even gone so far as to say Banff National Park, whose east gate is less than five kilometres from my front door, is "the world's finest national park."

Yet every time I try to suck it up and accept things unconditionally, it isn't long before I'm haunted by the idea that if you're not pissed off at the world then you must have your head rammed up your ... I mean ... you must not be paying attention. Before moving "out West" (after an extended stay in purgatory – sometimes referred to around here as Ontario), I envisioned a perfect existence against this stunning backdrop. But the truth is, I've found the interactions of everyday life to be a series of small deceptions and partial truths, glazed over with a weak smile and half-hearted, "Fine thanks, how are you?" Nothing *feels* real, and that commonly heard workingman's refrain "Same old, same old" just doesn't cut it anymore. Skyrocketing real estate prices, restaurants and bars heaving with impatient and impolite city types, and a cost of living that rivals any city or town, anywhere on the continent, are all a consequence of too many people stumbling into "paradise."

I understand it's a bit harsh to paint Canmore with a pessimistic brushstroke just because I'm in a bad mood, and it was also unfair to come here expecting Utopia, but to be perfectly honest, I expected more from this place, not just more of the same. The result of this simmering discontent is an internal conflict threatening to boil over any day now. But, whatever is ultimately responsible for these feelings is probably irrelevant in the end. I'm a fool, surrounded by so many other fools, all of us living a back-and-forth struggle between the ridiculous and the sublime, and I'm tired of the rollercoaster ride. John Mellencamp once sang, "I know there's a balance, I see it when I swing past," but he never mentions anything about how to avoid motion sickness.

So, while my personal Alcatraz in the Rockies may have a tremendous view, it still feels like a prison, and I think it's about time to get over the wall. I know it will take more than a day off to unravel this discontent, and more than a weekend away in the backcountry to decompress. It's not normally in my nature to just give up and quit, but something's got to give, and quick. Walt Whitman, in his ode to simple movement and possibility called "Song of the Open Road," shouts, "Allons! whoever you are, come travel with me!" Hold on a minute there, Walt, I've got a few things to pull together first, but I'm on my way.

• • •

Ever since I was a kid riding his first two-wheeler, I've thought of the bicycle as the modern-day horse. Like the cowboys of the Old West or Mongolian herders out on the steppe, a man with a bicycle has a low-impact way to travel and a measure of autonomy unattainable with motorized vehicles. Give a man a horse and a wide open prairie and he's good to go; give a man a bike and a long ribbon of road, and he is similarly blessed. Foot power excepted, a bike remains the world's most frequently used mode of transportation, and many countries in the developing world continue to embrace it because it's easier to obtain and cheaper to maintain than a car. In any urban setting, riding remains the fastest way to travel for distances less than five kilometres, and it also happens to be a superb form of exercise.

These practical considerations aside, my attraction to the pedal-powered steed remains largely romantic. I make a unique connection to people and landscape while riding a bike that I simply can't get with planes, trains or automobiles, and it has always been my favourite method of exploration and escape. Exhaustively planned trip or last-minute whim, the result is always the same – freedom. In this context, pedalling a bicycle well is a tremendously liberating experience, underrated in this day and age. With the sun on your face and the wind at your back, pedalling hard through beautiful country is almost like flying. The klicks skip by unnoticed as legs pump down rhythmically and lungs deliver an endless supply of oxygen without effort. On any rise in the road, the heart jumps in and produces a few dozen extra-powerful beats, and the mind is free to get lost in the wonders of a carefree day. It's magical. The world disappears and comes into bright focus all at the same time. Much like the better-known "runner's high," but on two wheels – and every good ride has a moment like that. On a great ride, the feeling may last minutes, or even an hour or two. I'd even be willing to say that a bad ride in shocking conditions will still offer a taste of that freedom at some point.

Simply cruising down Bow Valley Trail in Canmore, however, you probably aren't going to experience anything except boredom and a vague sense of déjà vu. The road is long, dead straight and flat, with hotels, motels and small businesses dotting its length. If you remove the mountain views, you could be on the outskirts of any city or town in North America, with all the familiar names homogenizing the landscape: A&W, Best Western, Dairy Queen, Boston Pizza and McDonald's, among others. Canmore's version of a suburban ride culminates at the north end of town with a sweeping right turn that leads to an overpass and interchange with the highway, where the Trans-Canada hustles vehicles along the valley bottom at a pace that defies the serenity of the surroundings.

While my legs are sufficiently steady beneath me, and my new road bike feels responsive after years of travelling around town on a mountain bike, everything seems sluggish and mushy when I'm called upon to jump a little. Getting up and over the overpass turns into more work than it probably should be, and the whirlwind of motion and noise generated by the traffic whipping past below is enough to put anyone off the idea of venturing out on that metaphorical endless highway. Fortunately, the other side of the overpass brings a secondary access road that turns northwest again and offers an easy, rolling and – dare I say? – fun ride to Harvie Heights, the last small hamlet you come to before passing into Banff National Park. As the pedal strokes modestly start to add up, I'm inspired to give a little shout of excitement to the travel gods between sips from my water bottle and begin to get drawn into the wilderness that now stretches out in every direction.

When you look at the area around Canmore on a map, it's impossible not to notice that the town, despite being nowhere near a significant body of water, is essentially at the head of a peninsula. It's the last bit of a small strip of unprotected land surrounded on all sides by a patchwork of national and provincial parks, wildlands, wilderness areas, recreation areas and ecological reserves. You can't travel for more than a few kilometres in any direction without crossing into an area that's under some form of stewardship: the Canmore Nordic Centre Provincial Park, just up the hill to the west of town; part of the Don Getty Wildland Provincial Park, due east as the crow flies; the Bow Valley Wildland Provincial Park, cut and pasted all around; and Banff National Park, to the north and west. All represented by different colours on my Alberta Parks and Protected Areas map. In fact, on the 2008 edition of the map, there is only a small sliver of unprotected white that extends roughly to the southeast, passing through Exshaw before slipping behind the dramatic south face of Mount Yamnuska and expanding out onto the Prairies.

In 1984, Banff, Jasper, Yoho and Kootenay national parks were collectively designated a United Nations Educational, Scientific and Cultural Organization World Heritage Site under the umbrella name Canadian Rocky Mountain Parks. The site was expanded in 1990 to include Hamber, Mount Robson and Mount Assiniboine provincial parks. The UNESCO designation means that this continuous string of parks has been internationally recognized as a site worth preserving for its natural wonders. Put together, the parks cover an impressive 2.3 million hectares, or roughly 23,000 square kilometres, and when you add the surrounding land that's not officially on the UNESCO radar, the number jumps to nearly 33,000 square kilometres – larger than Belgium. If the countryside surrounding and including the Canadian Rocky Mountain Parks were an American State, it would rank 42nd in overall size. It is one of the largest blocks of officially protected area on earth.

The entire World Heritage List includes 878 areas around the globe that are part of a cultural and natural tapestry the World Heritage Committee believes has outstanding universal value. Six hundred and seventy-nine of the sites are strictly cultural, 174 locations are natural, and 25 have dual designation. The natural list includes the Great Barrier Reef in Australia, the Sichuan Giant Panda Sanctuaries in China, the Central Amazon Conservation Complex in Brazil and Virunga National Park in the Democratic Republic of the Congo. It seems we keep good company out here in the mountains, and I am reminded of what a privilege it is to live in such a special place.

Pushing on to the park gates and joining the main highway, I may not yet be sure of where I want to go after today's little outing, but there is no denying that the Canadian Rocky Mountain Parks are a damn fine place for an adventure. And now, as a few spattery drops of rain hit my shorts, darkening the fabric with expanding blotches, I am immediately reminded of two sobering counterpoints to this tentative escape from my everyday. One, I'm not at all fit at the moment, and two, riding on highways means riding in close proximity to speeding cars and big, noisy trucks.

● ● ●

The Trans-Canada Highway is the longest paved highway in the world, at 7821 kilometres, Australia's Highway 1 and Russia's Trans-Siberian Highway are longer, at a mind boggling 14,500 and 11,000 kilometres respectively, but both still have sections of gravel and dirt and so technically cannot lay claim to the crown, in my book. Spanning the continent from the Pacific to the Atlantic, the TCH crosses all ten Canadian provinces and is at once a convenient short-distance commuter route, an avenue for greater exploration in a vast country and a vital part of Canada's transportation industry, and by extension, its economy. The Rocky Mountain section of the road was completed back in 1958, but the end-to-end link didn't come about until Rogers Pass in British Columbia's Selkirk Mountains was bridged in 1962. The TCH is monumental by any measure, a feat of engineering in some sections and not exactly uniform across its length.

In Canmore and Banff's vicinity, the road crosses wide open plains and foothills to the east, penetrates a dramatic wall of mountains that marks the beginning of the Front Ranges and passes beneath the lofty, glacier-strewn peaks of the Eastern Main Ranges farther west. Even further afield, it crosses BC's Interior Plateau before climbing up and over the Coast Mountains on its way to the Pacific. In the other direction, it shoots out across the flat sprawl of one of the largest interior plains in the world, wiggles across the top of Lake Superior and the ancient granite of the Canadian Shield, slides effortlessly down the mighty St. Lawrence Seaway, then barges across "the Rock" (Newfoundland) on its way to the Atlantic. For a dreamer, it's the perfect escape route. Free. Accessible. And full of endless possibility. In my day, I have pedalled, hitchhiked and/or been a keen passenger on nearly every inch of it.

Practically, it remains a challenge no matter what form of transportation you choose, and not just because of the distance. Some bits of the TCH in northwestern Ontario, rural Quebec and the Maritime provinces remain two-lane, undivided highway, with the occasional two-to-four-kilometre passing lane added on, and there are also sections that are four-lane and undivided through Calgary's central area. Across Ottawa, the road expands to four- and six-lane divided highway, and along the Metropolitan Expressway section in Montreal, it's an elevated-traffic nightmare. The $130-million redesign and replacement of Park Bridge near Ten Mile Hill in BC has removed a large portion of wild, winding and dangerous road through Kicking Horse Canyon, but there is still a section between the town of Golden and the Yoho Bridge that needs serious work.

Personally, it had been years since I've done any sort of bike tour on a major roadway, and I'd forgotten how easily a transport truck can sneak up on you, depending on the conditions. A headwind in your ears or heavy rain tapping on your helmet can muffle the sound of vehicles approaching from the rear, and depending on the gear being employed and the amount of work the engine is doing, a truck can be relatively quiet. Once one is upon you, however, there's no question about who would come out the worse for wear in any altercation. There's a sudden, chaotic burst of noise and motion to the cyclist's left, accompanied by a worrisome lateral push of displaced air as the truck plows forward. That push is followed almost instantaneously by an even more worrisome lateral suction toward the side of the vehicle as the displaced air tries to fill the recently vacated space. The most volatile air only extends two or three feet from the side of the truck, but for a cyclist, getting pushed off into the ditch is a dangerous and inconvenient proposition. Getting sucked into the rear wheels is death. Most truckers and bus drivers recognize this and as a courtesy drift toward the centre of the road when space is available or slow down when there is too much traffic.

Most truckers and bus drivers, most of the time.

Once, during a long ride that took me across the top of Lake Superior, an 18-wheeler came so close to hitting me that I could have touched it by simply taking my left hand off the handlebars and extending an arm. In fact, I probably could have tagged it with my elbow if I'd tried. Despite the scorching midsummer heat, I could feel an unnatural surge of warmth on my bare leg, arm and face from the engine's heat radiating up off the pavement. The noise was nearly deafening. At the time, that part of the TCH was still a two-lane undivided highway with no paved shoulder and nowhere to safely escape to in an emergency. I had been pedalling along the ridiculously narrow strip of pavement between the white line and the loose and unrideable gravel for over an hour, listening intently for the far-off air horn warning blast that was becoming ritual. When it came, I would glance quickly over my shoulder to judge the distance the truck still had to travel, then look ahead to see if any oncoming traffic would necessitate a tight fit on the narrow roadway.

It all reminded me of those silly arithmetic problems we used to have to do in grade school: truck A leaves New York travelling at 104.92 kilometres per hour, and truck B leaves Chicago travelling at 77.08 kilometres per hour; there are 1144.47 kilometres between the two cities; at what point will they meet? In this case, you don't want to be anywhere near the point where they meet. As a kid, I never thought I would need to use those hypothetical equations again, but it was working out pretty well. There were some nervy moments, but in the end there was always enough space for me and the vehicles I was sharing lanes with, until I got the math wrong.

On this one occasion, the truck ahead was moving slower than what I'd become used to, and the truck behind was moving too fast, throwing off the calculation of where I would be. Or maybe the truck behind was on a normal pace and the truck ahead was speeding. Maybe I just wasn't paying proper attention. Whatever the complication, the three of us ended up on the same piece of road at the same moment. I couldn't get away to the right, because I feared the soft gravel shoulder would swallow up my wheels and toss me in the path of the behemoth bearing down from behind. Muscles balled up in anticipation of disaster. Air horns blasted all around. If there had been time, I would have shit my pants with a certainty of purpose rarely experienced in this life.

Then, in a split second, it was all over, leaving a wake of tension and diesel fumes but no catastrophic incident. Other cyclists have not been so lucky.

On today's route between Canmore and Banff, the TCH is a standard and well-maintained four-lane divided highway with a wide paved shoulder that is smooth and free of gravel and debris. It handles roughly 16,000 vehicles a day on average and as far as busy roads go is a pretty good one to ride on, but that doesn't mean it's devoid of danger. On June 29, 2007, a one-ton U-Haul truck struck and killed 23-year-old cyclist Collin Cureatz while he was travelling eastbound along the wide paved shoulder, barely five kilometres from the eastern park gates. The impact sent Cureatz up and over the hood, and his head cracked the windshield before his body slid off the driver's side fender as the vehicle swerved right and slowed to a stop. His bike was destroyed and his body ended up close to 60 metres from the point of initial impact. In court, it was determined that the driver moved onto the shoulder while trying to retrieve sunglasses and diabetes medication that had slipped off the dashboard. His vehicle operator's licence was under suspension at the time, and there was a detectable but legal amount of alcohol in his system.

In another local incident, on July 14, 2003, a Valmar

Express Lines truck killed tandem cyclists Kathy Husband and John Stoltenberg near Lake Louise, and again witnesses reported that the vehicle simply drifted onto the shoulder for no apparent reason. The driver told police that he didn't realize anything was wrong until he demolished a road sign and that he was unaware of having killed the couple. He travelled 500 metres in the ditch before returning to the highway.

Between 1998 and 2002, according to Statistics Canada, an average of 62 cyclists a year died on Canadian roads in all kinds of accidents, but I couldn't find a breakdown showing the types of vehicles involved. What I did come across, in the same article in *Alberta Spin* that described the Valmar Express incident, is the sobering fact that Canada's Hours of Service regulations for truck drivers are the laxest of any country that bothers to keep up with that kind of thing. What's more, Alberta has the softest commercial carrier rules in the country. While it is possible that smaller vehicles are more numerous and more likely to hit the average cyclist, it certainly is the big transports that are more immediately frightening. And that's without even knowing about regulations that make it legal for carriers to "ask/allow" drivers to work 105 hours in any given week. An exhausted truck operator is something no cyclist ever wants to think too much about, believe me.

Looking back to my incident in northwestern Ontario, I wouldn't be surprised if both drivers' side mirrors actually touched in the middle of the road as the two trucks passed, and as a precautionary measure I spent the rest of the day wheeling unsteadily toward the ditch whenever I heard anything big coming, but what I'll never understand is why one or both of them didn't just slow down.

We were in a desolate area, after all, and sure, it's a pain in the ass to come up on some dumb kid riding his bike in the middle of nowhere while you're working, but is that extra 30 kilometres an hour going to make much difference? Will it ever be that important to get to Thunder Bay (of all places) quickly? And next time, after not being so lucky, would the driver simply claim he never saw me as he wrote up the accident report and pulled my spokes from his grill? Most importantly, did Cureatz and Husband and Stoltenberg even have a chance to move out of the way, or was there just a split second of surprise before they were gone?

These are the chilling questions that often come to mind at the beginning of a new tour – sometimes they even manage to crowd out worries about gear and money and time – but accidents and near-misses are not something you can dwell on, or you'll never put rubber to road. All you can do is try to beat the disturbing thoughts down or put them out of your mind completely. It's not always easy.

Fortunately, after the initial shock of the first couple of trucks bombing past, I'm finding the state of my fitness more troubling than the fear of sharing the road with 50 tons of rolling thunder on a deadline. The short hill just inside the park gates takes more wind than my searing lungs can produce, and when I bend down to cinch up my toe straps in a vain attempt to harness a little more power, my belly – which has been ever-expanding in the recent middle years of life – makes the effort noticeably uncomfortable. Sweat is pouring off my brow, and I can't seem to catch my breath unless I stop pedalling. As a lifelong athlete who has never been afraid of the inside of a gym, I am lean and mean at 205 pounds; 215 is a good playing weight, no matter the sport, and 225 is just big and mean, as long as I've been training properly. As a younger man, I focused my energy on playing and training for team sports whenever travelling was impossible or impractical, and my base level of fitness confirms that, even at 40.

But 237 pounds – which is what the scale said just hours before departure – is nothing short of slothful and sloppy. I feel like an ex-NFL player who took gruelling two-a-day practice schedules for granted and never adjusted his eating habits once the years of intense effort ended. I'm a gigantic shadow of my former self and fear I've become the kind of once-was-an-athlete who now lives on chicken wings, beer and the glories of accomplishments past. Maybe I should abandon this attempt to regain an active and adventurous life right here between Canmore and Banff, where it's relatively flat and easy going, and start driving a truck. It's probably safer, and lord knows I've developed a body type more suited to it.

3.

We need the possibility of escape as surely as we need hope; without it the life of the cities would drive all men into crime or drugs or psychoanalysis.

—Edward Abbey

Making a break for it can be one of life's more stimulating experiences, especially if you happen to be stuck in a rut and are desperate for change. When you're at your wits' end, it doesn't matter where you're breaking to or where you're breaking from. All that's really important is going somewhere. Anywhere, really. Travel, by its very definition, means there are destinations to explore in the near future and a purpose for your daily actions that are not part of some tired routine. Any new outing could even evolve into a grand, life-altering event, given the right set of circumstances. All it requires is a willingness to be open to the experience. Travel can be exciting and unpredictable and memorable, but it can also be an education in the world and an exploration of the self.

In 1964, Thomas Merton wrote, "the geographical pilgrimage is the symbolic acting out of an inner journey," and "the inner journey is the interpolation of the meaning and signs of the outer pilgrimage." The idea, I think, is to try and experience both simultaneously. A destination should be highly personal, but the final destination is not the entire raison d'être of the trip. Using an around-the-world ticket on a major airline with unlimited stopovers might stimulate and refresh the soul, but that can also happen if you emigrate to a new country, accept a job in a town that is at least one time zone away or take any trip to any destination where a foreign language is spoken. Such an experience could rattle your cage just enough to inspire you. It isn't always necessary, though, to go away in order to get away. Or so they say.

In Tim Cahill's adventure article "Fire and Ice and Everything Nice," he counsels us that "travel doesn't necessarily involve distance. It is a process of discovery, and could as easily be accomplished in one's hometown as in the Congo Basin." That advice may be true enough, but up until now I've always been lured "away." It's almost as if a long-haul flight or excruciating bus ride is a necessary part of the process, and if those details can't be factored in, the trip is not worth attempting. For as long as I can remember, I have been drawn to destinations outside my area code and to cultures and landscapes foreign to my own. As the trips accumulated, I would get pulled across oceans and continents looking for my newest version of distant and exotic. In those travels I came to realize that without the Congo Basin there is no remote point of reference, no strange customs to compare to your own and no far-off horizon to wonder about. Without Kathmandu and Timbuktu – or even Kalamazoo – there are no great mysteries of sight, sound, smell and flavour not yet savoured.

For some, the romance of travel in unfamiliar lands is an irresistible urge that cannot be ignored; for others, travelling amounts to nothing more than checking a destination off the life list. Early explorers chased fame and riches. Personally, I tend to disappear on a good journey in order to abandon the habitual and find the space to recalibrate my senses and beliefs. I believe the Australian Aborigines call it a walkabout.

Whatever the motivation, what young wannabe voyager hasn't lain in bed staring at a world map pinned to the bedroom wall, or pored over the best atlas in the school library instead of going to math class, or flipped avidly through *National Geographic* on a lazy afternoon at the cottage, searching for glimpses of another life? Who hasn't dreamed about what it would be like to dive into an ocean they have never seen, or wander a mountainside on a continent they have never been to? But when the plan is to go one town over in an effort covering the grand distance of about 25 kilometres between Canmore and Banff, the novelty and romance associated with travel fades, and Cahill's assertion that home could be as interesting as away – if looked at in the right frame of mind – can begin to feel a bit strained.

In the article "Somebody Else's Rum," Mark Jenkins contends that "adulthood is an insidious process of accretion. If you're not vigilant, you begin to grow a shell, a carapace that you are expected to carry lightly: the rigid, high-stress hull of security, status, status quo. The thicker the better, right up until it crushes you." I couldn't agree more. So despite a general malaise and a disturbing tendency to take my surroundings for granted, I am rededicating myself to the effort of shaking off the "carapace" that has grown so heavy and to attempting a "process of discovery" on home turf.

To up the ante – and I already regret saying this out loud because then it becomes real – I will do so in the best way I know how, which is under my own power. I am going to walk and ride my bicycle through the heart of the stunning landscape that I have neglected due to sheer distraction, and I absolutely, positively, refuse to engage in the use of motorized transportation to do it! I may not be able to replicate the experience of the Natives or the early explorers who were here before cars and roads and fast food restaurants, but I do plan on earning every mile. Maybe that will help rekindle a genuine love of the land that has been misplaced of late.

Energized by the decision, I pack up my things after a brief rest under the sign welcoming visitors to Banff, and with the sky now rolling and boiling over the summit of Cascade Mountain and threatening serious rain, push off on the last short stretch into town.

• • •

The approach to Banff Townsite from the first exit off the TCH begins with a long stretch of undeveloped roadside that many local animals use as a corridor when travelling between the mostly forested Tunnel Mountain area and the good grazing land on the flat valley bottom. Many of Banff's worst traffic jams occur along this bit of road, as motorists pull over wildly to catch a glimpse of an elk, deer or bear going about their daily business. Today, no one is home, so I continue along Banff Avenue, which turns into a prolonged strip of hotels and motels in dizzying succession: the Inns of Banff, the Spruce Grove Inn, the Rundlestone Lodge, the High Country Inn, the Banff International Hotel and many more.

I suppose I could call in a few favours and save myself the trouble of deciding where to sleep. Get a great deal somewhere, or find a friend's couch to crash on, but that would contradict the spirit of adventure somehow. So eventually I choose the Voyager Inn because: a) it's one of the first along the strip, so I expect it to be among the cheapest available; and b) the sign out front encourages me to ask about the walk-in special. Feeling a bit frisky after getting some exercise, I'm tempted to ask about the bike-up special but know the joke would be lost on the French-Canadian desk agent with marginal English-language skills, so I refrain. I sign in, leave the vehicle information portion of the registration card satisfyingly blank, offer up a polite "*merci*" and wander off to find out what my $120 "walk-in special" is going to get me.

Not much, as it turns out.

The key card for the door is an old-fashioned mechanical one, with holes punched straight through the hard grey plastic. It's a technology that probably lasted for 45 minutes between actual keys in the '80s and the electronic key cards of today, but it lives on at the Voy. The room is an average size, with two queen beds, which I expected. The TV is tiny, but everything is tidy, and there are plenty of towels, so I throw my gear down on what will be the vacant bed, flip on the Giants–Redskins NFL season opener and struggle through the ten push-ups and ten sit-ups that are part of my new "beat back the flab" fitness routine. But after a shower and a little more football, I quickly become bored. Pleased with the fact that I biked for an hour *and* have done a bit of resistance work, I figure it appropriate to head to the Voyager Lounge for happy hour.

I'm surprised to find it three-quarters full of locals. Only a handful of the 20 or so folks present are under 50 years old, but the conversations are lively, and I retire to a table in the back to take in the atmosphere. Video lottery terminals, Canada's answer to slot machines, are doing good business along one wall, and a huge stuffed bison head adorns the wall behind me, along with two televisions whose placement appears predicated merely on avoiding the fireplace – a task they manage only awkwardly. The far wall backs the bar, and off to my right are two large paintings that look like they were freshly painted in 1943, depicting the experiences of early explorers and settlers. One has cowboys crossing the prairies with pack horses in tow; the other features a huge canoe with a half-dozen men paddling a swift river. There is even an interesting attempt at wainscotting: five two-by-six-foot wood panels intricately carved with similar settler scenes, running along most of two walls. But my favourite of the retro decorations is the set of four elk antler chandeliers spaced evenly around the room. The place has the slight hint of decay and stale beer that is inevitable in all bars and taverns over 20 years old, but a mug of Kokanee draft is cold and only $3.75, so I stay and have two.

After about 45 minutes, the pleasantly sociable din that made up the background noise starts to sound more like an endless series of annoying squawks, so I decide to hit the street and a have a look around, wandering up Banff Avenue toward the centre of town. One side of the street is entirely hotels and the other is well-kept residential units and staff accommodation suites, and although the views are not much from this vantage point, everything is exceedingly clean and orderly. Not a single gum wrapper on the ground or candy wrapper fluttering on the breeze. You almost feel as if you could eat straight off the sidewalk, and for a brief moment I imagine this might even be a pleasant place to live. Until I almost trip over 60 suitcases plonked right there on the sidewalk and am reminded that a funny thing happens around here after Labour Day.

The endless stream of tourists that descend on the Rockies in campers and SUVs and rental cars over the summer months is replaced in September by what I like to call the Blue Hair Gang, a group that's sort of like the Hells Angels, but with less leather and minimal law-breaking. As hotels, tour companies and travel operators drop their full-season rates in anticipation of winter, an explosion of aging retirees invades in droves, snapping up any deals on offer. I actually don't mind that they're old and can't (or won't) carry their own bags; it's just that they are a big group, so I find them annoying. A group of teenagers would be similarly unwelcome in my life, and would certainly be louder, but would a like number of 30-somethings be any better? I doubt it and suspect it all comes back to a deep disdain for crowds.

At the Aspen Lodge, Banff Avenue veers left and the views begin to get better. The more photogenic side of Mount Rundle peeks out from behind Tunnel Mountain. At 9,675 feet, it is not the tallest local mountain, but it's certainly the most recognizable. Rundle is a classic example of an overthrust mountain, a feature common in the Front Ranges that came about when layers of rock along the edge of the McConnell Thrust Fault broke off and piled on top of the younger rocks on the eastern side. Most of these types of mountains have a tilted southwest-facing slope and precipitous northeast-facing cliffs, and if you can imagine a table with one leg broken off so the flat top sits at a 45-degree angle, then you get the idea. From Canmore, we see only Rundle's jagged cliff faces, which soar over a kilometre above the valley floor, and they stimulate the imagination in their own special way. But from Banff's northwestern vantage point, Rundle delivers a dramatic and stunning view of the overthrust formation, one that has been made world-famous over the last 100 years in postcards and picture books printed in dozens of languages.

It doesn't take long to become distracted from the views, however, as I'm amazed how busy the streets are on a chilly Thursday evening in the fall. There are people everywhere. Some are obviously locals just finishing work or beginning a night out on the town, but a disproportionate number are tourists shuffling around as if it were a sunny Saturday afternoon in July – except that they're wearing giant new parkas. All the shops are open, and as the natural light fades, the artificial glow coming from inside each beckons, but I am oblivious. I don't even really see the people, to be honest. I know they are there, but I don't want to acknowledge them, don't want to hear them and don't want to interact. Technically, I may also be on vacation, but I feel like I'm on a bigger mission as well, and for the moment it's making me largely blind to people who are simply visiting. If I want the tourist experience, I can just go back to my service industry job, where I'll get paid to endure them. Looking for an escape, I duck into Wild Bill's for a beer.

Wild Bill's Legendary Saloon is on the second floor of a building at the corner of Banff Avenue and Caribou Street, with (you guessed it) a Wild West motif. The irony of this of course is that Bill Peyto was more an outfitter and guide than a cowboy in the traditional understanding of the word. Many of the notable characters from this area of the west were hunters, trappers and prospectors who added guiding to their repertoires as visitors began coming to the Rockies late in the 19th century to explore, climb and sightsee. Born in England in 1869, Peyto left home at 18 and by the early 1890s was guiding for pioneering outfitter Tom Wilson in Banff. By the turn of the century, climbing fever was spreading fast, and it was Peyto who escorted James Outram, with climbing guides Christian Häsler and Christian Bohren, to the base of Mount Assiniboine in preparation for their historic first ascent. Eventually, Peyto became a park warden, and in addition to at least two businesses I know of, he has a mountain, a lake and a glacier named after him.

The bartender at Wild Bill's this evening was once a waitress at the Drake Inn in Canmore, back when my friends and I used to blow in from Calgary for the weekend. We would sit around drinking and playing cards and generally made a nuisance of ourselves. Whenever I see Alison, I'm reminded of those times, when I was the day-tripping tourist who spent a lot of money but probably got on all the locals' nerves.

Apart from Alison, there are a few vaguely familiar faces sitting at the bar, and the all-too-familiar off-duty bar staff conversations are going on. It's mostly inane banter about the weather, about how busy it was around here in the summer, how quiet it will be in winter. A good hike or mountain bike ride is occasionally mentioned, but most of the time drunken party gossip and boyfriend/girlfriend troubles dominate. I know it's important to the participants in the moment – and I have, in my younger years, complained vociferously about my social life in inappropriate ways – but today it all sounds like this to my ears.

Off-duty waitress No. 1: "Blah, blah, blah, blah."

Off-duty waitress No. 2: "Blah blah, blah blah blah."

Off-duty waitress No. 3: "Blah?"

Off-duty waitress No. 2: "Blah!"

Off-duty waitress No. 3: "Bastard!"

It doesn't take long to get tired of that, so I finish my beer, have a quick shot with my bartender, pay my tab and hit the street again.

I'm well lubricated by now, and dinner at the Maple

Leaf Grill seems like a smashing idea. I had planned to roam a little more, maybe even see something other than the inside of a bar or restaurant, but I'm hungry, and Banff isn't exactly going anywhere. Over a glass of Babich Pinot Noir, I realize I haven't spoken more than a couple of words to anyone all day, and have very much enjoyed the solitude even in the midst of so many people. My delicious prawn fritter appetizer is accompanied by a little small talk with my capable and professional bartender about the fourth quarter of the football game, but attempts at more meaningful dialogue just feel awkward. So I order another glass of wine, tuck into my apple-crusted pork tenderloin and go back to minding my own business.

After dinner and a rather large aperitif, I try once again to be inspired by the town but end up wandering the streets aimlessly. Eventually I make it back to the Voy, jam a buck fifty in the vending machine in the hotel lobby for a package of Reese's Peanut Butter Cups and fall asleep in front of the undersized TV, watching Craig Ferguson on *The Late Late Show* with my big fat belly hanging out. Content for the moment, because I have managed to go somewhere and do something meaningful with my day, even as the exact details of the coming adventure remain unclear.

• • •

Visiting a national park should go beyond simply driving up, snapping a few pics, purchasing a souvenir or two and driving away. I believe more effort should be put into it than that. I dare say enjoying a national park is both a privilege and a responsibility that requires a determined attempt on the part of the visitor simply because of what a park represents and protects. Canada's Rocky Mountain

National Parks have a vast history that not only predates human occupation but is diverse and expansive nearly beyond comprehension. A rich assortment of flora and fauna find refuge in the alpine, subalpine and montane ecoregions, and the diversity of local rock formations is a geologist's dream. The cultural component goes back 200 years to the arrival of the first white explorers and fur traders, and even further still to the final retreat of the Wisconsin glaciation some 8,000 to 13,000 years ago, when the first Native North Americans began hunting and trading in the area.

This is a proper park, not some Disney theme park.

As an example, the Burgess Shale in Yoho National Park is a fossil site on Mount Field that dates back 505 *million* years. Discovered in 1909 by American Charles Walcott, samples taken from the site and examined at the Smithsonian Institution indicate a level of biodiversity previously unsuspected for that time period, and there is evidence suggesting that animals began evolving the capacity for vision around this time. A UNESCO World Heritage Site, the Burgess Shale is perhaps the best place on earth to find trilobites, those early arthropods that appeared in the fossil record so suddenly and in such variety that paleontologists refer to the period as the Cambrian explosion. Somewhere in the vicinity of 60,000 specimens were eventually collected, representing 140 species, including the first know organism with a primitive spinal column. In addition to this early ancestor of all vertebrates alive today, including us, all current body types in use by all complex organisms not yet accounted for also made their debut on the biological stage. It was an important time in earth history.

More recently, Banff became the third national park

in the world (after Yellowstone and Australia's Royal). In 1883, hot springs were stumbled upon in the Banff area by three rail workers. (The springs had been known to Aboriginal people for generations, and they used them for ceremonial and healing purposes, but never took advantage of the warm water's economic potential). Unfortunately for the surveyors, they made a hash of their claim, and on November 28, 1885, Prime Minister Sir John A. Macdonald and the federal government stepped in and took the land, creating a 26-square-kilometre reserve on the side of Sulphur Mountain that would eventually grow to become Banff National Park.

And of course there are the plants and animals that live here. There is a myriad of rodents and rabbits and weasels, as well as mountain goats, bighorn sheep and three types of wildcat (bobcat, lynx and cougar). There are white-tailed and mule deer, moose and the increasingly rare woodland caribou, as well as 40 per cent of all the bird species native to North America. Both black and grizzly bears are common. The diminutive Banff Springs snail inhabits seven local springs and can be found nowhere else on earth.

The vast forests also contain various pines and spruces and a scattering of subalpine fir, while balsam and cottonwood poplars have found a niche in sporadic stands. There are also wildflowers, mosses, grasses and lichens too numerous to mention. Because of the extremes in elevation, temperature and wind, no less than 130 ecosites – areas that don't fall precisely into the three normal ecoregion classifications – have been identified, and plants and animals have adapted to fill them all. Upon reflection, the Canadian Rocky Mountain Parks World Heritage Site is nothing short of a giant living museum.

Unfortunately for this veritable Noah's ark of North American species, Jasper, Lake Louise, Field and Banff are all within national park boundaries and are becoming increasingly urbanized despite their relatively small sizes. That increasing cosmopolitanism is not only a strain on local resources but a challenge for animal awareness campaigns. Living in and visiting the Canadian Rockies means living with and visiting wildlife. While most precautionary measures for dealing with wild animals seem like common sense, common sense isn't always in great supply within the human animal. So, in an effort to educate the general public and reduce the number of wildlife conflicts that lead to human injury and the inevitable destruction of the offending animal, Parks Canada and the provincial government have issued informative pamphlets on how to behave outside. Again some points are obvious, some are extremely useful in understanding animal behaviour, but some are not much help at all.

The Parks Canada "Bare" Campsite Program pamphlet is pretty straightforward and deals with the issue of animals being attracted to sloppy campsites. It welcomes visitors and reminds them they will be camping in a very special place and in doing so will be sharing the landscape with all manner of wild animals, including grizzly bears, black bears and cougars. The pamphlet goes on to explain that all food and food-related items are to be stored in a hard-sided vehicle or in the campground food storage lockers and not in a tent or tent trailer.

It seems that a big mistake made by inexperienced campers is leaving coolers out and unattended during the daytime, thinking they are secure. The slightly blurry black and white photograph on the inside page of the pamphlet, which shows a very large black bear making short work of a plastic food storage container, with two coolers casually tossed aside after being ransacked, is reason enough to heed the Parks Canada warning. The determined bruin is on his hind legs and is clawing at the top of the box set on the seat of the picnic table. He appears extremely focused on the task, and the whole scene would be an unsettling sight to return to after a short walk with the family. The recommendation to not store food in your tent may seem obvious, but I have, on occasion, eaten in my tent when the bugs were so bad that I couldn't stand it anymore, or have forgotten a half-finished granola bar in my jacket pocket and then used the same jacket as a pillow. So I guess these warnings bear repeating from time to time. And please, excuse the pun.

On the back page of the pamphlet is some general info about sharing the ecosystem and viewing wildlife safely. There is mention that travel routes, food sources, mating grounds and resting sites do not follow arbitrary boundaries and that it is important to be vigilant and aware, especially at dawn and dusk, near streams or rivers, or in densely vegetated areas. It goes on to say that all wild animals are potentially dangerous, that you should never approach, feed or entice wildlife of any kind, and that you are encouraged to keep a safe viewing distance at all times – 30 to 100 metres is recommended.

I go outside to photograph sunrises and sunsets, to look at pretty rivers and streams and to get as far away from pavement as possible, so I find all this information at once helpful and a little vague. It's sort of like being told to be careful crossing the street as a child – look both ways, cross at an intersection etc. – but the reality is that the only way to be completely safe is to never venture outside and across the road in the first place. Not a realistic option for anyone except agoraphobics. It seems I also have a difficult time judging metres out there on the ground and wouldn't really know where to stand in order to be at a proper, respectful distance. Generally, I just try to determine whether the animal appears agitated or not, and I find that's usually a pretty good indicator of its mood. Clearly, more research is needed.

Fortunately, there is also in-depth literature about the larger, scarier beasts. Bears are the most obvious threat around here and subsequently get the most attention, but I will deal with them later. Elk and moose and other ungulates can be dangerous if approached or antagonized during rutting season – you could get kicked or stomped or gored – but they are unlikely to carry out a fatal attack. In fact, hitting them with your car is probably more dangerous than encountering them in the wild. Wolves and coyotes are present but aren't normally aggressive toward adult humans. It's the cougars that are the great enigma to me. Reclusive, solitary and nearly invisible, cougars actively avoid human contact most of the time but occasionally behave out of character and attack humans in a predatory way that is most disturbing. The vast majority of bear encounters that end in human injury or death result from a surprise meeting or a bear being drawn to unnatural food sources. The meeting is face to face as long as you resist the overwhelming urge to run, and I do realize that this fact is surely no comfort when confronting 500 pounds of grumpy grizzly.

Cougars, on the other hand, stalk you, sneaking up from behind in such a way that you don't even know they are there until you've been knocked on your ass. Imagine: You're wandering along a lovely, meandering trail on the banks of a river, or climbing steadily through a fragrant pine forest, dreaming happy daydreams and generally minding your own business, when wham! You've suddenly got a 170-pound cat attached to the back of your neck. That's how they get you, by surprise. They slink, close to the ground, to within 10 or 20 metres. Then they run and pounce on you from the back or side. After this initial contact, they dig their formidable claws into the shoulders, neck and flank of their prey and sever the spinal cord with a bite to the neck or throat. They are also patient and will follow a potential meal over long distances, waiting for the right moment to make a move.

Although cougar attacks remain rare, the thought of them does disturb me, so I went online before I began my travels, to search for information pertinent to my type of outing. Key words: *cougar, bicycle, hiking* and *attack*.

Close to home, Frances Frost was attacked and killed on January 2, 2001, while cross-country skiing on the Cascade Fire Road, five kilometres from Banff Townsite. I remember reading about it in the newspaper and feeling unnerved because I had skied in the general area many times before and had done so alone. It remains the only fatal attack on record in Alberta. Wardens believe that prey species' becoming habituated to human settlements have led them to spend more time close to town. Predators have followed, and that may have contributed to the unfortunate incident. Others suggest the attack was simply a case of a teenage cougar trying to find his way in the world and not knowing any better, or it was starving.

On February 8 of that same year Jon Nostdal was attacked while riding his bike in the dark near Port Alice, on Vancouver Island in British Columbia. The animal knocked him off his bike and went for the back of his neck before a passing motorist stopped and helped Nostdal fight the cougar off. They hit the animal with a bag filled with heavy binders, punched and kicked him and eventually pinned the big cat beneath Nostdal's bike before retreating to the nearby vehicle.

Most of the other cougar stories I tracked down were from Colorado, Washington State or Northern California and involved children or pets, since smaller creatures are a more manageable size for an adult cougar. But the account that really caught my attention comes from the Nuxalk Native reserve in British Columbia in 2000. In a perverse twist of fate, Clarence Hall, a hunter hired by the Canadian government to cull problem wildlife, was attacked by the very cougar he was assigned to kill. Hall was casually examining tracks on the banks of Tatsquan Creek when the cat appeared. He tried to get to his rifle from his car, but the cougar pinned him to the ground before he could get there. For a brief moment the hunter become the hunted – an unusual event, surely, but not one that eases my distrust of cougars. Eventually one of Hall's companions came to the rescue and shot the animal four times from point-blank range.

This is the country I'm venturing into, fraught with peril both real and imagined. Despite the accumulation of stories that begin to make it sound like there's a bloodbath going on in the mountain West, the odds remain overwhelmingly against having a negative encounter with any animal in the park. Still, it is prudent to remember there's a mighty fine line between civilized and wild around here. It can be way too easy to forget that danger could lurk just beyond the nearest stand of trees, no matter where you are in the valley. If the Appalachian woods in Bill Bryson's *A Walk in the Woods* are "spooky," and "may harbor wild beasts," and leave you feeling that "there is something innately sinister about them," then I'm standing at the gateway to a predator's paradise. A buffet zone filled with unwary targets made up of soft, pink flesh.

Not only that, since I've lived here we've had freak storms blow in unannounced that caused trees to fall over and kill people out on leisurely walks. Avalanches have claimed an average of 11 lives a year since 1978, and if you stand close enough to the base of any local mountain, then sooner or later gravity will hurl bits of said mountain down upon you. Climb too high or too steep and you run the risk of simply falling off, which also happens with notable frequency. Although unquestioningly beautiful, this place can be a dangerous menace if you don't pay attention.

Standing across from the Banff Park Lodge on Lynx Street, however, at the entrance to the venerable breakfast destination known as Melissa's, it is doubtful I'll be venturing too far into this deep, dark and dangerous wilderness today. This development can be attributed to the fact that I woke up this morning with a headache behind my eyes that was one part late-night television and two parts beer and wine with a Rusty Nail chaser. After a couple of plastic glasses (cellophane-wrapped – for my safety, I guess?) of water and some coffee, I am ready to get on with my day but not exactly inspired to do battle with the great outdoors. It seems I'm looking forward to a casual afternoon where I don't actually have to "do" anything. Perhaps I'll be inspired to take a quick ride out to Vermilion Lakes, or pedal around the Tunnel Mountain loop, but the bookies will have to call that one an even bet. No odds one way or the other.

On a completely unrelated topic, it must be noted here that a coffee maker in the room is one of the great advances in the hotel industry, as far as I'm concerned. It's nice having cable with HBO or Cinemax or Showcase, and in warmer climates air conditioning was a huge leap forward to be sure. But apart from cleanliness and comfort, and a door that locks properly, what more could I need from a room that will be home for only a night or two? Chocolate on my pillow and a turndown service? Please! As I've mentioned, I'm plenty fat enough already and mastered putting myself to bed somewhere around Grade 1. But being able to brew up a small pot while getting ready for the day without the bother of going outside is brilliant. Brilliant, I say! What's more, it can be done while wearing a shower cap and polishing your shoes, if ever you're struck by the need to use up the pointless amenities.

• • •

"More coffee?" my waitress asks, after standing beside my table for a moment doesn't have the desired effect on my attention, I look up absently from the book that was keeping me from further planning.

"Huh? Sorry?"

"More coffee?" the waitress repeats, pot in hand.

"Sure," I say as I push the half-full white porcelain cup to the middle of the table. I've actually had enough already, but moderation is not my strongest suit. She tops me up and I return to my book, but I can still see her in my peripheral vision. I look up.

"Enjoying the book?" she asks. I turn the tattered copy of Bill Bryson's *Neither Here Nor There: Travels in Europe* over to reveal the cover.

"Yes, actually – I've read it a few times before, but I love the way he makes checking into yet another hotel in yet another city seem fresh and interesting."

This usually throws people, the idea of reading

something more than once, unless many years have passed between readings. As someone who likes to scribble and fancies the idea of one day completing an entire manuscript, I can read a good book five or six times in the same calendar year. The first time is usually for pleasure. The second and third time, I pick up on passages and themes that escaped me the first time around, and after that I'm actively deconstructing the work: highlighting great lines, writing my own notes down in the margins and marvelling at a smooth or clever turn of phrase.

"So you're reading it again?" she says, in search of clarification.

"Yes," I say, "I've read them all more than once. *Down Under, Notes From a Small Island, The Lost Continent.*" The list goes on, but she gets the idea, and she's clearly familiar with the author and asks if I have a favourite.

"Not really. There are parts in each that I find especially intriguing, but I wouldn't be able to choose just one. And yourself?" I ask, in order to be polite. It's obvious she isn't just going to go away.

"*The Lost Continent*, I think." She nods toward the other book on the table. "But I haven't read *A Walk in the Woods*."

"Different kind of a journey for him," I say by way of one-line book review. "Definitely the one to choose if you like the outdoors."

She mentally files the recommendation and leaves to take care of her other tables. I try to return to my book, but my brain is spinning now. Suddenly, I can't get my favourite writers out of my head. Bill Bryson, Tim Cahill, Jon Krakauer, Mark Jenkins. As an athlete, I have always been impressed, envious even, of the Wayne Gretzkys and Michael Jordans and Joe Montanas and Tiger Woodses of the world, guys whose talent and single-minded determination redefined their sports. Whatever you may think of how they managed their personal lives, at work they dominated. I am similarly impressed with the select group of songwriters and musicians who can, in a single verse or riff, convey an entire thought or capture a powerful emotion, but it turns out these adventure writers are my true heroes. Although I started wandering off on my own little outings long before I ever read a book for pleasure, their tales from the road have always been a reminder that there's a big, interesting world out there. Whenever everyday life has got too ridiculous to bear, they have been revelation and salvation in equal measure. They are responsible – and please don't hold it against them – for my compulsively writing down whatever it is I see.

Cahill and Krakauer and Jenkins have been on my radar for years, but Bryson first came to my attention only recently, on a trip to Nepal. I was trekking to Mount Everest Base Camp with my girlfriend, Jocey, and was not having an easy time of it. We had taken a short acclimatizing foray up the Gokyo Valley, and I got altitude sickness in the small village of Machhermo. I had the classic symptoms of early cerebral edema: a headache that felt like a train had derailed in my frontal lobe, extreme sensitivity to light and sound, and vague nausea when I stood up too quickly. Abandoning the goal of climbing Gokyo Ri the next day, and descending to Phortse instead, relieved the immediate symptoms, but then it started to rain. It was a cold, persistent type of rain that lasted for two days, and it was while we were in Dingboche, waiting out this stubborn remnant of the monsoon, that an older American gentleman slid me a copy of *Down Under* (this is the one published in North America as *In a Sunburned Country*).

"Not his best work, in my opinion," the man said. "But it will give you something to do."

I was bored out of my mind and couldn't get close enough to the yak-dung-burning stove to stay warm, so I was grateful for the distraction. I had been reading a five-year-old copy of *Vogue*, in Spanish, that a previous trekker had abandoned, but seeing as I don't speak Spanish and my high-school-level French was only helping things by about 20 per cent, the new book was both revelation and godsend. To me, Bryson is funny and adventurous but simple and accessible in his approach as well, a regular guy doing regular shit who is obviously enjoying himself. It's almost like sharing the journey in print was an afterthought.

Now, I'm certainly not as extreme in my endeavours as Krakauer or Jenkins, nor as versatile or as funny as Bryson or Cahill. Truth be told, I'm not half as talented as any of them, but I can't help it. Emulating these guys is what I like to do and is the effort that brings the most pleasure to my life. So I guess it's either continue with this half-assed plan I've hatched, disorganized as it may be at the moment, or go back to the meaningless job that fills my pocket but drains my soul. And if those are the only viable options available, then I suppose it's no surprise to find me sitting in a restaurant 20 kilometres from my condo as the crow flies, with a lingering hangover, defacing books and pretending I'm on some grand adventure.

Better order up another cup of coffee – sorting this out might take a while.

4.

CANMORE

For all intents and purposes, the mini-trip to Banff was a success. Fuelled up on coffee, a little hero worship and a late breakfast, I did eventually decide to go out for a ride. There had been some thought of picking up where I left off the night before and doing a little wander around Banff – casually exploring the history and culture, visiting a few museums and historical landmarks, perhaps – but the call to action that had been missing an hour prior to breakfast was suddenly upon me. Cruel experience was also nagging most of the morning, trying to remind me that if you don't spend at least a few hours in the saddle for a few days in a row before embarking on a more ambitious outing, a high price will be paid somewhere down the line. So off I went.

The afternoon had turned breezy and chilly but was not exactly cold, and the uniform overcast didn't suggest anything more than light rain, so I zipped out to Vermilion Lakes along a well-worn, pothole-strewn access road that paralleled the main highway for a couple of kilometres. After a short spell in the trees, the largely deserted road hugs the lakeside on one side and the base of the hillside 20 metres below the highway on the other. It almost feels like you're alone in the wilderness, until a car or truck flashes past, at high speed, just up and out of sight. Many a famous photo has been snapped from the shores of the lakes, but in this overcast Mount Rundle was just another unremarkable lump in the distance, and there was no one around. The wind was whipping a low chop across the water and the surrounding wetlands smelled faintly of the sulphur that bubbles up from local springs. In all, the scene was moody, yet starkly beautiful.

Because the highway just above these wetlands, and the railway line on the opposite side, are such permanent fixtures in this valley, it's easy to imagine the passage through from Exshaw has always been the primary route of travel in the region, but that has not always been so. In fact, archaeologists have found evidence of hunter-gatherers setting up camp on the shores of these lakes 10,700 years ago. At Lake Minnewanka, just northwest of here, another site is believed to be 11,000 years old, yet sites farther down the Bow Valley toward Canmore get progressively younger, suggesting the primary route of early travel was through Devil's Gap and over Carrot Creek Pass, not along the now-familiar path I used yesterday.

After backtracking along the road, I popped out on the highway and caught a gathering tailwind and hammered it a bit, before looping up and around Tunnel Mountain Road and Tunnel Mountain Drive, eventually descending in a barely contained rush into Banff from the opposite side I had exited. It was embarrassing to contemplate that in all my years living here I had never visited the shores of Vermilion Lakes or travelled Tunnel Mountain Drive, but overall I felt surprisingly good. I was finally giving the bike and the legs a proper test and somewhere along the way was inspired with regards to a route for the rest of the journey, choosing Kananaskis Lakes and Jasper Townsite as bookend destinations. Combining whim (I enjoy visiting both) with practicality (the approximately 400 kilometres between the two is a reasonable yet challenging distance, with plenty of interesting things to see and do en route). With some time painstakingly carved out of my regular duties and responsibilities, I might even get into the backcountry now and again, and climbing a peak or two along the way is also not out of the question.

In an optimistic frame of mind, I returned to Canmore to collect my gear – a fast, easy ride fuelled by equal parts opportunity and possibility.

Now, just to be clear, my plan to escape from this place didn't come about because I don't like it anymore in a *point final*, end-of-story kind of way. In truth, a big part of me will always blindly love Canmore no matter what, but the effort involved in being a pleasant, upstanding member of society is obviously more than I can manage at the moment. I've also noticed that the cost of living in the Bow Valley has become too great when compared to the cost of making a living, and I've grown weary of punching the clock. I moved away from Ontario over a decade ago to escape the "live to work" mentality that prevailed, then left Calgary when the same illness began to spread west. Now I fear my own little slice of heaven might also be infected, and I don't even need to leave my back porch to see the evidence.

The spectacular view from my condo remains uninterrupted thanks, ironically enough, to the 24-space parking lot servicing my eight-unit condo complex, which is above a handful of ground-floor businesses. Collectively, thanks must also be extended to our next door neighbours,

Fas Gas, Enterprise Rent-a-Car and Simpson's Car Wash, whose parking lots conveniently keep any pesky trees from obscuring the view. I would also be remiss if I left out the lovely folks at the Canadian Pacific Railway (CPR), whose main line passes within 30 metres of my back door.

In reality, the train is not so bad. It thunders by at an obnoxious rate of speed, sure, and every couple of hours on average – though at night, when I'm trying to sleep, it seems more like every hour, and I'm convinced it comes through every five minutes when I want to watch TV with the balcony door open in the summer – but it also prevents further development along my sightlines, so I can't complain. Not too much, anyway. Lucky for me, I'm not a bear or an elk or a moose or a cougar – or even a drunken redneck in his pickup truck lingering at the railway crossing a few hundred metres down the track – because Lord knows, those cargo containers and grain cars have to get out to the coast *right now*! Heaven forbid the world should slow down and the precious cargo arrive a few hours later, or even tomorrow. But I am not especially well versed on the subjects of speed and death as they relate to the economics of freight transportation, so I guess it all makes sense in some alternate universe I am clearly too thick or too sensible to grasp.

Still, as hard as I try, I can't wrap my head around why it would be so difficult for trains to hit more rednecks and fewer bears. Or better yet, an arrogant developer or two. I could even nominate a few local candidates if need be.

Sitting at home, safe in the fact that I am not a hungry animal plucking grain spilled from poorly designed or maintained freight cars, I suppose it's also lucky for me that the tall trees on the far side of the railway line shield any hint of the 12,000 full-time and roughly 5,000 part-time residents that I know are out there at any given time, waiting to aggravate me to no end. It's not each individual in the 17,000 that gets on my nerves, nor is it a definable combination of people within the group that manages to get under my skin, but there is a weird chemistry floating around that shouldn't exist in a town so blessed in natural beauty. In the glossy travel brochures, Canmore is pretty, Canmore is clean and Canmore is friendly, which is all true – but Canmore is something less palatable as well, and I can't put my finger on exactly what that is. On the cover of a recent vacation planner I noticed the tag line read: "Do More, Play More, Live More." And I immediately wondered: *Who's got the time?*

But in an attempt to be thorough in my diagnosis of what is ailing this place, I think it behooves me to have a good look around before condemning it completely. It is my home, after all, and I should give it every chance.

• • •

Canmore, Alberta, was founded in 1883 to support the construction of the CPR. Siding 27, as it was known at the time, was just another short stretch of secondary track, a common feature along the new railway line, until it was designated a divisional point, where the company invested in additional infrastructure to store locomotives and house crews. In 1884 the name Canmore was adopted, and by that time the two-track siding boasted a 12-bay roundhouse with old-fashioned turntable, maintenance shed, water tower and fuel yard. When coal was discovered at the base of the mountains, mines were established, stimulating the growth of the settlement, which had developed a population of 450 souls by 1888.

Despite its proximity to Banff, which was already

nurturing its reputation as a world-class tourist destination, Canmore remained not much more than a sleepy little mining town for much of the next century. The best coal dug out of these mountains was a high quality semi-anthracite type found only in the Bow Valley and in the vast reserves of Pennsylvania, but production was never a steady proposition early on. The Cascade Coal Company got the ball rolling just east of Canmore, but their product was only used locally, for heating and cooking. It wasn't until 1887, when the Canadian Anthracite Coal Company opened Mine No. 1 (after securing a favourable shipping rate from the CPR), that mining became big business. Eight hundred and sixty-four tons were produced in the first month alone.

Mining hit an average of 1,118 tons *a day* during the First World War but suffered a number of fits and starts as international markets ebbed and flowed, and oil and gas became a significant player in the energy market by mid-century. An improved road system and changing locomotive designs also caused a drop in the CPR's demand for Canmore coal. New seams were opened up and in time abandoned, and production numbers reflected a volatile market that often meant feast or famine for those whose livelihoods depended on the mines. In 1979, the last mine shaft in Canmore, owned by the Dillingham Corporation, closed for good, and the future of the town was somewhat in question. Then the 1988 Winter Olympics in nearby Calgary came along, and everything began to change.

Canmore was selected as the site for the Nordic skiing events for those Olympics and set about constructing facilities and a series of cross-country ski trails on the shadowy lower slopes of Mount Rundle's eastern face. Even with the scarcity of snow that year (truckloads had to be hauled in from neighbouring British Columbia to ensure coverage at some venues), the Games were an international success. The world fell in love with Alberta, with figure-skating sweetheart Elizabeth Manley, with poorly prepared English ski jumper Eddie the Eagle and the Jamaican bobsled team, if only for a short while. In Canmore the tide had begun to turn, and even though the town was still all but invisible from the highway during the Games, the economic boom across the province in the following two decades ensured that the formerly unassuming little community would never again be in danger of fading away, coal or no coal. By 1983 the population had grown from its modest beginnings to a humble 2,763, but by 2006 that number had swelled exponentially to 16,417.

Local writer and historian Rob Alexander contends that even without the Olympics, Canmore was already taking steps down the path toward rapid expansion. In his book *The History of Canmore*, Alexander notes that as far back as 1972 the Dillingham Corporation had designs on transforming its extensive land holdings into an expansive resort-style community, but early plans never got off the ground. The land was sold to KGM Developments in 1980 and then resold to Patrician Land Corporation shortly afterward without any significant development taking place. When parent company Fidelity Trust collapsed in 1983, the property descended into limbo for more than a decade. But growth was all but inevitable on a piece of land surrounded on all sides by a national park and an extensive collection of provincially protected areas, and what was once mine holdings is now Three Sisters Mountain Village.

In his book *The Weekender Effect*, Robert W. Sandford

describes a phenomenon common all over western North America and in mountain towns specifically: loss of place. He contends that it is not what small town folks build that gives them a sense of community, but what they save. Unique history, the local environment and close personal relationships are what make living in a small town worthwhile for most, and the erosion of this sense of place is often brought on by rapid and poorly regulated growth, usually initiated by outside interests. In the book, Sandford never identifies the town he lives in, and it could be anywhere along the mountainous corridor that separates Aspen, Colorado, and Valemount, British Columbia. For its part, Canmore managed to mutate in just a few short decades from a retired coal mining community into one that dabbles in tourism and consumes real estate at a blistering pace. The effect that this has had on the local "community" remains up for debate.

If I step down the back stairs and out the door for a reconnaissance mission of my little mountain paradise, the walk takes me diagonally across my parking lot and leads directly to a well-worn path parallel to the rail line. A branch of the trail leads left across the tracks after 100 metres. If I continue straight ahead, the dirt and gravel give way to asphalt after I cross Railway Avenue, and both rails and path carry on for a couple of dead-straight kilometres across the wide valley bottom to the northern edge of town. The municipal campground, the visitor information centre and the Canadian institution that is Tim Hortons are located at that opposite edge, and the back side of business interests and various hotels fronting Bow Valley Trail are constant companions along the well-used paved pathway. But today I take a left turn before reaching Railway Avenue, as I almost always do, and come immediately to an obvious symbol of the growing conflict around here – namely, a chain-link fence.

This six-foot-high affront to natural travel patterns is new and theoretically deters pedestrians from the dangers of the railway tracks, which are technically private property owned by the CPR and illegal to cross except at designated points – official crossings with lights and bells, where sloppy rednecks have been known to lurk in their pickups on Friday and Saturday nights all across the West.

Curiously, the fence only appeared after the development of the old Restwell Trailer Park began on the opposite bank of Policeman's Creek, when this prime real estate was reborn as Spring Creek Mountain Village in a fit of expensive new condos. A coincidence, perhaps, because at about the same time, the CPR informed town council that the only way to stop train whistles at every crossing was to erect a fence. But Spring Creek is not the only large new development in my neighbourhood, and local foot traffic has increased as a result. The real problem with the fence is that the shiny black chain-links also restrict access to the Policeman's Creek boardwalk, a public park and short nature walk that is not only the quickest route downtown by foot from my part of town but a pleasant stroll that avoids the noisy traffic that has become ubiquitous on Railway Avenue.

In a gesture that would make the late Edward Abbey and his fictional Monkey Wrench Gang proud (and one I had nothing to do with, by the way, I swear) the original fence was bulled down within a month, repaired, then bulled down, repaired, then bulled down once again. But no matter what the final tally in the fence war ends up being, this town is definitely changing. Buildings and fences are going up as quickly as green spaces and wildlife corridors are being consumed. And as if that wasn't enough, a casual glance southeast to the base of Grotto Mountain reveals that it too is being consumed, in plain sight, by a strip mine operation – Graymont is scrambling to produce lime products destined for industrial markets with interests far away from these stately and stunning mountains. The kilometre-long scar carved out of Grotto's side grows a little every day but conveniently does so at a pace that doesn't seem to alarm anyone.

Farther down Highway 1A and out of sight of town, Burnco and Lafarge are rushing to carve up mountains of their own, supplying gravel and concrete to fuel the explosive skyscraper and infrastructure growth in Calgary, 100-odd kilometres away. There is some irony in the fact that one of the first things most visitors come across upon close inspection of this stunning landscape is heavy industry. But there you have it, and if you're ever in the neighbourhood of Lac des Arcs, the blatant disregard for the environment can be an amazing sight to behold. Over on Highway 1, an extensive pullout on the shoreline allows long-haul truckers a chance to rest before the exhausting task of getting out to the coast. This also happens to be a popular stop for tourists entering the mountains for the first time. On a warm summer day, dozens of them might be scattered around their cars, cameras in hand, awed by the scenery that towers above and apparently oblivious to the devastation nearer ground level.

It's a bit perverse to imagine a big chunk of mountain being chewed apart, ground down into little pieces, only to be hauled away and reformed into a city. But that's what's going on, and again, no one seems to care. Touted as the "Heart of the New West" in recent promotional material, Calgary is the Canadian poster child for physical and economic expansion, no question – and I am not against urban development as a blanket rule. Having lived there for eight years, I admit to enjoying Calgary's compact downtown core with its towering high-rises, extensive riverside park system and seemingly endless venues for the arts and entertainment. Many of the restaurants are also outstanding. What I don't like is that parts of the suburban "New West" look an awful lot like the shiny New East, and I'm shocked that no one out here seems to realize that urban sprawl and repetitive tract housing is just a tiresome eyesore with a crisp paint job and manicured front lawn.

Who isn't vaguely nauseated when they crest that final small hill on the way to Calgary while travelling east on Highway 1, only to be confronted by a sea of new rooftops packed onto the previously bare rolling hillsides, with only a couple of metres between each virtually identical home? David Byrne, of Talking Heads fame, says in his book *Bicycle Diaries*, "Cities are physical manifestations of our deepest beliefs and our often unconscious thoughts, not so much as individuals, but as the social animals we are." If this is true, then one has to wonder about the tendency in our urban growth that leads toward common and predictable and away from charming and interesting. As you roll up to Calgary from the west, the landscape gradually changes from ranches and farms, to large trophy homes on acre and half-acre lots, before disintegrating into subdivision hell. I distinctly remember feeling a similar sensation the first time I passed by Oshawa on Highway 401, heading to Toronto from my hometown of Montreal. I stared out the passenger window and thought: *Wow, repulsive.*

The common perception is that cramming these homes together reduces land costs and makes owning a home more affordable to the average buyer, but I suspect the practice has more to do with maximizing profits for developers and investors. I suppose trees and shrubs will continue to grow and mature, making the scene slightly more palatable, but it's never going to be attractive, especially in winter, when the shield of green is stripped away for the season. I have no architectural background or professional interest in urban planning but can't help feeling that how we build is the most public display of how we choose to live, and that choice appears to be growing increasingly uniform by the minute. The bottom line is that modern suburbs have no soul, my friends, and all you have to do is look and you know, somewhere in your gut, that it's true.

Local and regional growing pains aside, arriving on Canmore's Main Street at the top end of the boardwalk on a sunny fall day, with nothing to do, is still magical, and a big reason I moved here to begin with. Turning my attention up the street, I'm greeted with a pleasant small-town tableau: dozens of small shops and businesses collected in a central area that has not yet been abandoned for a SuperMall at the fringes of town. There are small trees that line the route. Artsy banners hanging from the light standards depict the favoured recreational options in the area – hiking, mountain biking, skiing – and hint at the yearly arts and entertainment festivals that are part of the growing local culture. All of it is framed in the near distance by the mass that is Mount Rundle. In winter, stunning blue Christmas lights hang everywhere and cast a cool yet welcoming glow, and after a big snowfall it takes a few days (and sometimes weeks) for crews to remove the snowbank plowed to the middle of the street. For some reason I find this little detail endlessly endearing, even though it impedes my jaywalking tendencies.

To the credit of town council and local businesses, the

three-block stretch of two- and three-storey buildings downtown has avoided the stripmallization common to development these days. A few older places have been torn down and replaced with new structures, but most are tasteful and appropriate to the setting. More importantly, the mishmash of existing buildings, both new and old, gives the main drag a small-town feel that is still decidedly Canmore. Or *not* Banff, if you will, and please, don't even get me started on what I think of Whistler these days.

The old North West Mounted Police barracks sits right at the bend that marks the true beginning of the main drag. It's a quaint little tourist attraction with a small, well-kept yard, a garden filled with flowers, a handful of benches crafted from thick local logs cut in half and a sturdy table for picnicking. An official Alberta Heritage Site, the structure was originally constructed in 1893 at a cost of $450 and is now a small museum housing the artifacts and rifles and uniforms used in the early policing of the Canadian West. It's all well-presented and interesting, and when I first visited I immediately noticed the short and narrow interior doorways that indicate how much the human physique has changed in just a few generations. But I'm a local now, so nine times out of ten I don't even give the quiet little white building a second glance as I pass.

Being local, and spiritual as opposed to religious, I tend not to notice the historic Ralph Connor Memorial Church a few doors down, either. But having recently visited Tibet, I find the architecture of the now-vacant Chinese food restaurant a little farther along a persistent reminder of the disappointing – and all too familiar – development model I witnessed in Lhasa.

I went to Tibet as a last-minute addition to the trekking vacation Jocey and I were taking in Nepal. After an awe-inspiring flight over the mighty Himalayas, I was shocked to land on "the roof of the world" and find a modern metropolis smack dab in the middle of nowhere. Lhasa has become a Han Chinese city, filled with dusty and charmless cinder-block mixed in with prefab glass and steel; its downtown core appears to have been slapped up in the last 15 or 20 minutes. Apart from the occasional Tibetan monastery or palace spared in the Cultural Revolution, little history has been incorporated into the design, which could be described as Red Square Functional meets Exploding Economy, with a little Keep a Few Landmarks to Attract Tourists mixed in.

The Chinese government has a lot to answer for with regard to human rights, labour practices and the environment across its entire sphere of influence, and when it comes to the Tibetan Autonomous Region the bad behaviour is manifold. The atrocities have been documented by monks, scholars and historians much wiser and more eloquent than I – including a fair number who were executed for their troubles. But as I stood there, dumbfounded, at the epicentre of an ancient culture being consumed by an occupying force drunk on its own version of runaway capitalism, all I could think was, *Wow, the fools in charge have made this look as cheap and tacky as Las Vegas.*

Okay, comparing it to Vegas is an exaggeration, but it certainly was not the quintessential wind-whipped mountain town, filled with a hard brand of proud people accustomed to living off the land, that I was hoping for. I immediately wished I could have seen the city 20 years ago.

Our local version of the Chinese style is made up of oversized red brick and is not gaudy enough to qualify as tacky but does have some funky red tile trim around the windows. The set-up is also punctuated with flashy orange-and-green pagoda-style roofing that is beginning to fade and peel badly and isn't structurally valid at all, merely added at the tail end of construction, as an accoutrement. It's simply a decoration meant to transport me to another time and place – and crave buffet, I presume – and I can't help but laugh and cry a little every time I see it. I honestly thought Chinese folks in North America were having us on with the decor of their restaurants and retail outlets and that they took details to the extreme in order to sell more trinkets and chicken fried rice, exaggerating 6,000 years of history and contributions to world culture simply for the kitsch of it all. My recent travels leave me unsure, and it's something I'll look at more closely on my next trip to Asia, but there certainly appears to be a mighty tight window between bland and bawdy these days.

On a side note, the local place abruptly relocated a few years back, to a vacant building a block off Main Street that was once a German/Swiss restaurant and has the architecture to match. I'm pretty sure Beijing had nothing to do with it, but without any significant redevelopment, the whole Swiss/Chinese set-up is a living embodiment of the term "clusterfuck," and yet the odd combination does scream "small town" in its own make-do-with-what's-available kind of a way.

Sometimes as I make my way up the first block of Main Street I'll pop across the street to the Grizzly Paw Brewing Company for a double Caesar in a pint glass, because they do the best garnish in town: the obvious lime wedge and celery-salt rim, of course, but with a sprig of pickled asparagus replacing the celery stalk and an extra-large olive and pepperoncini pickled pepper tossed in for good measure. Unfortunately, because the microbrewery is popular with tourists and day-trippers from Calgary, there are often a lot of said tourists and day-trippers about. I'm not up for that kind of company anymore, so the Paw is a winter diversion, given up in summer and fall.

What is intriguing about this end of Main Street is that the low-budget Bow Valley Motel continues to thrive on what must be extremely valuable land, with no extensive upgrades or renovations. What's more, it has a laundromat attached to it. A coin laundry on Main Street is the universal indicator of a true small town, isn't it? Once inflation and growth drive rental rates above what laundromats and movie stores can afford, then you've moved on as a community. You're no longer a hamlet or a burg or a charming small town. You're just another wannabe metropolis desperate for a Wal-Mart and a multiplex, and I think the inevitable transformation of Main Street in the next few years will be more indicative of the state of affairs around here than will the continued condo and golf course development up the valley walls.

Moving on to the second block of Main Street, I am often intrigued by its art galleries, the delightfully overstuffed second-hand book shop and the wide variety of bars and restaurants, from the downright grubby Canmore Hotel to the pleasantly upper-mid-scale Quarry Bistro and Murrieta's Bar & Grill. Sadly, the block also houses my bank, where I am only just barely in good standing, so I try to make my visits brief, if only to keep from being reminded of how much I owe.

The last block is also decorated in small-town charm and is the turnaround point on my weekend walking tours. With a credit union, an independently owned convenience store, a fine book store, two good cafés that aren't Starbucks and a fantastic patio at the Wood Restaurant, the reward is worth the effort, and the entire stretch is full of lazy-day diversions. Most notable among them, to my mind anyway, is the best damn wine shop in the valley, bar none: the Canmore Wine Merchants.

CWM could be the best damn wine shop in the entire world, for all I know about the subject, and the staff doesn't seem to mind that I get half-plastered whenever they have an in-store product tasting. I'm a beer man, generally, but have a growing appreciation for a good Pinot Noir, can't find the palate for Chardonnay unless it's unwooded, love just about any port I can get my hands on and find the new dry-style blush wines to be not so lady-like as they appear at first glance, though you probably still won't catch me drinking one in public. Thanks, guys, for the heads-up on what's good and for the late-afternoon hangover that's sure to follow.

These walking tours generally improve my overall outlook on life around here. Still, I can't quite shake the feeling that this town is becoming less a community to live in and more a destination to visit – or worse, a business opportunity – but I am trying. On many occasions, I've had a few, and as I weave my way home, suddenly Canmore *is* pretty, Canmore *is* clean and Canmore is none of the things that were bothering me just a couple of hours ago. And oh yeah, Canmore sure is friendly. I can't make it from one end of town to the other without at least one honk from a passing car or a wave from a familiar fellow pedestrian. That doesn't necessarily mean I'm all that and a bag of chips, so much as reinforce the idea that, despite the recent spate of flashy growth, this is still a small town that might one day be saved.

5.

GEAR UP, GET OUT

I've got an answer,
I'm going to fly away.
What have I got to lose?

—Stephen Stills (Crosby, Stills and Nash)

To say I feel uncomfortable would be a colossal understatement. Pulling out of the driveway we share with the Fas Gas, my bike is overloaded and hard to manoeuvre, and as I attempt to roll it onto Bow Valley Trail I'm growing increasingly uncertain of my packing job. Kicking a leg over the saddle is a big stretch because of the gear piled on the rear rack, and the whole set-up is heavy and unresponsive as I try to pedal up the minimal incline that leads to the road. Everything wobbles and leans when I'm not centred directly over the wheels, and there's an unsettling creak coming from somewhere in the vicinity of the bottom bracket when I dig into the pedals. Clearly, I have too much stuff.

It also doesn't help that it's Saturday afternoon, warm and sunny, and Fas Gas is one of the busiest stations in town. Looking like an incompetent boob is bad enough when there are no witnesses, but it is much worse when there are. Fortunately, I'm heading south this time and don't have to endure the indignity of pedalling ineptly across town. A kilometre, maybe two, and Bow Valley Trail turns into Highway 1A and leaves the industrial park at the edge of Canmore, where I can be alone with this awkwardness.

As I pedal past the last of the houses and businesses at the edge of the corporate limits, it's not long before I'm distracted from the task at hand by three important discoveries. One: inspiration is a naturally occurring phenomenon – sit quietly for a few minutes, and specific answers to troubling questions won't come, but it's a good bet a direction to start looking will present itself. Two: acting on that inspiration is hard – as it turns out, thinking about something is easier than doing it. Three: once the initial distress of being pushed out of your comfort zone passes, you always feel better – it might require going out for a drink to calm your nerves, or lying down in a dark hotel room where no one can find you until you get your bearings, but eventually you will feel better. I guarantee it. Now if I could just figure out how to keep the momentum going, I'd be set, but I've let the excitement of finally making a decision wane, and for reasons that defy explanation almost a week has passed since I left Banff and came back to Canmore to collect the bulk of my gear.

Part of the problem is that I'm fond of lists. Quite fond of them actually, which is strange because I'm not an especially organized or time-sensitive person, at least as it relates to my personal life. At work I am orderly, punctual and tidy, but on my own time everything falls apart and I become disorganized, lazy and sloppy. My home office looks like a two-megaton book bomb exploded and scattered hardcovers, paperbacks, journals, manuscripts and random scraps of paper everywhere. It's almost as if my orderly self gets used up between nine and five (or, as is the case for many service industry drones like myself, six p.m. to three a.m.) and whatever is left can't be bothered. On some level, making a list feels a bit like doing, without the sweat equity investment, and once the lists are done, I'm done.

At any rate, sometime in the spring – right around the time I started thinking about travel as a means of getting a fresh perspective – I typed out a message to myself, in big bold capital letters, that hung at my desk next to the computer all summer long. The list made me feel better and was supposed to inspire action toward the end goal that is this trip, but was, perhaps predictably, already being ignored by the time the ink was dry. It went something like this:

STEP 1 – CONSOLIDATE A PLAN

STEP 2 – ORGANIZE THE GEAR

STEP 3 – DO A COUPLE OF SHORT WARM-UP TRIPS

In August I scribbled in a fourth step in pen, hoping it would help.

STEP 4 – GET GOING BEFORE IT SNOWS YOU DUMB BASTARD

What I should have included early on was a specific date for departure, but I rationalized that idea away by claiming travel would feel too much like just another job if approached too systematically. Turns out I don't like being told what to do, even when it was me doing the telling, so for most of the summer I didn't do much of anything to make things easier on myself. As a result, this past week has been a chaotic mess of checking and rewriting lists, idle panic and not much else. If success is what happens when preparation meets opportunity, then I'm in big trouble.

Of all the equipment on these famous lists, the bike has been the easy part. It's over a year old now but practically brand new because I haven't bothered to ride it much. It's just been sitting out on the deck, waiting, because in a moment of impulse I decided I needed a touring bike. I do have a history with bicycle touring, so the purchase was not as impulsive as it sounds. It's not like I went out and bought a pet tiger and caged him in the spare room. But with the exception of two or three trips to Banff and back, I also hadn't ridden more than two or three kilometres at any one time in at least five years, so the new ride was not exactly a necessary purchase either. It's almost as if my subconscious was anticipating an existential meltdown and was predicting a need to return to a more simple and familiar way of approaching life. For me, that means riding a bike.

As kids, my friends and I rode everywhere – to school, to soccer practice, around the neighbourhood just for kicks – and I have had at least eight bikes in my lifetime, including a shiny red machine with high chopper-style handlebars and a banana seat that I got for my fourth or fifth birthday. It was so big I couldn't ride it at the beginning without blocks on the pedals, and I left a fair bit of skin out on the gravel road in front of the house before getting the hang of things. But I loved that bike; it represented freedom and mobility in a way that my young mind wasn't yet ready to understand. It was sturdy and it was powerful and, best of all at the time, it was very, very shiny.

I didn't get serious about riding a bike until I was 15 or 16, when I began thinking about it as something more than getting from point A to point B. In the way most kids that age start thinking about getting a car and cruising around on a hot summer day, I started romanticizing about getting a new bike and pedalling to the next province and then the next country after that. Maybe even to the next continent, eventually. I would buy the latest issue of *Bicycling* magazine with my paper-route money and pore over the ads as much as the articles. Coveting the bikes and the racks and the panniers in the same way gearheads covet a vintage Dodge Charger. Of course, this was the kind of nerdy behaviour that made people look at me funny and inspired close relatives to wonder out loud what I was going to do with my life, so mostly I kept those ambitions and dreams to myself. When asked what my fascination with the bike is all about, I still can't manage to explain it. It just is.

So if the bike was easy, then the rest of the equipment has been more problematic. My camping gear was a shambles when I dragged it out from deep in the back of the closet – all worn out or broken down – and I knew I didn't have a big enough budget to replace everything on the list. My pile of packs was similar, a large number of options and combinations but no best choice. Lately, I've taken a real shine to photography, and beyond the fact that a comprehensive selection of equipment suited to shooting wildlife and landscapes weighs a fair ton, jamming it all into a pack that fits on my back and straps onto a bike meant too much time staring down at piles of stuff and cursing. I would fill the available bags, try and get them strapped on the bike and then empty everything out on the floor again in new piles when the whole mess didn't sit right. And when the set-up was acceptable, it couldn't be transformed into a practical form for walking with.

Part of the appeal of going backcountry hiking or bicycle touring is the minimalism it requires. Bringing along only what is absolutely necessary for survival, and can be reasonably carried, is meant to rid a person of all the crap that accumulates in closets and cupboards and drawers.

Theoretically, freeing oneself from that clutter is meant to help free the mind of cluttered thought, but being unable to achieve that Zen state with my gear, let alone my life, I did what any reasonable North American does in a crisis. I went shopping.

Wandering around Valhalla Pure on Main Street, I probably looked as much like a vagrant as like a guy ready to drop 500 bucks. After quickly putting a couple of maps and a nifty combination emergency-whistle/compass/thermometer down on a discreet corner of the glass-top counter next to the cash register, I began to amble somewhat aimlessly through the racks of expensive new gear. There was a huge selection of sweaters and cozy fleece tops and all manner of high-tech clothing for every imaginable temperature variation, all in a rainbow of colours. There was also a comprehensive selection of climbing gear, books and camping equipment of every description. Not to mention packs and shoes and boots. It was all gorgeous, and a guy could get out of hand rather easily. In fact, I could feel my credit card heating up in my pocket, desperate to purchase unnecessary items. But I had one of my famous lists and was determined to stick to it for once. Everything I need and nothing extra, I kept telling myself. Yeah, right.

After countless attempts at narrowing down a dozen piles back at the condo, I finally figured out that the biggest priorities were a tent compact enough to strap comfortably to the outside of my pack and a sleeping bag that would keep me from freezing to death in October. Sure, my panniers are 20 years old and wearing thin at every edge, and my boots and favourite hiking clothes have seen better days, but the slow accumulation of small tools and miniature kitchen pots and utensils means I might be able to get away with the just the above items. And perhaps, because I'm afraid the beat-up old piece of junk I've got will blow up in my face, a new stove.

"Can I help you find something?" Skippy (or Braedon, or Carabineer, or something equally fitting and ridiculous), the young, way too fit and way too energetic sales associate, finally asks after watching me do three slow laps of the store.

"No thanks," I say. "Just resisting for now."

Skippy gives me a funny look, then shrugs and continues stocking some recently arrived items in men's outerwear.

I hate being bothered in a store by the sales staff. I want to take my time, look at everything on offer and weigh the pros and cons of the purchase. I am often afflicted with buyer's remorse and know I'm going to regret bringing home whatever I purchase no matter how necessary the item. So I need to talk myself into it. That takes time, and when I'm finally ready for help, I'll ask. I don't need to be prodded along by someone whose primary purpose is to get merchandise off the sales floor and out the door. I may be a cynic, but I've never had a salesperson say, "Oh no, sir, I don't think that item is right for you," unless it was to suggest an expensive upgrade. All I ever really need to know when I go in a store is "Do you have my size?" and "Do you take Visa?" Most of the rest of the time I can figure things out for myself, thank you very much.

After cruising through tents for the fourth time, I finally decide on a model that should suit my needs. It's incredibly compact when packed away, yet surprisingly spacious when pegged up. It's designed as a two-man, but the active outdoor folks this stuff is built for are often diminutive and lithe, so I always have to add a person to be comfortable. As a bonus, the vestibule is large enough to keep my camera bag, panniers and boots dry through any inclement weather, which is inevitable where I'm headed. I've also made a choice of stove, which only took two trips through stoves; a Jetboil that breaks down and packs up inside the cooking pot. It takes up about as much space as a one-litre water bottle and is convenient because no extra pots and pans are required. The fuel canister also screws directly to bottom of the unit, so there's no tiresome pumping and priming of the stove, and presumably no leaks.

I'm pretty pleased at this point, and all that's left to figure out is a sleeping bag.

"How's the bag?" Skippy asks without missing a beat, while on a trip to the stockroom at the back of the store. I'm lying on the floor in the corner, tucked deep into sumptuous layers of 800-fill goose down wrapped in sleek black and silver nylon.

"You know," I say, a bit surprised, "not bad at all. It's long enough, and the hood fits well." I cinch the whole thing up to full mummy mode, so only my face is poking out. Then roll around a bit for effect.

"It's a bit tight in the shoulders, but overall incredibly comfortable."

"That one's rated to minus-seven, but you can tack on a few more degrees if you're in the tent you were looking at earlier. If you take good care of it, it should last practically forever and..." Skippy's on a roll, I can feel the pièce de résistance of the sales pitch coming. "... it's on sale."

All good features and well presented, and I'm already almost sure I'm going to buy it, but now it's time to bring the pain.

"How much?" I ask, wincing. Anything this luxurious has got to cost a pretty penny.

"Three fifty, down from 500."

Yeeooow, talk about sticker shock! It's more than the tent, for Christ's sake.

I'm momentarily speechless, but instead of saying something rude when I do come to, I make some quick calculations in my head. Three hundred and fifty bucks is a lot to spend on a glorified blanket, but then again, sleeping outside in Canada in the fall can be a bracing experience. Besides, it's not always easy to find anything in my size in stock. Usually shoes are the issue – size 13 often only gets one order per style per season, and goes fast – but most items that need to be worn have some kind of awkward or annoying deficiency.

This bag, for instance, really is a little tight in the shoulders when I lie on my side, which is how I usually sleep, but overall the effect is minimal, and without special ordering I'm not going to find anything that fits better. On the plus side, it should be the last sleeping bag I own, ever. If I add the bag to the tent and the stove and a few other small amenities, then I'm over budget by nearly 300 bucks, but I will sleep well knowing my gear won't let me down. I'm going to regret it on the 20th of next month, when my credit card statement comes due, but I'm going for it, the whole lot. I give a resigned little nod and gather up my loot and make for the cash register. On the way, I realize that Skippy (his real name was Bob or Tim or something, I'm sure) has not been so bad after all. He was helpful and knowledgeable and not at all pushy, and as I leave the store with an armful of stuff I also take away the refreshing feeling that I haven't been had, or at least not completely had.

So after repeated forays to town to have a good look

around and clean up the final details prior to departure, I think I'm ready to go. It took six days instead of the intended two, in part because I still can't wrap my head around the idea. It seems that without the bolstering effect of adrenaline and the soothing touch of alcohol, there are moments when it's hard to accept an extended bike ride as the best choice of activity for a proper adult. In the sober light of day, I'm finding it difficult to admit that this is what I most want to do, right here, right now.

Still, there's no denying I'm sick and tired of working day after day for nothing more than a paycheque and am similarly uninspired to plan my retirement fund or build a small business out of my writing and photography. All the things I've been programmed to want as a grown-up person simply don't hold much appeal. I just want to go out and do. I want to go and see what's out there in my special little corner of the world. But it all seems a little ridiculous as well. Turns out I feel like a fool not so much because I've packed poorly, but because I'm a grown man who's putting his life and his future on hold to go for a bike ride. What am I, 17 all over again?

• • •

Fortunately, it doesn't take long to clear town and start to feel more confident about my decision. It's a gorgeous day, and apart from a few small stones and the occasional scattering of gravel on the shoulder, the road is in pretty good shape. Traffic is almost nonexistent. One car in either direction every five minutes, tops, and after a couple of kilometres the angle on the Three Sisters changes significantly. Even though I'm just underway, I can't resist the urge to pull over and take a picture. From home I've got an almost perpendicular angle of view on the mountain formation, but as I gradually travel in this direction the three distinct peaks are lining up in a row, smallest to largest in a roughly east-to-west orientation. I'm also slightly higher up the valley wall now, and that meagre shift in elevation results in a remarkable aspect change. I realize I don't get to this side of the valley often. I'm also reminded that I'm very lucky to live here, because it really does take only 15 or 20 minutes in any direction to get an entirely new perspective on my surroundings.

Barely clear of the incorporated town limits, I'm also finding it unusual to feel suddenly so free and unreachable. Detaching from the grid, with no phone and no email, and indeed no radio or anyone around to talk to, can be disconcerting at first. After a couple of pictures, a few notes in my notebook and a moment of pure awe as I take in the beauty of a flawless fall day, I'm suddenly uncomfortable all alone with myself, and I hope for a vehicle, or better yet another cyclist, to come along. But looking back the way I came, and then forward toward where I'm going, reveals only an empty highway, and I can't help but laugh out loud. I've stumbled and bumbled my way through months of dreaming and awkward planning, only to experience, within a half an hour, a bizarre longing for the security of everything left behind. Even without any direct intrusion at this moment, the sensation of the modern world being out there is unshakable, and I've yet to grow accustomed to this new-found silence. And I suppose that is not so strange, all things considered.

A long and deeply ingrained history of increasingly constant contact is a byproduct of our industrial and electronic ages, and does not easily switch off. But a funny thing happens as the minutes begin to tick away unnoticed and uninterrupted. As the background hum of

civilization fades, a quiet descends and you eventually realize how long it's been since you actually stopped, took a
deep breath and listened: not to the voice programmed
to execute a well-laid plan for social and economic success, but to the one yearning for more personal and intimate truths. Strip away the external noise, and you have
to pay attention to something deeper and infinitely more
profound than skyrocketing housing prices, idle gossip
and the price of gas at the pump. Eventually you begin to
think about the important things sitting at the back of
your mind that nag and linger and simply don't go away. I
suspect that this quiet corner is where art and poetry and
music come from, and paying attention is probably the
first step on the road back from who you're expected to be,
to who you really are.

The thing is, coming face to face with your true self can
be a scary proposition, so I quickly pack up my camera,
jump back on my bike and try to shake off the idea that I
might eventually have to learn something out here. Part of
me thinks that a mindless, booze-soaked week at the beach
is a much better idea than a month-long, effort-filled journey of self discovery, where I may not like what I find. As
I continue to ride with no great urgency, I grudgingly accept that taking a vacation from everyday life is going to
produce some uncomfortable moments, and as the miles
slowly accumulate, the cap that keeps everything in its
proper, orderly place is slowly going to rattle free. As time
and space lose some of their shape and structure, there will
be days where none of this makes any sense, and others
where all those bits and pieces will come together in a singular moment of clarity and purpose. Then, inevitably, it
will all come apart again, like so many fall leaves scattering on the wind. I guess that's one of the great joys and

terrifying challenges of solo travel: having the opportunity to be open to the place you're moving through, and to the pure thought and real experience that come with it.

Practically speaking, these early days will also mean getting used to the small details of touring, and for the moment I'm grateful for the distraction. For example, my seat post needs to be raised slightly the next time I stop, to take some pressure off my knees, and sooner or later some of the heavier items in the front panniers are going to have to go in the back because steering is a bit unresponsive at the moment. It will also take a few days of experimenting with different set-ups for the gear strapped to the rear rack before it all sits properly. But although it is excessive, the load is manageable. I'm also noticing a subtle yet encouraging shift in how my legs feel: a bit of strength has returned. I can't push with any force for long without gasping for breath or noticing the burning accumulation of lactic acid in my thighs, but I can push hard in short bursts, a good indicator that my former level of fitness is willing to at least try and make a comeback.

Swinging east around the southern end of Grotto Mountain, I have a couple of minor hills to contend with and often a resident flock of bighorn sheep to navigate around. The animals are by no means tame but are habituated to humans and are drawn to mineral licks near the road at fairly regular intervals along this route. Today, the usual spots early on are abandoned, however, so I pedal through, a little disappointed. Farther along, on one of the short, steep downslopes before Exshaw, I'm chugging away without a care in the world when I notice a dramatic change in the handling of my rolling rig. Suddenly, I'm back-heavy, and the rear of the bike wants to fishtail left, then right, then left again. Glancing over my shoulder, I notice the rack is hanging precariously off the back end. I've had this happen once before and realize quickly that four adjustment screws have come loose and the weight of the equipment has dragged everything back along the two stays linking the rack to the frame. Everything is still attached, but just barely, and I am travelling at 50 kilometres an hour!

It's the kind of situation disasters are made of, but fortunately the trouble is at the rear of the bike, not the front. The worst that can happen is some damaged equipment getting scattered across the road. Maybe a few broken spokes if something gets caught in the wheel. I suppose there's an off chance a loose strap could get tangled up in the brakes, the seat stays and the rapidly spinning spokes, inducing an inconvenient skid that would lay me out on the pavement, but I'm slowing down quickly, and as I glide to a stop on an old driveway that now seems to lead nowhere, I realize this could have been much, much worse.

Years ago, I rode through the Coast Mountains. I was bombing down into the Pemberton Valley in BC after a long slog up and over the pass on Highway 99, coming from Lillooet. The road was steep and wickedly fast, and near the bottom it was full of switchbacks. As today, my bike was fully loaded and not easy to manoeuvre at high speed, but I was feeling full of piss and vinegar after stomping up the mountain and was probably a little more tired than I was willing to admit. I managed the first few tight corners with ease and was amazed how quickly the bike gained momentum in the short straightaways between turns. I would hammer the brakes and then dive into each bend before accelerating out again simply by releasing the calipers on my handlebars. There was no traffic, and it was fast and fun.

Then, coming into a long, sweeping left-hander, I quickly realized I was in trouble. Lulled into complacency by the relatively gentle start of the turn, I had left the braking until too late, and the shoulder was covered in a fine, loose gravel. It didn't take a rocket scientist to figure out I was travelling way too fast to make it around, so I pulled the brakes as hard as I dared and tried to ease away from the danger of the ditch. Or more accurately, manage the danger. Fortunately, it was a shallow ditch with an easy ride in so I did the only thing I could and followed momentum into it.

There was actually a point where I thought I was going to make it out in one piece, escaping with no damage to body or bike, and with an exhilarating story to tell. Then the ditch narrowed abruptly. The last thing I remember is the front panniers getting wedged into the narrow space before being unceremoniously ripped from the bike. The panniers flew past in a blur, accelerated by the fact that I was launched over the handlebars and was travelling in exactly the opposite direction. It was one of those split seconds that are amazingly fast while still playing out in that strange kind of slow motion that has an underwater quality to it. One pannier flew by, followed closely by the second, and the thought *Hey, why are my handlebars below me and not in front, where they belong? Wait a second, am I flying?* flashed across my mind.

Then everything went dark.

The next thing I remember, amazingly, is hauling my bike into the woods five minutes later. There I was, stumbling around like a punch-drunk boxer, trying to hide evidence of the accident before anyone happened along, hoping against hope to sort it all out and carry on. No harm, no foul, as they say. Thing is, my helmet was smashed, and my front wheel looked more like a figure eight than a circle. The front panniers were easily ten feet away and ripped up so badly at key points that they would not attach to the front rack anymore. Clearly the bike was unrideable, and I wouldn't have been able to ride it safely even if I hadn't just mangled the entire front end (it would be over a month before I noticed that the head tube was bent where it attaches to the down tube, effectively reducing my wheel base by about a quarter of an inch).

After getting everything safely stowed from prying eyes, I finally began to properly come to. That entire ten minutes, from accident to full consciousness, is still just a couple of vague snapshots on the otherwise blank canvas of my memory. I was standing on the far side of the ditch with a pannier in my hand, wondering, *What am I doing? And why am I hiding my gear in the woods?* The human psyche is a bizarre thing. I wasn't frightened, or shocked at being in an accident (but looking back, was probably *in* shock). I wasn't worried about getting to a doctor, or even upset that my bike was bashed half to bits. My biggest concern was: *Did anyone see that bonehead move?* I was embarrassed at having been in an accident that was clearly my fault, and my first course of action, executed before I had even completely regained consciousness, was to try and minimize the fuss. What I wanted to do in my addled state was sit quietly and get my bearings, then pack up again and continue as if nothing had happened. A pretty strange reaction, when you think about it.

Fortunately, as my neural pathways began to rewire after the massive short circuit that is a knockout, it dawned on me that I was in no state to do anything except get to a hospital. So I began unpacking my stash from the cover of the woods. Just as I was dragging my bike back to the side of the road, a pickup truck happened by, headed down. I jumped out of the ditch to flag the driver, probably using my cracked helmet as makeshift signal, and as the truck slowed to a stop I poked my head in the open passenger window.

"Hey," I said a little wildly. "This is going to sound a bit strange, but I think I've been in an accident. I don't know what happened, exactly..."

I paused awkwardly in mid-sentence as a few more neurons made the leap to functionality, and realized I didn't know what province I was in, let alone what town might be nearby. "And I don't know where I am."

"Pemberton is just up the road," the guy at the wheel said hesitantly, as if I was putting him on. "If that's any help."

The bit of information did connect a few more dots.

"Yes, yes, okay. That makes sense. I was coming down from Duffey Lake and ended up in the ditch."

I took a minute to process the options going forward, something that would have taken a minute at the best of times, and I'm sure I was mumbling under my breath as I replayed recent events to try and get them straight. I probably didn't sound completely sane, because nothing in my head would travel in a direct line and only parts of sentences were being vocalized.

"Say," I finally said through my mental haze, "do you think you could drop me at a hospital? My head's not right and I'm not sure I can make it on my own."

I also waved vaguely at my gear, as if it was a clear explanation of everything, but it seemed to be enough.

"Sure," the guy said, "there's a clinic in Pemberton. Toss your stuff in the back."

"Thanks," I said, greatly relieved he didn't make fun of

my foolishness. As if crashing my bike was a direct indicator of my worth as a human being.

In the end, all was well. I didn't make a lick of sense in the truck on the way to town, and the doctor added a concussion to the growing list of sports-related injuries in my medical file, but by morning my head was clear enough to continue, and the local bike shop went above and beyond to make sure my equipment was also ready to go. I pedalled the short distance to Whistler cautiously and then navigated the old Sea to Sky Highway all the way to Vancouver without incident.

This time, as I make my way around Grotto Mountain east of Canmore, the unexpected interruption of a speedy downhill is far less dramatic. After wrestling the bike to the shoulder and affecting the appropriate repairs, I'm back on the road, and about 45 minutes after leaving Canmore I pull into the hamlet of Exshaw before stopping at the Heart Mountain convenience store.

I must admit I have a soft spot for little places like the Heart Mountain store. They have "character" as opposed to "style," they have junk food and they have interesting people passing through. What is most compelling about these kinds of shops is that they remain in the spirit of the small independent corner store – or general store, as it was known in the days before franchises began dominating the retail landscape. I've noticed this is becoming something of a rare breed in North America, but those that remain are places for browsing and marvelling at unusual combinations of products and services. Some are even hanging on to the idea of being a meeting place.

Many of the mom-and-pop shops of old were community centres in addition to places of commerce – a stark contrast to today's big boxes, built on vast wastelands of pavement, designed to move deeply discounted and/or grossly marked up luxury goods. One is an experience of sights and sounds and smells, and the other is a sterile transaction, in my humble opinion. What is that annoying tag line again? "Save money, live better"? I'm always amused by the insinuation that saving money is the deciding factor in a happy life. And all this time I've been wasting my energy caring about people and ideas, misguided soul that I am.

At any rate, I'm not sure I'd enjoy working here at Heart Mountain every day, but it's still a great place to people-watch if you happen to be in the neighbourhood. Even before they reach the door, you can almost pick out which customers are going to be demanding, polite or troublesome, and it's a pleasant experience to just sit outside for a while, taking it all in. As I relax into it, the warm Indian-summer sun shines with muted intensity, the high, wispy clouds drift by in a pleasant lazy fashion, and I notice that from here, Heart Mountain (the mountain) looks very much like a Valentine's Day rendition of a heart near its peak. After a while, I step inside to purchase two "mountain size" Kokanee cans, a small bag of cashews and a crappy prepackaged sandwich for dinner. The purchase stretches the absolute upper limits of my already strained packing system. I'm forced to jam the beers into the spare shoes dangling off the pile on top of the rear rack, and only hope I remember to rinse off the cans before putting the aluminum to my thirsty lips later this evening.

Another 20 or 30 minutes will get me to Bow Valley Provincial Park campground, where I plan to spend the night, and I find I'm anxious to get going now. I've had an encouraging tailwind and have spent the comfortable afternoon in shorts and shirtsleeves. Most of the stress that has been accumulating this summer is gone for the moment, and I'm curious about what I'm going to see in the coming weeks. I find I'm feeling a measure of cautious hope as well. Although it doesn't look like it yet, winter is coming, and with it snow and cold. Maybe the bad weather will show up next week, or maybe it will hold off at the lower elevations until the middle of next month, but it is coming. It's impossible to know how far I'll be able to go before the weather turns, but I feel like it will be an interesting adventure as I make my way to finding out, so I pedal off not so much in a specific direction but toward a place in time I have no control of.

Near the junction of Highway 1A and Highway 1X, I slip from the shadow of the mountains and am now staring at the edge of the foothills as they roll and gently fade away onto the prairie. This is the only real horizon anywhere close to where I live. I suppose I could just keep the wheels pointed east and would be home at my parents' home in Morin-Heights, Quebec, in about a month, if I really pushed it. A difficult trip, but doable, although in order to make the distance I'd have to dump about three-quarters of the junk I'm hauling around. The wind kicks up, as if encouraging me to give it a try, but I realize that suffering and ambition of this kind will have to wait until next time. I am gently reminded, however, that there is something compelling and inspiring about wide open spaces, and it can be easy to forget that these kinds of big spaces and persuasive journeys are here, and there, and everywhere, really. It also dawns on me that I'm now officially back out in the wider world, and I can't help but wonder what took so long.

● ● ●

It is said that he who ignores history is bound to repeat its mistakes, and there certainly are plenty of difficult moments from the past that had uncertain outcomes but predictable consequences. The Great Depression comes to mind because it is followed over the decades by any number of depressions, recessions and "market corrections" that have caused untold hardship and stress. I only mention it because I'm not sure I'd even be out here if my steady and well-paying job didn't make me nuts, but the economy, though volatile and unpredictable, appears to be the number one measure not only of an individual's place in society but of society itself. Just because I'm not savvy in the ways of the dollar doesn't mean money shouldn't be our most trusted appraisal of how things are going, but I do have my doubts about how well it evaluates "quality of life." And when the economic bubble bursts again, will we have the right to act surprised?

Cautionary tales aside, ignoring history also means missing the opportunity to be moved and inspired by those who have gone before. Prior to relocating to Alberta, I had an idealized and somewhat naive view of the mountain West. I saw it as an escape to simplicity in an uncrowded, wide open environment where people kind of did their own thing at their own pace. I probably watched too many Westerns on TV as a kid, but in my mind's eye I saw the Eastern Slopes of the Rockies as a rough-and-tumble kind of a place, where a man could challenge his wits and endurance in a vast natural setting. In Alberta and Montana, a man could fall in love with being out of doors, and inspiration and beauty meant more than careers and possessions.

Lately, however, I've been feeling a bit hoodwinked, as even my anonymous little town appears to be turning into nothing more than another outpost of commercialism and growth. Being unable to articulate why I came here to begin with, or express what I really believe is going to happen if we continue forward unchecked, has kind of poisoned my soul. I spend too many of my days waiting for the other shoe to drop, and that's not healthy. Yet accepting everything that's going on around here as normal and inevitable feels too much like giving up and giving in. As a college-educated white male with a good job and the appropriate amount of personal debt, I may be complicit in the system, but I do not believe in it. It is not a path that soothes the soul.

The Reverend Doctor Chief John Snow, an accomplished leader from the local Stoney Nakoda First Nation, cuts through the mire swirling around my mind in a few simple sentences:

> These mountains are our sacred places. They are
> our temples, our sanctuaries, and our resting places.
> They are places of hope, a place of vision, a place
> of refuge, a very special and holy place where the
> Great Spirit speaks with us.

Hallelujah! Snow was a controversial character around here, no question, and like so many political leaders was accused of using his power and influence for personal gain, but I believe that the spirit and power of those words still resonates, even if they were too carefully chosen to serve his own needs when he spoke them. Chief John Snow lived most of his life on the Stoney Nakoda reserve just to the east of here and passed away in 2006.

After negotiating the obnoxiously long access road leading to the actual tent sites at Bow Valley Provincial

Park – and getting stuck in a crappy hookup site in an open area away from the water because of all the car campers taking advantage of the last long weekend of the season – I shed my gear, set up my tent, eat my sandwich and wander down to the river with my beers to watch the sunset. The campground is full but not as noisy as you would expect. The season is winding down and everyone appears content to let it go quietly. If it was the May long weekend, there would be pickup trucks and beer coolers and portable stereos going full blast. As it stands, it's couples and families and campfires, and that suits me just fine.

Along the river, there's a nice walking path that runs the length of the campground, and at odd intervals a cut in the bank drops down to the water's edge. I pick one at random and find a suitable log for wasting away the final two hours of the day. The Bow is about 40 metres wide at this point and drifts by at a sedate yet powerful pace. Yamnuska is there, directly across the river from my perch, and with my telephoto lens I imagine I can pick out a few of the climbing routes up the famous crag, but can't be entirely sure. At odd intervals, trucks rumble by on their way to or from the Graymont and Lafarge plants along the 1A on the far bank, filling the air with the heavy drone of rubber on pavement, but the sound dissipates quickly into the surrounding forest. Every once in a while, somebody walking a dog passes by on the path behind me, and just before the sun drops behind the mountains to the west, a pair of kayakers drifts by and stops chatting just long enough to wave. I wave back.

In the stillness after the kayakers' voices follow them down the river, I listen for a continuation to the lessons hinted at earlier in the ride today. A successful trip will not be x number of miles covered or y amount of peaks bagged, but success could be defined by days filled with challenge and effort, followed by evenings of relaxation and reflection. Lately I've been noticing that I don't even know what it looks like to live in that kind of calm or exist with that kind of certainty of purpose. To just be and do is as foreign to my psyche at the moment as German or Japanese or Mandarin would surely be to my ears. But I know that some of the answers on how to achieve a level of peace and purpose are out here, and even though it's going to be an awkward search, I will find them. I realize I can't go back empty-handed. I won't go back empty-handed.

In Sid Marty's book *Switchbacks*, about his life in the Rockies, he captures the essence of this feeling quite eloquently at the end of the first chapter. In that final paragraph, he's looking back at a younger, more innocent and perhaps naive version of himself: one who, in a fit of youthful exuberance, is determined to "climb that peak at the end of the valley," and who thinks that "if you could do that, you would learn something about life and about yourself that could be found no other way." I'm not young, innocent or naive anymore, and I'm not a climber either, but I understand. I've experienced the same certainty and sense of accomplishment in my own visions and in the subsequent efforts designed to make those singular dreams come true. The point, I think, is not to achieve the goal but to undertake the effort that is most a reflection of you. The rest will take care of itself.

Tim Cahill, in "Professor Cahill's Travel 101," explains that in all adventures there needs to be a quest, a reason to step into the unknown, and that these days we all get to be the protagonists in our own mythologies. The trick is simply to figure what your quest is and then go. I guess mine is to retrieve the feeling Marty talks about in *Switchbacks*, and I want to retrieve it because it belongs to me. Maybe if I'd been a little wiser in my life choices along the way, I never would have got so lost, but I can't change where I'm at any more than I can change what I want. My rational mind still resists this idea of wandering somewhat aimlessly through these mountains, but instinctively I know for sure that I've got to do something worth believing in, even if it appears at first glance to be pointless or irrational. It might be that I have to do it *because* it's pointless and irrational. Maybe I need to do it because my life needs some life.

So, as brown trout and mountain whitefish surface to strike at caddis fly larvae and insects unlucky enough to fall in the river, I realize that a driven man overcomes all obstacles, a smart man avoids the obstacles in his path, and a desperate man does the best he can.

6.

KANANASKIS COUNTRY

Spent some time feeling inferior, standing in front of my mirror
Comb my hair in a thousand ways, but I came out looking just
the same.

—Rod Stewart, Ron Wood

The Front Ranges of the Rocky Mountains are an incredibly dramatic physical feature, and there are few spots where the striking transition from foothills to mountain range is more evident than the Morley Flats. Even after passing hundreds of times through the gateway cut by the flow of the Bow River, I'm still awed by the view from along this stretch of highway. I'm not talking about my little part of the valley anymore. Technically, yes, all the mountains I can see from Canmore are part of the Front Ranges, but I live there, and since it appears to be human nature to take our immediate surroundings for granted, I have often looked around and – I'm now embarrassed to admit – muttered, "Yeah it's beautiful, but so what?"

Out here, however, I'm fortunate to be a little less blasé.

Moving out onto the flats created by the modest flood plain, I rip off ten kilometres rather easily, thanks in part to a continuation of yesterday afternoon's building tailwind. I did have to retrace my steps along the winding access road to get out of the campsite, and that made it hard to settle into a rhythm, but once I was on the main artery the wind practically blew me forward. Soon I will be abandoning

Highway 1 eastbound in favour of Highway 40 south and will have to climb slowly back into the mountains, where the easy miles will undoubtedly end. And as predicted, the minute I begin to move south, the wind slams into me from the side and confirms that the next little section is not going to be a pleasant Sunday morning pedal. I drop from a smooth and steady 30 kilometres per hour to about 15 in the time it takes to turn right 45 degrees.

On a trip of any significant distance, there will always be some fun, easy miles, and exceptionally hard miles are also to be expected if the plan is to ride up the spine of a mountain chain, but I find the annoying filler miles like these to be the most difficult of all. They're not enough of a challenge to get the adrenaline flowing, which at least helps in the effort, and too few of them accumulate early on to allow you to pound out a few dozen more without noticing. Once the thrill wears off of finally being away, nearly everything is an effort, at first. Filler miles are simply an inevitable feature of getting from where you are to where the real action is, and there often appears to be no obvious purpose beyond the mindless, awkward grind. A week to ten days is a generally how long it takes to be truly immersed in a new adventure, even with the inspiring words of Cahill and Marty and Snow fresh in your mind.

I find roadside attractions to be the perfect antidote to these uninspired moments, and when it comes to good places to stop while riding a bike, privatized spots are the obvious option. They are inexplicably alluring, despite being tacky or flashy more often than not, but the downside is you're probably going to be charged admission if you want to see what all the fuss is about. Inevitably someone is going to catch you wandering around aimlessly, introduce themselves pleasantly enough and then try and sell you a ticket and a souvenir and a sandwich.

Points of interest and rest areas, on the other hand, are free and relatively common on most major and intermediate roadways in North America. In a car they aren't as compelling because they come and go too quickly – and don't have any neon signage to draw attention – but on a bike they provide a great excuse to stop and have a look around. I admit they may not always be as informative or interesting as you would expect, but someone went to the trouble and expense of creating a pullout, erecting signage and installing garbage cans, so the least I can do is try and appreciate them. And let's face it, when the miles are not rolling by at a comfortable pace, any excuse for a break will do. So I coast to a stop just down the road from the recently completed Stoney Nakoda Resort & Casino, curse the infernal wind and prop my bike against the improbably sturdy information board that suggests that if I'd been unfortunate enough to rest here 20,000 years ago, I'd have been pinned beneath close to 2,000 feet of solid ice.

The Wisconsin Glacial Episode was the last major advance of ice associated with the North American Laurentide ice sheet. According to the eggheads, this particular glaciation was made of three glacial maxima, often mistakenly called ice ages, and these were separated by interglacial warm periods. The Tioga was the last and least severe glacial maximum of the Wisconsin Episode and began about 30,000 years ago, ending roughly 10,000 years ago, when the first native North Americans began hunting here for mammoth and mastodon and beavers the size of bears. The entire episode had a profound effect on the geography the region. Poking my head around the edge of the sign into the teeth of the wind, I can imagine an immense river of ice pouring down out of the Bow Valley at two or three feet a day, carving away rock and sharpening the profile of many of the peaks. Before the Wisconsin, the Rockies were more like high, rounded domes – though, looking at them now, that's hard to imagine.

Come to think of it, from a distance these Front Ranges don't seem plausible at all. They just erupt out of the ground in what appears to be a random location, along a straight line drawn in the dirt where God said, "Right, how about some mountains here." The foothills do roll right up to the edge of the formation, but in my mind's eye, before I had ever actually seen the Rockies, I imagined that the lowest of the snow covered peaks would flow seamlessly out of the highest of the hills. Looking east from around this area does give that general impression, but from a distance of more than 50 kilometres, looking west, the peaks are sharp and abrupt. Not necessarily massive, because they are so far away, but very obviously different from the surrounding countryside.

The other thing I slowly began to notice about the Front Ranges after I first moved to Calgary was how atmospheric conditions dramatically altered their appearance. When I first settled in the northeastern part of the city, I had to commute on the C-Train every day to get to my job downtown. I was staying with friends of my family, and the trip was a necessary evil endured for a few months until I could get a place of my own in the downtown core. It was a pretty typical commute, I suppose. The train was often crowded, and a lot of immigrants lived up in that neighbourhood, so it was a virtual melting pot of cultures. Having grown up with Montreal's cosmopolitan, almost European undertones, I quite enjoyed that aspect: the strange languages being spoken, the unusual dress, the working class ethos carved into many of the faces.

Of course, those strange folks who are an inevitable fixture on public transit were present too. People who talk to themselves, people who make everyone else vaguely uncomfortable with their wild eyes and sudden outbursts – but that was all part of living in a city, and I tried to take the fringe behaviour in stride. Admittedly there were also too many teenagers with the backs of their pants hanging way too low for my taste, but what can you do? We were all young and stylistically challenged once. I was fortunate to be working in the service industry, and as soon as I graduated from the less lucrative day shift, I often rode in non-peak hours, when it was much less crowded. But what passes for exotic in the conservative West slowly began to lose its charm, and I ended up feeling like just another schmuck, riding along with everyone else to a day that was virtually identical to yesterday. And so I daydreamed.

The most interesting part – by far – of my C-Train ride downtown was always the right-hand bend coming into Max Bell Station. The tunnel after Franklin Station would deposit the train near the top of a hill that afforded a stunning view of the city, with the Saddledome and the venerable Stampede Grounds – home to the greatest outdoor show on earth – leading the eye smoothly to the Calgary Tower and a growing number of skyscrapers stretching east to west along the corridor between the Bow River and Ninth Avenue. Highway 2 (or the Deerfoot 500, as it is affectionately referred to by locals) was perpetually rushing by in the foreground, and the Rocky Mountains provided a sturdy backdrop, about 70 kilometres distant to the northwest. I realize there are country folk and there are city folk and not everybody should be expected to share the same passion and interest in wilderness, but to me the view was always entrancing, enthralling, compelling and beautiful, and not because of the cityscape below.

As time went by, I began to notice a strange phenomenon as I made my way to work. I would look forward to the view even as I began to dread my daily destination, and was intrigued to find the mountains never appeared to be the same distance away two days in a row, or even twice in the same month. On days with heavy cloud, they didn't appear to exist at all, of course, obscured as they were by rain or snow, but I still found that I missed seeing them. When the weather was warm and hazy, the mountains appeared to be very far away, aloof in their distance, and when it was windy and dry and dusty, the experience was much the same.

When it was clear and cool, however, the range advanced like an approaching army, and on cold winter mornings it appeared to be standing just beyond the city limits – until the temperature dropped those extra few degrees and ice crystals formed in the atmosphere, pushing the mountains back to a ghostly middle distance. It was an ever-changing marvel that always had me questioning my perceptions. I know it's physically impossible to move a mountain chain (at least without a very big shovel), but I wasn't about to start arguing with my senses in public. Enough weirdos were already riding around aimlessly on the C-Train without me joining the ranks.

My very favourite view of the Front Ranges, however, is quite a bit closer to Canmore, on the long, sweeping downhill after Scott Lake Hill, in the general area where the legendary explorer and mapmaker David Thompson described his first encounter with these mountains back in 1787:

The Rocky Mountains came in sight like shining white clouds on the horizon. As we proceeded, they rose in height; their immense masses of snow appeared above the clouds forming an impassable barrier, even to an eagle. About thirty miles from the mountains, we crossed the Bow River on gravel shoals near four feet in depth and two hundred yards wide.

Born in 1770 in London, England, Thompson appeared destined for service in the navy but instead found himself an apprentice at the Hudson's Bay Company at just 14 years old. After a successful spell as a fur trader, Thompson defected to the rival North West Company in 1797, where his duties focused more on surveying and map-making. Over his career, Thompson mapped fully one-fifth of North America, covering 80,000 kilometres from Hudson Bay to the Pacific, mostly on foot, by dogsled and by canoe. His early years in the West were spent north of the Bow Valley Corridor, establishing fur trading routes through the Rockies at Howse and Athabasca passes, and later he explored the length of the Columbia River, from its headwaters all the way to the Pacific. Although he never did discover a pass from along the Bow River, he was in all likelihood the first European to enter the valley.

Thanks to the highway, a traveller headed west is not required to ford the river anymore, and after cresting the rounded peak of Scott Lake Hill – which is, in one of the those strange statistical anomalies that can barely be believed, higher than any other road pass on the Trans-Canada between Calgary and Vancouver – the road drops steeply and gathers speed before gradually veering left. There are tunnel-vision-type views of the mountains to the north, and a textbook foothills landscape dominates the foreground. Or what might be considered a textbook Hollywood-style foothills landscape, as scenes from *Legends of the Fall*, *Unforgiven* and *Dances with Wolves* were all filmed in the general area. Three-quarters of the way around the bend, you clear the trees and are suddenly faced with the seemingly impenetrable wall of mountains that now stands before me. It's a beautiful and soul-stirring sight in the way major transitions in landscape have a tendency to be, and the atmospheric interference works its shimmering magic from that advanced vantage point as well, pulling the mountains closer or shrinking them into the distance depending on the mood of the day. It is almost always splendid.

• • •

After the short break behind the information sign at the Morley Flats, I suddenly find I want to go, go, go, as if the next big glaciation was suddenly threatening. But it's difficult to keep any speed or momentum against the stiff crosswind and gradual incline of the road. I know it's my ego hammering on me as much as the actual conditions – I should be fitter, I should be better prepared, I should be 20 years younger and able to jump back into a high-energy existence without missing a beat – but even knowing that a radical change in lifestyle is going to take a little time to adjust to doesn't help me feel any better. I long to get past the physical discomfort of muscles unaccustomed to heavy use, and desperately need to move beyond the doubt surrounding a radical change in routine, but I'm stuck with this annoying pattern of fits and starts.

Clearly there is a transformation ahead that I'm not

ready to make, even as these first steps lead in that direction. My old self resists naturally thanks to the lack of physical preparation, but in time my body will adjust. The worry is that I continue to resist deeper down. Exasperation has pushed me to act, but a big part of me doesn't want to let go of my creature comforts, even though so many lie at the root of my everyday anxiety. Earlier this morning I had an experience that reveals just how precarious my moods have been of late. As I went through the new and somewhat awkward process of breaking camp, my tent decided to make a break for Saskatchewan on the strong westerly wind the minute I pulled up the pegs anchoring it to the earth. It's a bit aggravating, not to mention mildly ridiculous, to find yourself chasing your new home down the road even before you've finished breakfast, but at least I could find the humour in it. "Man pursues dwelling" is always good for a laugh, and after catching up to the wannabe parasail two tent sites over, I made a mental note to keep hold of the pesky bugger whenever the wind was up.

Fifteen minutes later, the tent was stowed, breakfast was finished and my panniers were packed and ready to go. Suddenly I felt good, and in an uncharacteristically proactive act, I abruptly got it in my head to top up the tires with air, feeling that if the bike was so helplessly overloaded, the least I could do was minimize rolling resistance. After encountering no problem on the front, I began to force a dozen or so blasts from the hand pump into the valve on the rear wheel, and after a brief pause decided to top it up with two or three more, which of course was a big mistake. Three seconds after detaching the pump, I heard a faint "pop," followed by the unmistakable hiss of air escaping a confined space. Less than five seconds later, the tire was flat. At first I couldn't believe I'd done something so stupid, and for a moment I just stared at my bike, as if it owed me an explanation. For a split second I even imagined it was excuse enough to abandon the whole trip and go home already. Then abruptly I sat down and began to cry.

Imagine it, a grown man sitting at a wooden picnic table, openly weeping, suddenly desperate to just turn around and go home. It did not bode well that I couldn't manage the stress of a flat tire, especially with the high probability of bigger challenges ahead, and now, as the wind batters without mercy from the right side, I feel useless, I feel slow and I feel vaguely lost, even though I could easily pinpoint my location on any map. Thankful for another bit of distraction, I stop again, just up the highway at the Barrier Lake Information Centre.

Folks are steaming in and out at a healthy clip, and the interior is well presented, with maps, guidebooks and posters championing the highlights of the area. After last night's close call at Bow Valley Provincial Park, where I was lucky enough to secure the second-to-last site in the entire place, I'm nervous about not getting a camping spot, even though it's Sunday, so I call Mount Kidd campground from the number I find in one of the handy brochures. I'm assured a spot but am also informed it will be $60 for two nights, payable by credit card at booking, thank you very much. Thirty bucks a night, for a meagre patch of uncomfortable gravel? Are you kidding? I can get a cheap motel room in Canmore in the off-season (complete with private bath and cable TV) for less than 50. I don't need a water hookup, or electricity, or even a washroom that I don't have to share with any number of strangers, but such is the state of "camping" these days that commercial campgrounds have expansive infrastructures to accommodate RVs and car campers. To the point where a simple tent platform, wooden picnic table and metal fire pit require a credit card reservation.

I almost feel as if I'm paying a subsidy that helps ownership resist the urge to pave the whole property over and install neat rows of hookups to better accommodate the air-conditioned and satellite-dish-equipped rolling mansions that are common around here in the summer months. The real kicker is that if I wanted to forgo the car camping experience and just pitch a tent any old place I pleased, I'd risk a fine for illegal camping in a protected area. Reluctantly, I read off the numbers from my card.

In an attempt to avoid getting unduly aggravated about this particular brand of roadside robbery, I endeavour to wander around the info centre a little bit more, and end up, quite by accident, picking up a handy bit of information about bears. One of the Alberta Parks employees on duty is talking to a group of tourists about Kananaskis Country. It's a fairly standard info centre lecture, and two other parks employees are standing at a discreet distance on each side, fielding specific questions from the assembled masses. A few of the people gathered are obviously experienced outdoor enthusiasts in search of practical information on bear sightings, fishing options or availability of backcountry campsites, but most of the crowd appear to be raw recruits to the outdoor scene, and I'm not feeling particularly generous or patient. In fact, I'm still so annoyed by the Mount Kidd phone call that I doubt I'll be able to do anything but find fault.

At the moment, nobody is asking anything ridiculous, but I am reminded of an incident from just the other day that exemplifies how diverse the knowledge base is when it comes to wildlife. I was walking in Canmore when I overheard a kid of about 13 say to his dad, "Wow, look at the size of that bird, he's enormous." It wasn't the words that caught my attention so much as the tone in his voice. This teenager was obviously a city boy and had that unique inflection laced with awe, excitement and wonder usually reserved for the osprey, owls and bald eagles that can be found in the Bow Valley at certain times of the year. Bird-of-prey and wildlife sightings are not unheard of where I live, and one night last year, walking home from work, I startled a small herd of elk not 50 feet from where this kid was now marvelling over a raven in the parking lot of the A&W.

Granted, the close cousins to the common crow that hang around many of the fast food joints in town are disturbingly large and not terribly shy. But anyone who's lived here for any amount of time has a story about stupid questions or asinine comments that reveal a whole segment of the general population with absolutely no regular contact with the natural world. Some of these people have obviously never even watched the Nature Channel. Not a character flaw, exactly, but perhaps a bit dangerous if you happen to be visiting an area where wild animals roam free without borders or fences.

Jocey worked for four summers in various jobs at a resort in Moraine Lake, near Lake Louise, and she has some pretty hilarious stories to tell about what tourists have said over the years. Most reflect on the body of water in question rather than wildlife, but "When do you take the ice off the lake?" "Does the lake go all the way around?" and "How long is an hour canoe rental?" are still amazing things to hear. The questions defy logic and common sense and can stop you in your tracks when you hear them first-hand. These bon mots were all jotted neatly in a notebook Jocey kept (and are scribbled on the wall in the canoe shed, I hear). Although they're funny at face value, I find the stories she tells to be scary as well. After all, many of the people who utter these gems have children who are most likely following in these footsteps of brilliance (if I had a nickel for every time I hear "children are the future"). These Mensa candidates also probably operated a motor vehicle in order to get to the lake – a solid ton of glass and steel driven by someone who doesn't know that an hour is 60 minutes or that ice melts. Our collective gene pool may be getting broader every day, but it doesn't appear to be getting much deeper.

Were these kinds of incidents unique – or even rare – that would be one thing, but the frequency with which these observations get verbalized makes you wonder about general IQ levels. Part of me just assumes that with the continued growth and education of a culture comes a certain amount of accumulated knowledge, and that with experience and opportunity, a general level of understanding about the world develops among the populace. Under this theory, my generation should be the wisest and most educated group of humans ever to exist. My friends, who appear to be stumbling over themselves to reproduce, should be contributing to a group of advanced humans that raises the bar to higher levels than my parents and their parents would ever have dared to imagine.

Not so, it seems, at least as accumulated knowledge relates to the great outdoors. Michael Kerr has gone to the trouble of gathering up some of the more startling examples of intellectual progress gone awry in *When Do You Let the Animals Out?*, his collection of all things ridiculous that go on in the Canadian Rockies. In addition to the brain teaser from the title, Kerr has compiled some of the best – or worst, depending on your mood and point of view – questions and stories gathered from locals, parks employees and other service staff over the years. And yes, foreign visitor with your hard currency, a lot of the time we are laughing at you and not with you. The almighty tourist dollar may be a good thing for the local economy, but the secret no one is letting you in on is that actual tourists often get in the way of the scenery and can be painfully dumb.

Here are some of my favourites from Kerr's book, with appropriate answers added by yours truly: "At what elevation does an elk become a moose?" *Different species, elevation not applicable. Sort of like asking at what age a baby chimpanzee becomes a human being with a valid passport.* "What kinds of monkeys are found in this park?" *Just the ones whose ancestors didn't make that crucial leap hundreds of thousand years ago.* And finally: "How many people are eaten by grizzlies a year?" *Not nearly enough.* Of course I don't mean that last one, but if the question is rephrased as how many *tourists* are eaten by grizzlies every year, well then, it would be a scenario worth pondering.

To be fair, these lovely folks crowded in front of me may be just a little too clean and pressed and shiny for my liking, and a few might even drift toward the naive end of the intelligence scale, but deep down I wish them no real harm. Besides, the information being given at the moment is good, and I manage to park my I'm-a-local-and-have-slept-outside-on-the-ground-recently-and-you're-just-a-weekend-warrior brand of snobbery long enough to absorb what's being said. It seems the bears are eating like mad in preparation for hibernation and not really paying attention to anything else. As a result, normal caution is advised, especially in areas where ripe buffalo berries are prevalent, but there don't appear to be any troublesome animals in the direction I'm headed. Which I do admit is comforting to hear.

Back outside, I'm snacking on some trail mix and find my energy is slowly coming back after the erratic beginning to the day. I'm not in a race, and this little adventure will unfold at its own pace, no matter how hard I fight to impose my will on events – if I can manage to get out of the way and accept that, I just might enjoy the experience. But I am stubborn, and I expect it will be a few days before the idea really begins to sink in. As I pack up my snacks, notebook and credit card, a couple stops on their way into the info centre to look at my bike. They're a handsome pair, middle-aged and fit, and are the only people to give me a second glance in the ten minutes it's taken to rearrange my gear.

"Is that a touring bike?" the man asks, taking a sudden detour from the doors.

"Sure is," I reply with a little more enthusiasm than I actually feel.

"Don't see many of them anymore. Most people tour on hybrid mountain bikes these days," he says.

I'm simultaneously surprised and impressed that anyone would even notice what kind of bike I'm riding, and as the man's wife joins him for a quick look, we all stand with arms crossed and nod appreciatively at the subtle sophistication of my ride, which apparently is becoming something of a rarity.

"I didn't know Garneau even made a touring bike," the woman adds, reinforcing the point.

"Me neither. But there it was in the window of my local bike shop, and I couldn't resist." What I fail to mention is I always thought of Louis Garneau as more of a sports clothing manufacturer, as opposed to a bike maker of any kind. I just stumbled onto the thing, to be honest.

"Where you headed?" the man asks.

"Right now I'm on my way to Kananaskis Lakes. Then I plan to loop around on Spray Lakes Road back to Canmore. After that, weather permitting, on to Jasper."

The man quickly does the math, imagines the route and takes one last long look at the rolling pile of gear in front of him before wishing me well.

"Good luck to you, then. It sounds like fun."

Yeah, right, fun, I think to myself. That's exactly what I've been having all morning, fun. Self-loathing and crippling doubt always make for a party.

"Thanks," I manage to say.

In a flash of self-awareness, I realize I'm still desperate for conversation and reassurance after the first 24 hours of my self-imposed exile, and I nearly blurt out the idea that Jasper, Alberta, might as well be Jasper, End of the Known Universe, for how I'm feeling about actually making it that far, but the couple are already moving toward the doors. It's often easy to pick out a fellow bicycling nut of the long-distance variety, even if you don't talk bikes or routes or anything else related to cycle touring, and I suspect this couple has undertaken an extended trip or two in their day. They've done me a favour by taking an interest in my trip, and I don't want to ruin the moment by coming across as needy or unsure. British alpinist Christian Bonington once said, "The true adventurer is one who escapes the treadmill of the obvious," and it is decidedly uncool to break out on your own and then promptly ask someone if they can call your mommy, bring you your childhood blankie or stay and chat for just a few minutes more because you're terrified you've bitten off more than you can chew.

I may not be the picture of fitness or confidence or motivation at the moment, but I must remind myself that even wobbling along and cursing an unrelenting cross-breeze beats the shit right out of going to work, and I remain amazed at how often these kinds of inspirational people turn up just when you're feeling doubtful about pedalling off into the distance. These little chats help make you feel like you're not crazy, because other people do this too. Not a lot of other people, but they are out there. I once bumped into a man of 72, somewhere in the middle of Saskatchewan, pedalling his way west as I made my way east. Turned out his wife of over 40 years had died, and he couldn't think of anything better to do with his time and so decided to bike across the country. How great is that? Imagine taking on an adventure into the unknown at the spritely young age of 72, with the whole of Canada available to be explored, no less. Given the right motivation and an industrial-sized dose of Geritol, something like that could turn out to be the trip of a lifetime.

Granted, it's a tremendous undertaking at any age, but it certainly sounds more interesting than playing shuffle-board in Florida or watching endless hours of daytime television in some assisted-living facility. The old bugger was out there doing it, living life. I was duly impressed and am newly inspired. Instead of clinging onto the nice couple who have unknowingly given me so much, I slap on my helmet the minute the info doors swing shut, tuck my feet into my toe clips and get on with it without another word.

• • •

After I take leave of my fast friends, mid-morning turns out to be a lot better than the shaky start to the day ever would have indicated. Mentally, I've stabilized once again, and the weather appears to be calming down as well. The wind has died off and the temperature is creeping into the high teens. I make a point of stopping to snap some pictures and take notes whenever the mood hits me, even though breaking stride feels awkward to my more goal-oriented self, and the road is now also peppered with a handful of other cyclists out enjoying the weather.

These fellow riders are of the speedy variety, however, with outrageously expensive bikes executing well-planned training runs between strategically parked vehicles, and again I feel like a bit of a fraud as they approach from the opposite direction at what appears to be an impossible pace. It's true we are on different missions and don't really have much in common beyond our choice in transportation, but compared to these well-trained athletes I'm completely out of place. I might as well be riding a donkey as I lumber along, which should actually come as no surprise whatsoever, given my limited physical gifts.

Once, while doing research for a story that appeared in a now defunct local online magazine, I participated in a virtual bike race at one of the Canmore gyms. Winter and spring spin classes were all the rage at the time, and I fancied myself something of an all-around athlete, so I agreed to do the assignment even though I hadn't been on a bike for quite a long while. I showed up at the appointed time, full of poise and confidence; had a few pictures taken on a borrowed bike attached to the appropriate technical equipment; and then preceded to get my ass kicked. Granted, I didn't expect to *win* the virtual race set out for us on a projection screen across the room. But I had once ridden 5000 kilometres across Canada during a summer vacation – the distance between Kingston, Ontario, and Vancouver, British Columbia – so I did at least expect to keep up. But there is clearly a difference between a long-distance touring cyclist and a bike racer, and the two guys I was riding with were fast. In fact they were very fast.

Once the CompuTrainer program started and we began spinning our wheels, it didn't take long to recognize my folly. It was only a matter of minutes before I was sweating buckets just trying to keep up, and certain aspects of the course were actually painful – notably the simulated hills, where the computer instructed the apparatus to increase resistance to the pedals as gravity would in the real world. The whole thing was embarrassing and demoralizing, and worst of all, the program was set up so that all racers had to finish before the results could be properly tabulated. If one racer quit before the end of the course, all the results would be lost, not just those belonging to the abandoning cyclist. The other two riders, who had just taught me a lesson about playing with the big boys, graciously sat on their bikes and waited for me to limp along to the finish line, 15 minutes behind the winner.

My ego properly chastened, I did come away from the experience with some interesting information about my physiology. Amid all the complicated squiggles and spikes for each individual measurement, there was one constant in my case, and that was cadence. No matter the situation on the screen or how my fellow riders were performing according to benchmarks measured in watts, RPMs and left/right power splits, I was only able to compare to those trained athletes when cadence was the measure. It appears that I can push the pedals consistently and repetitively over any landscape in any conditions, but that is the extent

of my skills as a cyclist. I was never going to outrace anybody in that room, at any distance, over any terrain, but I
can still plod with the best of them.

So on this fine sunny morning I am tortoise among
hares, and in an act of good faith I offer up the obligatory courtesy wave every time a real cyclist zips past, even
though I feel more inspired to flip 'em the bird, the fit
bastards. Just off to my left, traffic remains steady and
distracting.

• • •

In the early 1800s, European explorers sought out the high
passes across the Rocky Mountains in support of the fur
trade, and many of these trails had already been established by Kootenay, Snake, Blackfoot and Stoney Indians
as hunting and trading routes. A growing concern over the
fate of the Oregon territories, however, shifted the focus
south to what is now Kananaskis Country, as the government hoped to strengthen its claims on the lands west of
the Continental Divide.

James Sinclair was the first to pioneer a new route in
Kananaskis Country. Sinclair was actually Métis (a mix of
European and Native bloodlines), and the year was 1841,
but the approach he took was through the Spray Valley,
just west of Canmore, and the pass they crossed is now
known as White Man Pass. It wasn't until 1854 – when
Sinclair returned with a trusted guide, the Cree chief
Maskepetoon and a second group of emigrants – that
the Kananaskis Valley was first explored as a viable way
to travel through the mountains. For that second group,
the going was uncommonly difficult, and the journey
from Old Bow Fort (also known as Peigan Post), east of
the confluence of the Bow and Kananaskis rivers to what

is now North Kananaskis Pass, took 30 gruelling days, whereas the White Man Pass trip took no more than ten.

By the time the Palliser Expedition of 1857 to 1860 descended on the southern Rockies, the focus of exploration had shifted once again, this time to finding a suitable route through the mountains for a railway line designed to unite Canada from coast to coast. The success of such an endeavour would further weaken any US claim to what is now British Columbia. Led by 42-year-old Irishman Captain John Palliser, the expedition was sent by the British government and the Royal Geographical Society to give a detailed account of all the lands north of the 49th parallel, up to the North Saskatchewan River and all the way from Lake Superior to the Rocky Mountains, and then to investigate possible routes across that rather formidable barrier.

Along the way, they were also expected to record details on climate, geography, geology, flora and fauna, as well as to explore the potential for agriculture. In support of those goals, Palliser had guide and interpreter Peter Erasmus, doctor and geologist James Hector, botanist Eugène Bourgeau, surveyor Thomas Blakiston and astronomer and secretary John William Sullivan at his disposal. In August 1858, Palliser left Old Bow Fort and entered this valley on his way to a pass he named in honour of a local Aboriginal man who was reputed to have survived a blow to the head with an axe near what is now known as Boundary Flats. Eventually, two passes, two lakes, the river and the valley all took on the name Kananaskis.

Following in Palliser's footsteps, it's easy to imagine his teams' wonder at moving deeper into these mountains. Despite the inherently slow nature of this type of travel, you are quickly absorbed, and the individual peaks gain a stature that was only hinted at from out on the flats adjacent to the Bow River. It is an experience that stimulates the senses and stirs the emotions, to the point where you almost feel like an early pioneer, plunging headlong into your own personal unknown. If you can manage not to be distracted by all the cars, that is.

Of all the things you notice after forsaking modern comfort and convenience for a while, I find vehicular volume to be the most obvious disturbance at first. TV and home telephones drift from consciousness remarkably quickly, and I know iPhone lovers will find this hard to believe, but cell phones are not especially missed either – it's a joy not be a constant slave to the ring tone. But not having the latest device seems to make you something of a Luddite these days. I had a cell phone once, for about three months, but the damn thing just kept ringing, and I couldn't come to terms with being that wired in, so I got rid of it. I don't know how people do it, to be honest, and I remain endlessly amazed that they pay for the privilege. But to each his own, I guess.

It has also been my experience that sleeping outside is not so bad in the short term, once you get used to it – as long as it's not constantly raining, of course, and your tent doesn't decide to make an impromptu break for the Saskatchewan border. But people seem to drive everywhere these days, and travel of any sort in North America is practically impossible without bumping into the internal combustion engine. Bryson claims, in *A Walk in the Woods*, that the average distance an American walks these days is 1.4 miles, *in a week*. I don't know how well Canadians would do in a comparable study, but even if you opt to go without, a vehicle will undoubtedly rip past you at some point in your travels, often at a terrifying pace.

Cars are inescapable, and with compressed schedules and appointment-oriented lives, most people even drive to commune with nature or to go exercise, it seems – but this is not a current development, by any means.

Over the course of the last century, the human race has developed an unshakable love affair with the car. "Obsession" might be a more accurate descriptor, but there is no denying that Henry Ford's introduction of the Model T in 1908 set in motion a string of events that forever altered how we travel between various destinations, and indeed how we perceive both time and distance. For the early settlers and explorers, just getting to the edge of these mountains was an arduous task. At the end of the 19th century, it took days to travel from Calgary's western edge, instead of the hour it takes today. If the plan was to head south through Kananaskis, along my intended route, you'd need about another week to navigate the labyrinth of mountains and valleys on the path toward the Continental Divide. It wasn't just the rough track that made for slow going; snags, deadfall, high water and landslides all played a part. You really did have to *want* to get somewhere back then.

On a bike in the 21st century, the trip is a bit easier and certainly faster, but it still requires a commitment of time and effort that doesn't fit modern day life. A cyclist on a casual tour can comfortably average 50 to 60 kilometres in a day, and 100 klicks a day averaged over a week will cover a lot of ground, but the effort still needs an available block of time and that same force of will exhibited by the early travellers who went on foot and by horseback. Compared to these now archaic means of transportation, a car is almost instantaneous. When the first motor carriages came onto the scene, the idea was to introduce ease, comfort and affordability to a rapidly modernizing North American and European lifestyle, though I find it difficult to imagine that this goal has been accomplished as advertised.

In the August 13, 1898, edition of *Scientific American*, the Winton Motor Carriage Company of Cleveland, Ohio, flogged their early vehicle in the following manner: "Dispense with a horse, and save the care and anxiety of keeping it." The company's new horseless carriage was said to travel at speeds between 3 and 20 miles per hour and cost $1,000, or roughly $28,000 in adjusted dollars. The claim at the time was that a motor carriage required about half a cent a mile to operate and maintain, and presumably a garage didn't smell as bad as a stable. The numbers may have changed since 1898, but the relative difference in cost in adjusted dollars is negligible. The underlying message remains the same: a car makes life better.

There are an estimated 275 million passenger vehicles out on the road in Canada and the United States, which theoretically translates into a lot of comfort, ease and affordability. Or does it? We now spend more time than ever using our cars for relatively short trips. In fact, the average Canadian spends an entire month out of every year commuting to and from work, according to an article written by Andrew Coyne in the January 17, 2011, issue of *Maclean's* magazine. Because a vehicle also requires a tremendous investment in time and money just to keep on the road, the average North American now also spends eight weeks a year working to pay for their cars, a stat cited in Colin Beavan's book *No Impact Man*, about trying to live for a year in New York City without harming the environment. Eight weeks of toil for the privilege of owning a conveyance whose primary purpose appears to be facilitating another four weeks of transporting the user back and forth from home to that place of toil.

In the sober light of day, these numbers are nothing short of insane, and they don't even include trips to the grocery store, to kids' soccer/karate/choir practice, or even the occasional day trip to the country – uses that I assume were among the original motivations for owning a private vehicle in the first place. But to drive is an inalienable right in our culture, a habit of convenience that few can seriously imagine living without, at any cost. And nowhere does this strange obsession appear more overwhelming than when you travel in the country by foot or on a bicycle as car after car whistles past. While I certainly appreciate these smooth and well-kept roadways that have sprung up to accommodate and encourage vehicular demand, when the sheer volume of traffic on a secondary highway reaches the level expected of a major artery in a city suburb, it does tend to take away from the experience of actually being outside.

When a disproportionate number of said vehicles on that secondary mountain road are Corvettes, Ferraris and Hummers – and a common raven in the parking lot of a fast food restaurant is cause for wonder – then it may be time to entertain the idea that we may have lost our way just a little bit, don't you think?

Fortunately, the mountains seem to be ejecting vehicles of all makes and models as the afternoon crowds begin to head back home, and by the time I roll up to the sign for the Mount Kidd campground, the flood of traffic has diminished to a mere trickle.

• • •

It's now scorching hot out – 23 degrees Celsius being scorching hot for this elevation at this time of year – and the campground is largely deserted, even though the sign at the entrance still said "campground full" when I pulled in. It turns out the sign just hadn't been changed yet. I check in at the office and am given a paper map highlighted with a green marker showing me the directions to my home for the evening: a cozy, heavily treed spot with just enough space cleared for a tent, picnic table, fire pit and vehicle.

It's surrounded by other campsites, but the tree cover is dense enough to allow privacy. Still, I'm hoping that the five or six empty sites in the immediate vicinity stay that way. The area meant for the tent is rock hard. Even though it's firmly in the protection of the trees and it would take a hurricane to cause much wind disturbance here, I make a mental note to find a suitable stone and pound my pegs in deep. Even with that extra effort, set-up has already been cut down to about half the time it took yesterday. Overall, Mount Kidd is the best you can hope for in a public drive-up campsite. It's clean, well laid out and, at the moment, not too busy.

I feel remarkably chipper as I head off to complete the registration process. The front desk and reception at Mount Kidd turns out to be an interesting mishmash of amenities. Right inside the door are racks selling postcards and knick-knacks beside an out-of-order ATM, and to the right is the general store. Directly to the left, tucked in a little alcove, is the campground registration office. In what would otherwise be the main lobby, they have erected a small snack-bar-style café, with a '70s-brown Formica countertop and '70s-brown faux-leather swivel stools, with seating for ten. I call it "'70s-brown" because

I spent my formative years trapped in that interesting decade, and I've never seen an interior done in that particular shade that didn't originate between 1970 and 1979. They certainly don't produce that colour anymore, as far as I know, and my particular stool has the added bonus of sounding remarkably like a small, agitated woodland creature every time I shift even an ounce of weight. There is no grill or other restaurant-style cooking equipment, but in high season it is possible to get popcorn, hot dogs and microwave burritos, along with soft-serve ice cream, fruit Slushies and all manner of prepackaged cookies and cakes.

Naturally, all but the coffee and the cakes (which last pretty much forever) are now shut up until spring, and that doesn't leave much for the poor guy behind the counter to do, so he's drinking coffee and trying to stay busy by organizing the merchandise in the café and general store. Everything is already tidy and orderly, so mostly he just looks bored. Occasionally, someone will wander in and buy a chocolate bar or a bottle of water, but for the most part concessions are doing less than brisk business. As I sit and observe the scene, I can't help but wonder what's going through his mind at the moment. I wonder if he's wondering, *How did I get stuck here, doing this?* I know that when I'm at work slinging drinks at the Rose & Crown, there's an inevitable burst of clarity at some point in every shift, where I stand still after a particularly chaotic or mindless collection of minutes and think, *What the fuck? This is my life?*

The moment inevitably passes, and at the end of the night I count up my tips and thank God that at least I don't work retail, but the accumulated experience has me feeling like an automaton performing tasks, not a human being experiencing life. Temporarily sprung from that purgatory, I desperately want to ask this fellow counter jockey (my bar and the product I sell may be different, but the service we offer is essentially the same) what he thinks, what his dreams are and whether he enjoys schlepping candy and trinkets for a living, but I'm sure he'd look around at the chips, pop, Kananaskis Country T-shirts and boxer shorts strategically adorned with an elk on the ass, and say, "Come on, man, what do you think?"

Or worse, look over with a blank stare and uninspired "Huh?"

Although painfully curious, I decide not to impugn both of our dignities by asking what is dangerously close to being a stupid-tourist question, and instead amuse myself by flipping through my *Canadian Rockies SuperGuide*. After about an hour, I finish up the dregs of my cold coffee and pack up my things before giving my kindred spirit a polite nod on my way back to my blissfully quiet campsite.

7.

MOUNT KIDD AND THE VILLAGE

Here comes the sun, doo nnh doo doo, here comes the sun,
And I say, it's all right.

—George Harrison (The Beatles)

I woke up this morning a little after eight-thirty, physically tired but mentally refreshed for the first time in a very long time. The troubles and concerns of early yesterday eventually burned away completely with my evening campfire, and for the moment I'm travelling in the opposite direction of my habits and my struggles and my disappointments. In a small but important way, I realize I'm beginning to feel free. I still long for the day when I'll leap out of my sleeping bag feeling physically and mentally alert at the same time, but it's finally sinking in that this is a process, so I'll take whatever I can get. The important thing to do is to keep the momentum going without falling into that familiar Western trap of "needing to accomplish something," an attitude that will surely disrupt the natural flow that's developing.

Sitting down to breakfast, I'm again visited by two resident chipmunks who dropped by last evening to explore my gear and beg for some dinner, and who have decided that persistence is the surest way to a free meal. There's no way I'm going to encourage them by giving up any food, but they are very nearly irresistible as they carry out their reconnaissance of the new guy in town, sniffing the ground relentlessly in search of any morsel and occasionally rearing up on their haunches to have a better look at what I'm eating. The bolder of the two goes so far as to patrol the ground at my feet beneath the picnic table and at one point forgets I'm even there. In an impressive feat of athleticism for an animal smaller than my hand, he leaps from the ground, bounces lightly off the bench seat attached to the table and lands in a comfortable four-point stance less than a foot from my right elbow. The move is a surprise to us both, and the leap to the table is nothing compared to the dismount, a single-motion 180-degree turn and a rifle-shot long jump halfway across the clearing that also sends his startled little buddy scurrying into the surrounding underbrush. When you've got kamikaze chipmunks in your campsite, coffee seems redundant.

Although they're frightened for the moment, I know my little friends will be back, and before long a half-hearted repacking of my food bag turns into a serious attempt to organize things in a way that will ensure that a) the little buggers don't get at my rations and b) I don't get caught needing a corner store farther down the road, where there are no longer stores around every corner. The first thing I notice upon opening the black pannier marked "kitchen" at the top in silver magic marker is that the cinnamon raisin bagels I bought a few days ago at Safeway are a bit too fragrant for comfort. Instinctively, I cast sidelong glances over each shoulder, half expecting to see a predator drawn to the savoury bouquet of cinnamon. I enjoy bagels on the road and trail because they're compact and dense and stay relatively fresh for days after regular bread has turned green and porridge becomes an absolute bore. But if the stories of the olfactory capabilities of the average bear are to be believed, then Yogi and Boo-Boo should be dropping by for a snack any minute now.

Then again, on the way to the washroom this morning I did notice that my tent site is less than 40 metres from the big dumpster that services this corner of the campground. It is designed, like all garbage cans in and around the mountain parks, to be bear-proof, but that's of little comfort, because at close range it stinks to high heaven. Here, I'm more likely to get a visitor drawn to the subtle stench of old coffee grounds and mouldy potato salad than the heady aroma of cinnamon. But I will still have to re-evaluate my choice of food once I get further away from civilization. I've yet to hear of a bear travelling miles over rough terrain to ransack a campsite in order to get to a plain bagel, so that might be a better choice going forward, and I make a mental note of it.

Digging deeper in the bag, I find I'm also on the fence about including my water filter on this part of the trip – after all, just beyond the dumpster is the communal washroom with toilets and hot and cold running water – but I will eventually need it and the camp stove for trips into the backcountry, so I should get used to carrying and using both pieces of equipment. In the opposite pannier, also marked "kitchen," I find peanut butter, mixed nuts and the obligatory bag of trail mix, which ensures that even if I don't stock up before moving on, I'll be able to live for a week on the rations already on hand. It's not exactly gourmet fare, but I can always travel to France for steak tartar and crème brûlée next time I'm desperate to get out of town. A big bag of beef jerky from the camp store is not an entirely bad idea, though.

Wandering down my driveway and across the gravel road quickly leads to a set of marked nature trails that meander through the forest on the way to the shallow late-season waters of the Kananaskis River. Upstream, gravel bars split the flow into multiple channels, and where the river narrows just downstream, a single surge picks up speed but never appears to get more than knee-deep. The sun remains remarkably low in the southern sky – a clear indicator that technically fall has arrived – but despite the occasional splash of pale green and yellow from scattered balsam poplar on the far bank, it's clear that summer is not ready to give up the fight. It is a peaceful scene, in an environment where it's impossible not to feel both mindful and connected.

For the last few nights, I've been drifting off to sleep with the Peter Matthiessen classic *The Snow Leopard* drooped across my chest. The book is about Matthiessen's trekking experiences in western Nepal in 1973 with Dr. George Schaller, and their quest to record the behaviour of the bharal, a rare Himalayan blue sheep, in that remote and largely uninhabited part of Asia. Similar to my unexplainable attraction to the Canadian Rockies, I've always been fascinated by the Himalayas, and the book is a remarkable tale of perseverance, adventure and discovery. Already a keen student of the Buddhist philosophy, Matthiessen not only recounts the challenges and hardships of their travels and records their scientific achievements but also manages to observe his own inner workings in a way that is raw, open and at times brutally honest. He doesn't sugar-coat the journey or glamorize the hardships but simply documents the expedition while attempting, in true Buddhist form, to remain detached from the experience enough to actually experience it. Free of the distractions of the mind. I love that about the book and wonder if the detachment that is a cornerstone of the

Buddhist philosophy is part of what I'm ultimately searching for here in my own travels, thousands of miles away and decades removed.

It is a thought worthy of further study, and as I make my way back to the campsite along the narrow trail, there's no denying that one of my favourite things about getting away for a few weeks is being free to do a little casual wandering. In this simple, largely directionless roaming through unfamiliar territory, everything suddenly feels right in a way that's difficult to quantify but impossible to ignore. I may not be exploring a remote region of a foreign country in search of empirical evidence to help explain the behaviour of a little-known species, nor am I seeking to fill in the blank spots on a half-finished map (I ask, does a place like that even exist anymore?), but that hardly seems to matter. What I am doing is clearing the decks of tired patterns, shifting my perspective and allowing experience that hasn't been forced into any number of predetermined pathways the opportunity to be explored.

Theoretically, this experience is possible back home, I suppose, but when I'm there I'm responsible for all the things that are associated with having a life in the traditional Western sense. Jocey and I are now married under the law in Alberta, having lived together under the same roof for many years, and I do have a job and friends and social obligations that seem to fill most of my waking hours. Don't get me wrong, on balance these are all good things – but I'm also responsible for my rent and heating bills as well as my behaviour and abilities at work, and these relationships and friendships I'm lucky enough to have don't maintain themselves. Just like most things in life, they require time and effort to be of any value. As a result, I always feel that in order to keep up I have to be *doing* something, and lately there have not been enough hours in a week to get it all done. Worse still, I can't seem to find the energy to try.

Stopping to take a deep breath before returning to the campsite, I am helpless to do anything but to take it all in; the river, the forest, the sun and the gentle breeze have all conspired to ground me. After the chaos that is a summer tourist season in the Rockies, the outdoors is offering a free course in attention to detail, or in my case any kind of attention at all. In allowing it to do so, I am refilled with the simplicity I don't experience often enough. Here, my ambitions seem pointless, selfish and self-serving. My anger and frustration are a waste of energy. Still, I am only able to sink into it for a few stolen moments at a time before my conscious mind sabotages the process and drags me back to a reality that doesn't quite fit, like a poorly chosen pair of shoes, and I find myself once again in that endless battle between, on the one hand, what I know the world to be and what I've been taught to believe, and on the other hand how I'm expected to act.

That there is any beauty here at all to appreciate is something of a surprising thing when you step back and have a look at it. Kananaskis Country in its current incarnation is designated a multi-use recreation area administered by the provincial government. The 4000 square kilometres that make up K-Country are divided into eight distinct areas based on landscape features, and 51 different parks within the outer boundaries offer a wide range of allowable activities, from hiking, mountain biking and cross-country skiing to fishing, snowmobiling and ATV riding. There are 39 provincial recreation areas, 6 provincial parks, 4 wildland provincial parks, an ecological reserve and a designated natural area available to be explored, and regulations on use in each of these have attempted to create something of a balance between conservation, recreation and industry.

In the first half of the 20th century, however, that balance was considerably less sure. Prospecting was rampant in the first three decades, and a working coal mine began operation on Mount Allan in 1947. In this valley alone, hydroelectric projects sprang up at Kananaskis Falls, Kananaskis Lakes and Barrier Lake. But the most obvious blight on the landscape in those early years of development was forestry. For the better part of half a century, great big chunks of virgin timber were cut, mostly for use in Calgary home-building, and the land was significantly degraded as a result. The dams remain, but there has been no mining since 1952, and nature, in its remarkable capacity to heal, has erased most of the early logging damage inflicted on this beautiful setting.

Back at the site, I also realize that where you actually are for this kind of exercise in liberation is largely irrelevant, as long as it's not at home, propped up in front of the boob tube. I must confess that being in a foreign city is almost as accommodating to the state of grace I'm searching for as mountains and lakes and streams are. I can easily while away an afternoon exploring the grubby backstreets, funky bookshops and kitschy tourist bars of Kathmandu as the paved roadways, stunning mountains and meandering backcountry trails of the Canadian Rockies. I'm also fond of Portland, Hong Kong, Sydney, Montreal and Dublin, and could easily waste away days or weeks at a time exploring any one of those urban landscapes. It's just that this time around, my small town is beginning to remind me too much of a big town, so I've decided to go outside.

In puttering around the campsite and surrounding

trails here at Mount Kidd, I am grateful to attain the desired state, if only for a few hours, and the world is now in balance in a way I can more easily relate to. In this relaxed manner I am no longer a cog in the wheel, doing my part and fitting in. All of sudden I'm living at a different speed, on a revised and relaxed schedule, and am experiencing a different way of processing information. In turn I am interacting with the world in a way that is more natural. I am at once reminded of the movie *One Week*, where Joshua Jackson's character, Ben, after a devastating cancer diagnosis, sets off across Canada on his motorcycle. The film celebrates Canada's beauty and diversity, but more striking than the visual imagery is how Ben finds a measure of peace by embracing randomness and lunacy as an alternative to structure and judgment. He has an outdated map, no thought of consequence, and direction without a destination – a relief from our single-minded direction of growth at all cost. Progress does not always equal growth, and growth is not automatically progress, and yet we stumble forward regardless, while the effort to maintain that lifestyle consumes our lives.

Still, our pop culture remains littered with the alternative idea that we might be travelling headlong into a dead end and that what is good for the group in the short term might ultimately be damaging to the individual spirit. It is among the most powerful and endearing of our shared images, in my opinion. Our collective actions, however well intentioned, tend toward an army of paid slaves who are simultaneously thankful and resentful for the opportunity to participate. In stepping out, even in this small way, I find I'm now engaged in a process of pure discovery, even in those places that have been "discovered and explored" many times over. As a result, the small things in life become a revelation. The simple details, like how a trickle of water helps shape a stream bed, or how a mountain wildflower gains purchase in the most unlikely terrain, become important once again.

Maybe this is what Cahill meant when he spoke about travel being a process of discovery, not a destination. My question is, why is it we often wait for crisis or heartbreak or desperation before we set out toward a more liberated kind of life – toward the kind of life we really want to live?

• • •

It's still too early for a beer, so in the absence of anything better to do I head for a soak in the fantastically oversized indoor hot tub. Half an hour later, inexplicably, I find myself bombing along the Evan Thomas Bike Path. Even though I had no plans of doing any real exercise today, the path turns out to be an absolute delight. Freshly paved, with brand new bridges and an ever-so-slight downhill grade, it winds its way through a mixed forest and along a broad river valley back toward Kananaskis Village. I am also headed back toward Highway 1, and even though I detest backtracking even on a day trip, the conditions translate into a rocket-fast journey. I find myself involuntarily hooting and hollering like a fool, and don't much care. In what can only be described as a remarkable recovery, my legs feel great, the sun is shining, and the world is a beautiful place once again.

Once I'm out of the protection of the trees, the spectacular 360-degree views on the flats bring to mind yet again that this is prime bear country, and I can almost picture a big old grizzly ambling through the underbrush toward my stash of unattended bagels. But even with the ever-present worry of running headlong into one on the narrow trail, I can't actually bring myself to slow down. A word of warning is in order, however. Riding a bike is probably the worst way to travel in bear country, because bikes are quiet compared to cars and fast compared to hikers, and few things are more dangerous than a startled bear. A mother bear with cubs is still the granddaddy of bear encounters to avoid, but coming up quickly on a bear with little or no warning is a close second, just ahead of wandering the woods with a medium-rare steak tucked in your pocket. There are different schools of thought on alerting bears to your presence in the wild.

Bear bells are widely sold in western Alberta, but some researchers believe that the bells' unnatural sounds might actually attract a curious bruin. Others believe the bells are crap and don't work at all. In groups, loud conversation is encouraged, as well as occasional clapping and shouting, but no matter how hard I try, I can't make myself carry on a dialogue with the trees or play one-man patty cake without feeling like a dork. Some people suggest singing, but anyone who's heard my rendition of U2's "Angel of Harlem" will realize a bear would probably go out of his way to maul me just to silence the racket.

Since I've thoughtfully left my bear spray back at the campsite but don't want to be completely irresponsible, I eventually settle on a modified version of the excited whoop-whooping that I sometimes use to alert other cyclists when coming around blind corners too fast. Today it goes something like this: "Heeeey bears, hoooo bears, how are you doing there, bears. Nothing good to eat here, bears." This is shouted with varying tones and inflections, depending on the mood that hits me. Sometimes slight variations in the lyrics present themselves from out of the blue: "Hey hey bears, ho bears, no steaks in my pockets here, bears." Not exactly Grammy material, but it will do in a pinch.

About halfway back to the road junction that leads up to Kananaskis Village, I fly past – and I mean absolutely fly past – a couple casually puttering along on rented mountain bikes, and as I go by I make a point of digging in just a little deeper on the pedals to bleed out one or two extra kilometres an hour. It's a bit childish, but I can't resist pretending to be an accomplished and talented cyclist. Suddenly I'm one of those slim speedy guys in tight Lycra I saw yesterday, ripping across big chunks of ground without breaking a sweat. Suddenly I'm a hopped-up Lance Armstrong, destroying the field on the Alpe d'Huez during one of his tainted Tour de France victories. Suddenly I'm ... All right, big guy, settle down. I'm not suddenly anything different than I was ten minutes ago, except I'm not the slowest lump on the road anymore, and this development feeds my ego and makes my legs feel just that much less heavy again. More importantly, it allows me to apply the first rule in safe travel through bear country, which is: you don't need to be fast, you just need to be faster than the guy next to you. And that's worth a hearty "hey bears, ho bears" shout all its own.

After the fast easy miles along the flats, I don't much appreciate the short, steep climb to Kananaskis Village, but I split the effort into two parts with a brief rest in the middle and make the best of it before locking up the bike and looking for a place to have lunch. And maybe that beer I didn't end up having with breakfast.

• • •

Kananaskis Village is one of those purpose-built communities that was never anything before mining, large-scale farming, forestry or tourism came along and necessitated building a town to support a fledgling industry. In other words, it's not a natural place to settle. Yet here it is nonetheless, all glossy and pretty with its solid landscaping and man-made ponds – complete with tiny waterfalls – set against a gorgeous natural backdrop. The valley here is relatively broad, with Mount McDougall and Old Baldy to the east, and Mounts Allan, Sparrowhawk and Bogart due west. Much like the Canmore Nordic Centre, Kananaskis Village owes its current existence to the Winter Olympics in 1988. Plans for an alpine village development up on the natural bench overlooking the valley had been floating around for years, but with the development of the nearby Nakiska ski area and the decision to use Mount Allan for the alpine events during the Olympiad, work on the site began in 1986 and was completed in time for the Games. By all accounts, a spectacular feat of speed and efficiency for the construction industry in an ecologically sensitive area.

The village now has all the expected amenities and is also a step beyond Mount Kidd's basic offerings. Boutique shops filled with high-ticket art and clothing complement the restaurants and bars, and Ribbon Creek Groceries is a convenient place to get basic supplies and completes what should be an ideal mini-community. Even the typical cheap tourist tat appears shiny and beguiling. Yet with everything seemingly in the right place, something still seems to be missing here; something is fundamentally wrong with the scene.

Surprisingly, I actually like the idea of purpose-built communities. The concept of building a place to accentuate the positives of urban life while minimizing the negatives certainly has its appeal. After all, organized and tidy should trump random and rundown every time. But as David Byrne says in *Bicycle Diaries*, "There once existed natural geographical reasons for most towns to come into being," and he lists a meeting of rivers and a sheltered harbour among the reasons humans, as social animals, congregate in one place. I would contend that the list has expanded to include anywhere that large-scale agriculture and mineral extraction opportunities exist. There certainly can be plenty of charm in some of those communities, but I don't know if the end result of purpose-built-for-tourism ever really comes off. The concept works well enough in theory – and is in evidence right here in front of me – but in practice there just isn't enough dirt under the nails for my taste. Plus it's always ridiculously expensive. I enjoy a little style and class as much as the next guy, but it had better be anchored with solid legs and a sturdy back, and I'm not sure I see those foundations here.

Come to think of it, an eroding core foundation is probably the biggest beef I have with Canmore. Talking to a number of long-time locals, I've learned that Canmore was a workingman's town for much of its existence. Somewhere where you knew your neighbours, worked hard and played hard and didn't worry too much about the accumulated value of your house. Nothing in life is ever perfect, I know, and I have also heard whispers of drug and alcohol problems from those quieter days, but now there's just too much gloss creeping in at the edges. There is a working class for sure, but it's overshadowed by the multi-million-dollar homes and big new development projects. I want to live in my town, not just invest in it, and I also get the distinct sensation that many of this new generation of working class are just in it for the buck. If it dries up, they'll simply move on to the next thing. For over 100 years, Canmore was a working-class town with solid roots, and now it appears to be for sale to the highest bidder. But alas, I'm probably the one who's going to have to adjust my thinking of what a community is. It could be that Canmore is simply a microcosm of a larger trend, and the world certainly doesn't look like it's going to be changing direction anytime soon. Capitalism or crime? You be the judge – but I think it's a shame that my town is losing some of its charm as a result.

A flawless bluebird day, with two Coronas and a big glass of water in the 30-degree heat of a sheltered southwest-facing patio at one of the major hotel chains, should be an experience to allay all concerns and doubts about the direction my wilderness and my town are talking in the attempt to draw commerce. This is the new me, after all: rejuvenated, energetic, outgoing and freshly open-minded. It shouldn't take more than 20 or 30 minutes to pedal back to Mount Kidd, so I have the whole afternoon ahead to relax, enjoy the sunshine and take in the day at one of the premier resort destinations in the Rockies. I might even go so far as to contemplate my own shortcomings, including a distressing lack of patience that's been developing these last years. My immediate environment may have a lot to answer for, but I haven't exactly been gracious in how I've been reacting to the stress of trying to fit in. A vacation can be more than just an opportunity to get away from it all – you also have the option of doing a bit of personal work if you are so inclined, and I am determined to continue with the effort.

But after what feels like a month of Sundays, my first Corona has finally arrived – with the requested water conspicuously absent – and as the sun slowly blazes across the sky, the thirst for that life-sustaining liquid arises as it might for a pilgrim crossing the Sahara desert on foot, and my patience and objectivity begin to drain away. As I repeatedly attempt to get my server's attention, two couples leave (one after 10 minutes, the other after 12) because none of the staff on duty have even said hello to them as they sat there, let alone offered menus or thought it wise to take a drink order. Normally I wouldn't care about such things as long as my table was being looked after, but I'm very thirsty, and the clumsy performance playing out in front of me is akin to watching a car wreck out on the highway as you pass. You know you shouldn't rubberneck, but you just can't help yourself, and as a service industry veteran I don't stand a chance. Rare indeed is the aging server who can resist the urge to critique when they're out in public as a civilian.

If you've worked any amount of time in the service industry, then you've undoubtedly had some experiences that would astonish and mortify the average human being. At first glance, the hospitality industry is an orderly and professional environment like any other (indeed, cluttered tables notwithstanding, the patio I'm sitting on looks like a functioning place of business), but bars and restaurants also attract more than their fair share of unusual and slightly damaged characters in need of employment. Although it's regulated to a certain degree, I doubt there's another profession on the planet (prostitution notwithstanding) where these "patients" so thoroughly participate in running the asylum. A bar job is the best job in the world for young single people who don't yet know what they want to do with their lives, and as a result there are stories. Oh boy, are there stories. Health insurance and pension funds are a pipe dream if you wear an apron or carry a tray, but stories about illegal activities, stories about violence and danger, and stories that start with "Dear Penthouse Forum..." are all part of the stock in trade. It's what draws some of us to the life.

Unfortunately, inexperience and ineptitude are also chronic in the world I work in, and employers are often forced to take what they can get, as is in evidence here. I think the only way this service could be worse is if the staff were all smoking cigarettes just outside the glass fence while we all waited for our drinks. Accepting that shocking service is not unheard of, I will usually give my fellow industry professionals the benefit of the doubt, but with only three other tables on the patio apart from myself – two three-tops and a five-top – it's hard to imagine what the holdup is. My now-empty Corona bottle has been sitting in front of me for nearly 18 minutes, and two dirty tables have remained uncleared for my entire visit. I finally have to beg for my second drink and that glass of water from a new server who came on shift mid-visit, and on the way to the washroom I decide to have a look around inside just in case it's busy in another area of the restaurant and I'm just being hypercritical.

But nope, there are only two two-tops inside.

Back at my table, my second drink finally arrives (again with no water), and another couple has come and gone without anyone even acknowledging their presence. I do concede that early afternoon can be a bad time to visit any establishment, because lunch service is over and dinner needs to be prepared for, but the lines are becoming increasing blurred. Gone are the days when restaurants close between two and five in order to take care of the prep work necessary for evening service. Full service all the time is the new norm, and is a double-edged sword. A waiter on a split shift doesn't want to hang around serving a table or two here and there; he just wants get away for a couple of hours before having to do it all over again. A typical day shift for a waiter goes something like this: set up, serve, clear, set up for shift change. A night shift is similar but will usually be longer and busier. A good manager directs the action and asks what needs to be done next during a big push, and a good busboy fills all the holes in the service experience by taking care of the small details and doing the grunt work. A good server makes sure the customers have what they want when they want it. Higher up the food chain, a good owner makes sure the people hired are able to execute their jobs and act as the face of the establishment. It's not rocket science but is harder than it looks and does manage to go wrong more often than you would expect.

It's difficult to tell who should shoulder the blame for the poor experience in this case – the servers, for being largely incompetent, or the manager, for being invisible on a nice day when it's probably going to be busy – but I almost want to apologize for all of them now as yet another two-top comes in, sits down, waits and then leaves. Perhaps I should start taking tables, or apply for the general manager position, which appears to be vacant at present. At the very least I should fill in one of those customer feedback cards that invariably end up in the trash, or exercise the most powerful tool in the customer arsenal and refuse to tip.

But because I work in the business, and as a result must pray to Saint Gratuity, the patron saint of tips-are-a-substantial-portion-of-my-income, I know I will still leave two bucks a drink anyway. I also manage to refrain from offering any advice on my way out. Although the following seems appropriate: "Pssst, here's an idea: every time you go near your section for anything, *anything at all*, do the tour, clear some dishes and check on your active tables. You might find someone who needs something else."

Or in this case, needs something to begin with.

Exasperated yet slightly amused in my new attempt at detachment (as well as sympathetic because I was once new to the business and incapable of doing two or three things at once), I eventually leave my empty bottle and my tip in the middle of the table, where it will probably remain until spring, and head off in search of somewhere to have a glass of water and maybe a late lunch.

8.

NOTHING LIKE AN EPIPHANY
TO RUIN A PERFECTLY GOOD DAY

Go confidently in the direction of your dreams! Live the life you have imagined.

—Henry David Thoreau

Fucking Thoreau! Stupid quotes like that have just about ruined me. As an angry teenager I lived off them, along with pizza, song lyrics, sports, clever Nike and Patagonia advertising and chasing women. As a matter of fact, I still have many of these uplifting and inspiring phrases pinned to the walls in my workspace, and lately I have wanted to strangle their authors. Some of them are already dead, of course, but I would still enjoy giving them a good smack, because they encouraged the idea that responsibility didn't matter, the future didn't matter and money didn't matter if you ended up spiritually bankrupt. Take a leap of faith, they collectively said, and you will be saved. I can't blame Thoreau and his impossibly optimistic cohorts entirely for the predicament I now find myself in, but there's no denying that believing has left me at the edge of being bankrupt in the more practical and literal sense.

It is true that along the way I have made some half-hearted attempts at being responsible in the Western careerist sense, despite the seduction of art and the wild romantic allure of the bohemian life. I went to and graduated from college and university, had a couple of live-in girlfriends who made me toy with the idea of kids and the white picket fence, and have even managed to keep a few jobs for more than six months at a time, when the mood struck me. But in the end, all that has proven important over the years has been the here and now, and pursuing the dreams. In the grand scheme of things, even the nature of the dreams was irrelevant; as long as they were *my* dreams, I believed they were valid pursuits. In fact they were the only worthy pursuits. Everything else was an irritant and a bore.

Most people grow out of their teenage idealism, of course, or have it unceremoniously beaten out of them by life, but I'm remarkably stubborn, and things didn't improve much in my 20s or in my 30s. I began to read books instead of just the back of the cereal box, devoured movies as fast as they could be produced and continued to listen to music constantly, gravitating toward any sentiment that inspired the imagination, like a drunken freshman tracking down a keg party during frosh week. Come to think of it, the overall experience was eerily similar. A barely controlled buildup of energy and anticipation at the thought of upcoming possibilities, an absolutely over-the-top explosion of activity and emotion, followed closely by that lowest of lows that comes when the tank has been run dangerously past empty. I envy people who don't have a creative bone in their body and aren't easily seduced by the drink, but this is who I am, apparently.

> The desire for safety stands against every great and noble enterprise.
>
> —Tacitus

Tough to bother with a proper job, RRSPs and life

insurance with that kind of thought rattling around in your head. And if Tacitus's idea gets the blood flowing, then all the conventions of a normal life in our society won't hold much appeal, or manage to placate for long. Marriage, and that white picket fence everyone is talking about? Pleasant enough thought; never going to happen.

> Black-eyed man he took the blame for the poi-
> soning of the well.
> They found his shoes by the pulley, they found
> his fingerprints all over the pail.
> With a noose around his neck, cicadas trilling
> everywhere, he says to the people
> gathered around him,
> "It ain't the water that's not right around here."
> —Michael Timmins (Cowboy Junkies)

Hhhmmm, maybe, just maybe, things aren't always what they seem, or as they are so cleverly presented by politicians, industry leaders and the mass media.

> Knowing is not enough; we must act. Willing is
> not enough; we must do.
> —Goethe

Shit! Guess I better do.

Collectively the inspiration said, "Go for it; do whatever you want in this life and don't be swayed. Go before it's too late." But as my 40th birthday approaches, I have decidedly mixed feelings about how this particular brand of Kerouackian philosophy has paid out. On the one hand, most of my dreams have been fulfilled, and I am grateful for that. As a young man, I wanted to travel and explore, and by the time I was 20 I had hiked in the

Green and White Mountains of New England and bicycled solo across the Canadian Rockies from just outside Hope, British Columbia, all the way to Portage La Prairie, Manitoba. A hunger for a taste of the tropics meant visiting remote beaches in Hawaii and Fiji and Australia, and eventually spending a memorable afternoon standing and staring out toward the vast Western Desert from the top of Uluru, a.k.a. Ayers Rock.

In my 20s I graduated from university with a degree in physical education, visited Japan and Ireland and Mexico, and hiked the length of British Columbia's West Coast Trail with my family. Somewhere along the way I also managed to ride the Rockies on two more occasions along completely different routes and paddled a kayak with orcas in Johnstone Strait. In my 30s I revived a long-standing dream of playing professional sports and managed a couple of years in North America's United Soccer Leagues' top division, became a regular finisher of the Canadian Ski Marathon and stood at Everest Base Camp long enough to realize that high altitude is simply not for me.

We all have a personal highlight reel, a set of events and adventures we hold dear, and this is mine. If the old adage, "Nobody ever lay on their deathbed wishing they'd spent more time at the office," is true, then I've done well. But it's still not enough. To any reasonable degree, I have accomplished everything I set out to do, and yet I still don't feel satisfied with the idea of settling down. There is always another adventure out there, another town to visit, another set of mountains to gaze upon, another lesson to learn. Genetically I appear to have the gene to roam and have absolutely no idea what I want to do with my life when I grow up. The question is, what do you do when you realize this is what you're good at, this is what you love and this is who you are? How do you reconcile the sensibilities of a vagabond with the demands and expectations of modern-day life?

Thoreau is absolutely right, it is important to live the life you imagine, or else why bother? But the last time I checked, they don't give out university degrees for cruising around, and "Jobs.com" didn't have a listing for happy wanderer posted this month. Fucking Thoreau – if he wasn't already dust, I'd throttle him.

• • •

With the experience at Kananaskis Village fresh in my mind, I resolve to take another step away from constructed comfort and the inevitable disappointment that comes with too much interaction with other people. After making my way back to Mount Kidd and spending a relaxed evening by the campfire, I have woken up feeling vaguely optimistic once again, with the intent of travelling to Kananaskis Lakes. It's not exactly a remote destination but is off the casual tourists' beaten path, and now that the Calgary weekenders have presumably all made tracks back to the city, it should grow increasingly quiet the farther south I get.

Morning proves uneventful – if a bit difficult to warm to with what now feel like perpetually achy legs – but a gradual incline along a winding mountain road, with no wind, is a perfect place to continue to work out the kinks of active travel. I'm not especially spry or speedy but am gradually becoming steadier as all the little balancing muscles begin to find their shape under my skin. There are no trauma-inducing hills along this stretch of road, and stunning peaks on both sides of the valley counterpoint the occasional glimpse of the Kananaskis River flowing gracefully past. Each pedal stroke makes me feel that much more liberated, as if little bits of a persona that is not really me are continuing to fall away, to be replaced by genuine hopes and wishes and desires. As I gradually make my way up the valley toward the headwaters of the river, the whole world is suddenly in front of me, waiting to be discovered anew.

At Fortress Junction – a lonely outpost that is decidedly busier in summer than fall or winter – I was hoping for a café with cooked food but settle instead for a well-stocked convenience and grocery store, complete with booze and magazines. This will be the last proper store for the next four or five days, so I casually browse the aisles in search of anything I may still need. My map shows a symbol for a restaurant at the Boulton Creek campground, but the odds are overwhelming that it will now be closed for the season. So instead of fried chicken with mashed potatoes and gravy complemented by the mellow sounds of Muzak wafting from unseen speakers hidden in the ceiling tiles, it will be trail mix, a six pack of beer, the sounds of the forest and Stagg Chili cooked right in the can over an open campfire. Tomorrow evening will be much the same, with a 375-millilitre mini-bottle of Gallo Cabernet Sauvignon standing in for the beer, but I've done worse. Pedalling back out to the road after a sandwich eaten out on the lawn, I notice in passing that gas is $1.40 a litre, and that gives me a perverse sense of joy in not driving this route.

In the afternoon the air develops the clean, clear feel that can only be found in autumn in the Rockies. The sky is painfully blue, with only the occasional whisper of cloud, and at fairly regular intervals an airplane contrail streaks slowly across the sky. Highway 40 bisects a primary flight path from Calgary out to the coast, but every successive contrail dissipates quickly into the high atmosphere like the one before, and after each disappears I am left with the feeling that I am the only man left on earth. There are no cars, there are no airplanes and, apart from the actual pavement beneath my wheels and the occasional road sign, there is no indication of any other human presence.

After three weeks on the trail, Matthiessen remarks in *The Snow Leopard* on the inevitable conflict every pilgrim, no matter the nature of the journey, must face. The moment of realization where the life you have been living and the life you are beginning to live suddenly strike a hard contrast, a contrast that has grown so obvious as to be unavoidable and has to be addressed. "Between clinging and letting go, I feel a terrific struggle. This is a fine chance to let go, to 'win my life by losing it,' which means not recklessness but acceptance, not passivity but nonattachment."

It's an interesting concept, and I wonder why I can't manage it myself. I don't fit into my community comfortably, as much as I may sometimes want to. There is too much pettiness, too much self-interest and too much greed. While not always overt, these traits taint modern life like the bad aftertaste of aspartame. I admit it's subtle, but it's there. To participate in that life requires a compromise I feel uncomfortable making, yet I find myself making that compromise every day, with the bizarre hope that someday everything will change. That one day everything really will be okay. There is no doubt I'm happier here at the periphery, not living there in what amounts to my version of Joseph Conrad's "heart of darkness," and to "win my life" I will have no choice but to get rid of everything that no longer works for me. At the very least I need to reverse the ratio of time spent in each of these environments if there is any hope of retaining any hint of sanity. But I remain addicted to fitting in to the modern lifestyle, even as it slowly chips away at the edges of my soul. Why do I cling? Why can't I let go?

I don't know.

As I carry on at a leisurely, almost thoughtful pace, I can't help but stop in at the visitor centre before making my way to the Boulton Creek campground. The centre is well laid out and maintained, with plenty of information and interactive displays, but for some reason I can't find a way to get into the whole scene. I try to strike a spark by lingering on the topographic maps tucked under glass at the main desk (maps usually have a way of lighting up my imagination) but am strangely uninspired. Apart from the cast of a gigantic grizzly paw print that is easily as large as my outstretched hand and nearly twice as wide, there is little to hold my attention, and I end up leaving the centre vaguely disappointed, through no fault of its own.

In a fit of obstinacy, I pedal all the way to the top of Boulton Creek upon arriving at the campground proper. This isn't necessary – there are open sites all over the place – but it's been a strong afternoon in every respect. It's been a good ride through beautiful country that has stirred up strong emotions, and every once in a while you've got to do things "just because." Getting to the upper reaches of the campground requires a short, stiff climb, but I have a sudden burst of energy for an effort that would have been improbable only a week ago. Unfortunately, the gate is closed for Sites 58 to 118, as the campground is being shut down in stages for the season. After casually tooling around in search of the perfect spot I eventually settle on Site 50, high up the slope and tucked off the far end of a sweeping bend, where it's unlikely I'll have much company. In among the tall, straight pines, I can't see the lakes as I had hoped, but there is a nice view down my drive-way and along the access road to the already snowy upper slopes of Mount Fox. Or maybe it's Tyrwhitt; I can't be entirely sure which.

After taking a moment to assess my new surroundings, I crack a beer, set up my tent quickly and spread my gear out just as two big fifth-wheels (or whatever you call those rolling monstrosities you drag behind an oversized pickup truck) pull into the two sites directly to the south of mine. Fifty metres of forest separates us, so I doubt it'll be much of an issue in terms of crowding, but I'm still annoyed. I had anticipated having this place all to myself, and social-ization of any kind wasn't part of the plan. One of the cou-ples waves and says hello in a perfectly friendly manner as they amble down to use the facilities, and despite being ag-gravated by the intrusion, I return the gesture as pleasantly as humanly possible.

As dinnertime approaches, most of my fire and brim-stone bleeds away, and the evening transforms into one of those warm summer nights I was so fond of as a kid. Wandering down through the campground, looking for a suitable place to take some sunset shots, I can almost hear the crack of the bat at the neighbourhood ball diamond back in the suburbs of Montreal. I could also swear I hear my friends shouting and laughing as we ride our bikes home wildly from an afternoon at the pool. A man could get reckless in these circumstances and engage in what Cahill called "an invitation to commit poetry or philoso-phy or any number of the higher aesthetic or contempla-tive crimes." Part of the reason the memories are so com-pelling is that there was nothing to do back then but just "be." Much like little bits and pieces of today, those days were carefree, full of raw energy and very nearly perfect. I realize we were, in our youth and innocence, mindful. A state I'm desperately trying to reach once again.

After revelling sufficiently in the past, I find myself over by the dumpster near Site 44, which ironically offers the best view of the Opals unless you wheel all the way down to the lakes or back to the highway. Having arrived too early for the sunset, however, I end up draining my traveller and realize there's time to get back to the site for another beer before late afternoon spills peacefully into twilight. I'm walking along, still thinking of long, lazy afternoons with no responsibilities, and generally feeling pretty pleased with life, when a subtle movement catches my eye from off to the left. Being right at the edge of my peripheral vision, the motion isn't enough to immediately trigger a physical reaction, but my senses are instantly on high alert. A million possibilities flash past simultaneously, and after discarding a large number of reasonable options, I eventually settle on, "Why is there a dog up in that tree?"

The initial impression doesn't make any sense, of course, but the animal in question is clearly too small to be a bear and too big to be a cat, or a bird, or anything else that comes easily to mind, so my subconscious settles on the simplest, if least plausible, explanation. Whatever it is, rough calculations suggest something spaniel-sized, and as I hold my breath and turn my head slowly, the canine in question reveals itself in the end to be an improbably large bird. An owl, actually, or more precisely a great grey owl, the second-largest species in the owl family – a great grey can grow to the approximate size of a small springer spaniel.

This particular dog-imposter, a magnificent creature with a round face and an intense, penetrating gaze, is sitting head-high in an immature evergreen 20 metres away and doesn't appear even vaguely concerned by my presence. I figure he'll bolt the minute I turn to have a proper look or raise my camera for a couple of shots. But he's on the hunt and pays me no mind as I continue to hold my breath and train the camera lens on him. Snapping off a few frames, I can feel myself slip into photographer mode (even though I don't know what the hell I'm doing most of the time) and eventually try a number of settings and exposures to help ensure I get the picture I want – all the while figuring that with every click of the shutter the owl will grow tired of my company and fly off to find more peaceful hunting grounds. But he never does. After a quick glance to figure out if I'm a threat to his potential meal, he just stares with unwavering concentration at a patch of undergrowth somewhere between us, fixated on prey I can neither see nor hear.

Peering into the display at the back of my camera for a moment confirms that I have the best possible shot under the circumstances, but as I try to get my excited breathing under control, I also realize I don't have the right lens for a proper close-up. My 17–85 mm lens is a good general zoom, but the 100–400 mm that would have made it much easier to get in tight on the action is back at the site and would take a few minutes to retrieve. By then the unfolding drama would surely have been played out, and walking past would also probably annoy the bird enough for it to abandon the hunt. In winter, great greys have been known to plunge headlong into the snow when mice or voles are detected, and disappear completely in the effort if the snow is fresh and powdery. I don't want to miss the chance to capture this owl mid-hunt, and I find myself holding my breath once again in anticipation of the moment he zeroes in on his target and takes flight.

Naturally it isn't until I drop the camera to my side and take in a panic-stricken suck of air and rest my arms that the owl halves the distance between us in an instant and plunges into the underbrush and long grass, disappearing in a fit of rooting and digging. Cursing, I yank the camera back up to eye level, but the moment has passed.

My friend the owl eventually comes up from the scrub vegetation empty-handed – or empty-beaked, if you will – and takes off on silent wings to continue the hunt, presumably in a location without an audience. He passes within five metres as he flies along the treeless corridor created by the narrow road, and again I'm torn between trying to get the shot and simply watching a beautiful and powerful animal operating in his element. The whole experience leaves me simultaneously breathless and amazed.

• • •

Having put in a respectable physical effort over the last few days, I nod off early with thoughts of owls and other woodland creatures dancing in my head and end up sleeping in late. I had planned on getting up before dawn to make my way down to the lakes for some sunrise shots, but instead I doze until nearly nine and then lie in the comfort and warmth of my sleeping bag for another half an hour. To say I'm not a morning person would be an incredible understatement, and these frosty mornings, when the sun doesn't clear the surrounding mountains and hit the campsite until after eight, aren't helping. I haven't woken up to a frozen water bottle just yet, but I can see my breath as a subtle puff of condensation every day at breakfast.

After poking around an uninspired bowl of porridge with my spoon, I manage to beat back the chill and pedal the two or three kilometres to Upper Kananaskis Lake but am not really feeling it. The temperature is finally coming around, but I'm still trying to find the pace of the day and perhaps a plan for it that doesn't involve riding a bike. Although a rhythm for this trip is certainly developing – one that includes endlessly spinning wheels and pedals that turn relentlessly to produce not only distance from the start back in Canmore but a separation from the life I was living there – that doesn't mean I'm ready to face the idea of riding any kind of serious distance today. The exertion of pedalling may be growing into something soothing and hypnotic that I will soon accept without complaint, but the fact is that an unavoidable byproduct of this change of routine is an ass that is killing me.

For all its inherent benefits as a mode of transportation, the bicycle has one glaring design flaw: a large portion of the rider's body weight sits directly on the saddle. The ischial tuberosities are not a part of the human anatomy commonly referenced in casual conversation, but these sit-bones can become a sudden focus to a cyclist not accustomed to long hours in the saddle. Not a big deal to the casual rider, for sure, and after a week or two of consistent riding the area affectively goes numb to the abuse, but for those few days in transition it can be an ordeal. I'm fine walking around the campsite, and even sitting at the picnic table causes no undue hardship, but place the precious cargo in direct contact with the faux leather of my cheap seat, and pow, an instant pain-response rattles through my system. The predicament is less a stabbing pain and more like putting heavy pressure on a bad bruise, but depositing my tender backside on a bike for a couple of hours just to come back to where I started has zero appeal at present, no matter the emotional, physical or metaphysical benefit.

So it appears I've got to find something else to do. The question is, what?

A scramble up one of the surrounding peaks seems the obvious choice, but in addition to being sore, I'm also tired and not sure I'm up for a six-hour round trip. I gaze toward the northwest and the Continental Divide, but the trail that hugs Upper Kananaskis Lake and runs along the western shore is not beckoning either, being largely in cool shadows at the moment. Normally, this would be a time to panic. Being pointless, goalless or helpless carries a certain stigma in our culture, so I have to force myself to stop, take a deep breath and settle into the indecision. Fortunately the beauty here is very nearly immeasurable and provides easy distraction, with the peaks to the north and west reflecting off the blue waters of the lake in a rippling psychedelic fashion, while the sun has begun to radiate an unseasonable amount of heat once again.

As I tilt my head to absorb the energy-giving rays, it strikes me that Mother Nature is perpetual, if a little tormented at present, and if I want to be more than just another tourist, I will need to continue to find ways to appropriately interact with these surroundings. Generations of indoor living have taken their toll, but my more primal self is determined. Even though I now spend the majority of my days nestled right at the edge of these great outdoors, formidable barriers remain between us. Physically there are walls and fences as well as homes and businesses, not to mention roads and railway lines that fragment the landscape on the valley bottoms. More damning are the routines and excuses and time constraints that keep a metaphorical window pane between me and what remains just out of reach much of the time.

Granted, beyond that barrier there is an unusually

attractive view, but I might as well just look at a postcard or watch a nature documentary. A couch with a remote control in hand is a comfortable proposition, after all. But I've made the effort to get away from all that, and there still needs to be a reason for being here beyond just admiring scenery, because that takes all of two minutes and I've got all day. In the end I simply decide not to decide, and instead content myself with reading the information placards about the geology and geography of the area.

It turns out that the Continental Divide, just across the lake, creates something of a barrier to weather patterns moving from west to east, and these mountains are responsible for the relatively dry climate in Alberta. As warm, wet Pacific air rises on its way across the Divide, it cools and condenses before falling as rain or snow, leaving in its wake a "rain shadow" that affects the climate all the way across the prairies, encouraging grasslands and discouraging the thick forest common on other parts of the continent. Despite this relative lack of moisture, the lakes here are made possible by the bowl shape of the surrounding mountain ranges and the deep, hard-packed gravel deposits that make up the bottom of this basin. A cool mountain climate also keeps evaporation to a minimum. Hydroelectric projects have expanded the size of both lakes significantly, yet they remain an unusual feature on the Eastern Slopes of the Rockies.

Newly educated on how the Kananaskis Lakes came to be, a gaggle of nervous high school kids is disgorged from a yellow school bus that sounds like it could be slipping a few gears, and the silence is disrupted. Judging by the time of day, this is probably a Calgary school group on a field trip, and while awaiting instruction from their teacher and adult chaperones, they chatter endlessly at exaggerated volume and subtly compete with each other for attention. They're just being kids, overconfident and desperately insecure at the same time, but they're disturbing my puttering, and as they spread out in small groups across the parking lot, I kind of drift off the edge, like elk do when humans venture too close. A few of them begin to walk past in their loud and largely oblivious manner, and after the bulk of the group finally wanders out across the earthen dam separating the upper and lower lakes, it is dead quiet once again, except for the birds and the gathering wind. When a second school bus shows up five minutes later, however, and the new group of teens begins to toss a football around the parking lot, I develop the sudden need to go.

I quickly make my way back to the campsite for sunscreen, a refill for my water bottle and a bag lunch for later. It is, I now understand, time to walk. Different muscles and no contact with a seat of any kind should translate into a different experience, and something with more vertical and less horizontal might even be in order. Back at the site I have a quick look around for my friend the great grey owl and am disappointed when he's not sitting on his perch by the road. Checking my map, I take an educated guess that the trail leading to the Kananaskis fire lookout can be found near the top end of the campground, through the now-closed section, so I head off in that direction with new-found determination.

Drifting off on your own in the wilderness is exactly the kind of thing parks employees and search-and-rescue professionals warn against, but nobody knows exactly where I am anyway, so in the end it probably won't make much difference if I trip and break a leg here, or while taking a whiz in the woods ten yards off the road anywhere along my planned route over the next three weeks. Besides, I pick up the trail immediately, which turns out to be an old fire road that's just beginning to get overgrown and could only be missed by a blind man or a complete idiot. By the looks of it, I doubt there's been a vehicle on this track in the last decade, and it's much cooler here in the forest than down by the lake, not to mention remarkably quiet. Even the light wind I experienced at the water's edge can't penetrate the dense tree cover, and after about 20 minutes of steady uphill walking, I scare up a pair of spruce grouse.

These medium-sized birds with mottled brown colouring are remarkably well camouflaged when sitting on the forest floor and have a startling habit of remaining perfectly still in the face of a potential threat and then, if the predator is not fooled, launching into action in a last-second bid to escape. Lost in my own thoughts, I nearly jump out of my skin when they explode into the space right in front of me in a fit of shrieking and flying feathers. Like a squirrel who freezes a quarter of the way across the road and then inexplicably darts the full distance in front of an oncoming vehicle, they insist on flying across my path instead of to the left and away from my direction of travel. After the initial shock, however, they don't seem to be too perturbed by my presence. Their demeanour is almost tame as I stop to take a couple of pictures, and after continuing on with my walk I make sure to practise my "hey bear, ho bear" routine quite diligently, as much for grouse as for any bears that might be foraging in the area.

After about 45 minutes, the trail finally meets up with the main dirt fire road, which is not nearly in danger of being overgrown, and I sit for a spell at a park bench positioned just off the intersection, soaking up the sunshine. For the fifth day in a row, it's unusually hot as morning drifts toward noon, and the metal bench feels a little out of place here in the woods, but it is a welcome alternative to sitting on the ground. I stretch out, have a sip or two of water and imagine that I might not see anyone else for the rest of the day, which strikes me as a fabulous notion.

But then, as if on some demented cue, a Suzuki Sidekick with an elderly couple inside rumbles slowly toward me, headed down, and I can hardly believe my eyes. Their car is jammed with gear, and when they stop at the intersection of what I thought were two old gravel roads now used only as footpaths, we exchange pleasantries as if it were the most natural thing in the world. A few hellos and what-a-nice-days pass between us, and for some reason I can't bring myself to ask what they're doing up here in a car. Eventually it dawns on me that they've been manning the fire lookout for the summer, but the vehicle still seems completely out of place here in the woods. An old-fashioned cowboy on a horse stopped at the traffic lights on Main Street in Canmore might be as odd, but only just. As they resume bouncing down the road at no better than 15 kilometres an hour, I wonder if the exchange was nothing more than a heat-induced hallucination.

Beyond the intersection, the main trail turns south and the steady upward slog gets just a little bit steeper. At a switchback cut into the side of the hill by a small stream, I nearly step in a pile of scat that is distressingly large, but lacking any expertise in the matter, I write it off as evidence of giant bunnies in the area and carry on upward. That clumps of hair appear to have passed through another animal before being deposited here is something I try not to think too much about.

Eventually, and with determined effort, I find myself looking down at the lakes far below. It's now clear that this has been a respectable walk, and I'm struck by a surge of energy that can only be described as pride. This little bump in the landscape is not any great height compared to the surrounding mountains but is enough for today. Mount Lyautey and Mount Indefatigable dominate the foreground, and I can see many of the peaks that make up the border with BC tucked in behind, as well as a good 20 or 30 kilometres up the Smith–Dorrien Creek drainage just to the right, where it stretches out in the direction of travel set for tomorrow.

It was up the drainage directly between Lyautey and Indefatigable that John Palliser is said to have crossed North Kananaskis Pass, but there is some discussion about whether this actually happened as history records. Ernie Lakusta, in *Canmore & Kananaskis History Explorer*, revisits the evidence and suggests that Elk Pass, just off to my left, is the real Kananaskis Pass crossed and subsequently named by Palliser. Among other bits of evidence supporting this new theory is Palliser's description of two conspicuous mountains he sighted from an early campsite near Boundary Flats and identified as the obvious gateway to the western watershed – that line of sight points toward Elk, not Kananaskis, Pass. Barometric pressure readings taken at the pass by Palliser also suggest a height roughly equal to that of Elk Pass but 600 metres short of Kananaskis Pass, and Palliser himself describes an easy crossing for man and horse, which could be upgraded with little effort and expense to accommodate carts as well. By all accounts, that would be an overly ambitious plan to put in place at either North or South Kananaskis Pass.

The identity of the true route taken by the Palliser Expedition 150 years ago may be interesting to contemplate, but getting to the fire lookout has just about knocked me out, and after a half-litre of water, a few pictures and some chocolate-covered almonds, I find a bit of shade and prop up my daypack as a makeshift pillow before passing out stone cold from the morning's adventures.

• • •

I wake up 20 minutes later, after a bout of vivid dreams about words – which should probably come as no surprise, because I love words almost as much as I love this wilderness. As a form of communication, words are handy, of course, but as a form of expression I believe they have the power to become so much more than that. Combining words and getting them down on paper has an entrancing and compelling quality that cannot be ignored. Wars have been started over simple misunderstandings, and unfortunately hatred can be quickly spread by a clever, if misdirected, wordsmith, but love, passion and understanding are also expressed and shared with uncommon depth by combining everyday words.

I suppose there are as many uses for language as there are users out there, but it is the act of capturing that language and writing it down that encourages me to explore the threads that spin out from both my conscious and unconscious minds – and that's a powerful thing to have dancing around at the tips of your fingers. Good words have the ability to cut through uncertainty and doubt and can change the world as surely as actions do. The pen is mightier than any sword. At least that's what I believe.

With that in mind, I begin my casual descent back to the campsite, lost in a reverie of optimism. Life is good, full of hope and possibility. On the way down, I find that my grouse friends have moved off into the forest somewhere, and the middle part of the afternoon remains pleasantly warm as I settle deeper into the idea that it's okay to just relax and be a traveller in this vast wilderness, open to its lessons. This is where the magic that is life happens for me. Walking around an unfamiliar mountainside is inspiring, and wandering around the edges of a vast wilderness is comfortable. Ideas that need to get out require time to percolate, germinate and process, and that is decidedly more difficult to achieve back home when I'm stuck in my routine of eat/work/get drunk/sleep/repeat.

I admit it would be picture-perfect to see a deer or a wolf or some other wildlife in the occasional clearing as I pass, but it's not essential to the experience – and for a change, I'm quick to accept that it's just not to be today. I worried early on about this trip being a pointless exercise is escapism, but thankfully that doesn't appear to be the case. As the hours lose their shape and the days blend into an indistinguishable mass, the journey is developing into the calming and life-affirming reconnect with the natural world I was hoping for, and I thank God for that.

Back at the campsite I make my way down to the dumpster with the last of my beers and my camera for another attempt at sunset shots. Once again, they fail to turn out the way I envision them. But that's okay, I don't really care – for the moment, I believe in the process and know there are plenty of sunsets ahead that I can practise shooting until I get it right. Or maybe I never will, and this wish for capturing a moment of purity and beauty will remain unrealized. Just having the chance is enough. After all, I don't imagine myself a photographer any more than I imagine myself a writer. They're just convenient labels, used in polite company to avoid sounding long-winded, unsure or self-important. The fact is I don't know what I want to be when I grow up, and putting a label on it isn't going to help.

Susan Shaughnessy once wrote a book of meditations for writers called *Walking on Alligators*. In it, artistic people of every type are quoted on the process of creating, and in a few paragraphs Shaughnessy offers an interpretation of each quote. One of my favourites is from actor Nick Nolte, who once said, "I was never able to define the concept of happiness. All I'm looking for is to be engaged and not self-indulged." That sounds pretty good to me.

After dinner I let the campfire die a natural death, and as the coals fade, a chill gathers, so I crawl into my high-tech cocoon. Inside, I'm warm and comfortable with a headlamp and a good book, and the subtle sounds of the forest night beyond the nylon envelop me. Outside, a gentle breeze tries and fails to add a bit of oomph to the evening as it massages the very tops of the lodgepole pines that surround me on all sides. The billions of stars overhead have been narrowed to a long strip of dark littered with points of light in the gap in the tree cover above my tent site. Under those stars, I'm just another being in the universe, searching for an appropriate way to interact, and for the moment it's okay to truly relax, because there appears to be balance in the cosmos.

Besides, I'm too physically tired to be stressed out anyway, and as I slowly drift off to sleep, my weary muscles ache in a way that is not altogether unpleasant. They say your troubles cannot climb, walk or roam, and that statement has never been as true as it is right here, right now. As consciousness fades, a little bit of the nervous tension I've been carrying around for years is released and bleeds into the earth beneath me. It's all right if I do things my way. It's perfectly normal to be peaceful and curious. It doesn't matter if these actions and efforts don't make any sense or apply to the everyday world I've left behind. This remains worth doing, and I am inspired.

It could be I owe that Thoreau fellow an apology.

9

MOUNT ENGADINE

In this world I often think you'll understand me,
In these words I often think you'll recognize me.
—Jim Moginie, Peter Garrett (Midnight Oil)

It isn't long before the concept of total relaxation and the thought of becoming one with the universe are put firmly to the test. Overnight, or more accurately in the murky hour before first light, I am gradually dragged to consciousness by the shrill yip and howl of a small group of coyotes. I am in the deepest part of the nightly sleep cycle when I first begin to feel a strange force pull me from the depths as a recurring set of distant calls slowly gain in volume somewhere out in the physical world. It's unsettling at the best of times to be woken up in unfamiliar surroundings. The muddy, seemingly incoherent nature of a brain that's been in shutdown mode; the physical incapacity common in dreams; the bizarre tangents the mind takes as it warms up – these can make for a disagreeable way to start the day. Add to the mix a pack of wild dogs and a thermometer approaching the freezing mark, and an alarm clock at full volume would positively be a treat by comparison.

It is a mountain tradition and the belief of many Aboriginal cultures that there was a time when man and animal could communicate. Folklore speaks of spirit guides that were thought to protect individuals and clans, and members of the animal kingdom were also thought to possess power and wisdom not often recognized in our modern times. A power animal represented an individual's connection to all life and was believed to be a rough reflection of that person's character. The spirit that occupies the physical form of the chosen animal was also thought to empower the individual and protect them from harm, like a guardian angel would.

I'm fond of animals because I envy their simple and direct way of being and because their behaviour often makes more sense to me than the often erratic behaviour of other people. I don't spend enough time outdoors to have had a vision guide me, however, nor have I put much time into figuring out what my spirit animal might actually be, until now. I desperately want it to be a grizzly bear of course, because they are a symbol of the wildness of this land as surely as any craggy, wind-ravaged peak is. But under the circumstances I'm going to go with coyote, and it seems I have not fallen so far from my animal ancestry as to be completely unaware of my surroundings, even at the edges of sleep. At the moment I am at the periphery of the action and remain caught somewhere between dreams and reality as the coyotes move through the valley. Although I sense their presence, they remain difficult to locate or understand clearly through my mental haze. The different howls are all just chatter in a foreign language that seems to be coming from everywhere, until a call from only a few hundred yards away jerks me unceremoniously from my fog.

Suddenly, I'm as wide awake as if I'd been touched by a live electrical wire, and the coyotes give the impression of being all around. A short howl is again let loose from close by and is answered from a considerable distance away before other yips and barks are asked and answered by different members of the pack along the hillside above and below the campground. The experience is not scary, exactly, but does get the adrenaline pumping in a way good European espresso and a Danish never could, and there's little doubt that there are small animals out in the forest that are not having an enjoyable morning.

It's all a reminder that despite the amenities and conveniences set up for campers and travellers to this region, I am still essentially in the wilderness, and after this unusual wake-up call I can't get back to sleep. So I lie there instead, listening to my brothers of the land slowly fade into the distance on a bearing I can't exactly put my finger on, although they do seem to be heading south, in the general direction of Elk Pass. Getting up for a pee out the back of my site 20 minutes later, I can't help but notice a little-used walking path, which in light of my recent visitors now appears to be a game trail, not ten metres from my tent. I did take note of it yesterday but failed to recognize it as an animal highway. I'm pretty sure none of the coyotes used it today, but just the same I am glad I hung my food bag far from my site and followed proper backcountry cooking etiquette for all my meals.

A half-hour later, I get up for good and am greeted to an overcast start to the morning. It has remained cool, but I break camp easily now that I've had a few practice rounds. Following my standard procedure, I fill my water bottles in the public washroom on the way out of the campground before rolling out toward the highway, and the first few kilometres glide by with good energy – absorbed from my passing guests, no doubt. I'm now headed back toward Canmore via a different route than I came in on and will inevitably have to try and interact with the regular world for a few days before continuing north toward Jasper. Canmore, Banff and Lake Louise are all between where I am and where I want to go, and I'm worried. After a little bit of time away, I'm not sure how I'm going to react to human company again. I'm getting comfortable being alone and am not in much of a rush to get back to society.

The incident with the coyotes this morning is a simple reminder that we are pack animals, not herd animals. Humans are the direct descendants of hunter-gatherers, nomads, clans and small groups. We're not cows. We're coyotes. We're wolves. A few of us are even bears, accustomed to physical effort and a life lived in contact with the outdoors. Over hundreds of thousands of years, we've evolved in a system of close personal ties and have interacted with wide open spaces, and yet in the last 100 years we've been drawn to the congestion and chaos of increasingly large cities and towns. Ironically, we've distanced ourselves from each other even as we've got together in larger numbers. Single-family homes in sprawling suburbs, long work hours and brutal daily commutes have in a short time usurped our connection to the natural processes – and to each other – that took millennia to develop. Add the fatigue associated to the effort of keeping up, and even when we're together there is often little connection. We are now humans doing, not humans being.

The social problems attendant to those changes are obvious and enormous, yet are accepted with few questions as the byproducts of progress: pollution, overpopulation, crime, violence, divorce and chronic stress all appear to be consequences in the "growth" of our urbanized culture. Most frightening of all, we imagine and accept this change as normal, a simple outcome in the business of doing business. An inevitable side effect of modern life, if you will. And for the most part we don't even notice what's going on anymore; we simply consent to the changes unconsciously. But not me – not today, at least. I am in touch with my inner wild once again.

Feeling cocky and self-righteous in equal measure, I attack the pedals and create a chilling wind with my progress along the deserted roadway as the energy of my core begins pulsing up through layers of accumulated sloth and casual indifference. The trees whip by in a pine-scented blur, and I am a powerful presence in the universe, a force to be reckoned with in a great, wide natural environment. I am capable and potent, yet light as air gliding over the surface of the earth, and for a few precious moments I truly belong. I am an animal in the best sense of the word.

I settle back in to a sustainable rhythm a couple of kilometres farther on, the adrenalin coursing through my veins ebbs, and I am left to ponder the possibility that the way we live may in fact be part of the new natural process, one that I may not understand but that is nevertheless inevitable. Urbanization is an unstoppable force, and we are drawn to it like (and please excuse the obvious cliché) moths to the flame. A reasonable argument could also be made that human beings are simply progressing to the next phase of evolution, and as I pedal along, I'm one of the last dinosaurs, clinging desperately to a way of life that's about to get clobbered by a meteor. It could be that I'm merely attempting to visit a place we can never truly get back to. Seekers and pilgrims are vanishing from the collective landscape, and as the decades pass there will be more pavement and land management and less actual wilderness to get properly engaged in. Lessons will come in different forms, and a link to our ancestral past will be cut, a part of us hopelessly lost.

Whatever the future, I do know that in just a few days of operating in this new environment, with its different set of challenges and different day-to-day requirements, I have uncovered another version of myself. I like to think it's a truer version, but even if that's not the case, there is no doubt it's a happier one. By removing the needless pressures and expectations that have become commonplace in my existence, I am no longer envious or greedy or angry or bossy, all traits that I'm afraid come rather too easily when I'm in my regular routine. Out here, pedalling along with no set destination and a very loose time frame, I am simply me, and that fills me with an indescribable type of joy. Not to mention a notable amount of inner peace.

Approaching the junction to Spray Trail, I'm tempted once again to chuck it all and just disappear. Let the bill collectors and the taxmen try and find me as I drift across North America's back roads with no fixed address and no bitter attachments. It would be easy enough. All I have to do is backtrack a few kilometres along Kananaskis Lakes Trail to Highway 40, turn south and go. But instead I make two lazy and uncertain circles on the empty pavement before veering left, digging into my pedals and, with a curious mix of energy, anxiety and disappointment, beginning the journey back to Canmore. After a few hundred solid uphill pedal strokes, the thought of maybe even making the distance all in one go does cross my more orderly mind. With the ground already covered this morning, the effort would easily constitute the biggest day of the trip so far and a victory according to my old, shallow way of thinking.

And so the battle continues.

• • •

Spray Trail, which is often referred to as the Smith–Dorrien Highway at this southern end, starts with a long climb on deteriorating pavement littered with potholes and haphazard patch jobs. But it's still early, and I continue to feel remarkably strong. Bypassing the northern end of Lower Kananaskis Lake requires a long, lazy S along the lower reaches of Mount Kent. After the initial shock of travelling straight uphill, I find there's a hidden reserve of energy in my legs that wasn't there even a few days ago. A burst is no longer painful, nor embarrassingly short-lived. In fact, there's a remarkable feeling of power and endurance hidden deep in the old bones and tissues. I get up out of the saddle to stomp this early challenge, testing just how much gas is in the tank. The heavy burn of lactic acid buildup is slow in coming and washes away quickly when I settle back to a comfortable pace.

This has turned into an interesting-looking morning. Moody clouds split the sky into a left and a right as the sun desperately tries to break through high above the Opal and Elk ranges, with a mirror image of the scene reflected off a small pond midway up the climb. Up around the corner from the pond, the pavement gives way to gravel, which by this time of year has usually been driven into definable grooves. In winter, this road is better maintained than many of the suburban streets of Calgary, oddly enough – it is plowed wide, with packed snow filling many of the washboard ruts. In summer, vehicular traffic tends to cut the gravel down to the hard, bare clay. Recently, however, a new layer of aggregate has been laid that makes the cycling exceptionally difficult. The road appears smooth, but the new layer is a fraction too deep for narrow tires to run along without digging in, so a hill that would normally be a little test is now bordering on an impossible task as I sink and swerve and teeter with every pedal stroke.

Nowhere is momentum more important than on a difficult climb. Every time I break stride, everything grinds to a halt, including my will. Twice already I've jumped off to push my overloaded rig – but each time, after only a few steps, I cursed my lack of determination, and the hill, and the world at large, and reluctantly clambered back on my bike to struggle upward. It seems like every time I stop paying attention to the task at hand and try to drift off into a mindless rhythm, another awkward swerve upsets the equilibrium as my tires dig in with an audible crunch and swish of gravel. After such an energetic start to the morning, it's incredibly frustrating.

I do have a personal grading system for just such an occasion, which helps put some perspective on the task at hand, and it goes something like this: *An easy grade* is barely noticeable, and *an easy hill* is taken in full stride by simply pushing a little harder or shifting a couple of gears. *A challenge* usually requires a few more gear changes, and *an ass kicker* will produce at least a bucket of sweat. *A gut check* generally takes more than an hour to climb, and *impossible* translates into walking uphill, which is a great indignity to most cyclists. I use the system to occupy my mind as much as to accurately score a climb. This little gem is not long enough to qualify as *a gut check* but, thanks to the steepness and poor surface, certainly rates as *an ass kicker*.

As I finally hit the midway point, to a chorus of grunts and creative curses, an ancient-looking tour bus labours slowly past, swirling up dust and belching out a thick cloud of diesel exhaust. I should be amused that even the almighty internal combustion engine is struggling on this hill, but that offers little comfort. Suddenly a pleasant, if challenging, morning has turned ugly. Riding unsteadily at a ridiculously slow pace, all I can think is: *How many more kilometres are there to go like this?* And: *There's no way I'll ever make it.* If the trip down to Kananaskis Lakes has been a glimpse of the positive, travelling back toward Canmore suddenly feels poisonous, and every uninspired turn of the pedals and uncomfortable step feels both pointless and redundant as I grow increasingly tense about moving in this direction.

After what seems like hours but is probably closer to 25 minutes, I finally make it up around the corner and on to flatter ground, where I am greeted by a gorgeous moon-set over the mountains. Temporarily exhausted by the awkward struggle, I stop and lean the bike against a signpost to gather my thoughts and pull out my point-and-shoot camera for some quick snapshots. It's a handsome scene as the moon slowly sinks lower in the sky above the Spray Mountains. Before long, the moon will disappear altogether, and the ridiculousness of my fit becomes apparent as I calm down enough to watch it go. Taking a long pull from my water bottle, I can't help but laugh at my own hubris. Here I am tooling around in an area of the world most people on the planet will never have the privilege to see, and too often still I've got my head down to the point where I don't see much of anything at all.

I mean, really, so what if I'm forced to slow down because the road's been recently gravelled? So what if I've got to walk up a couple of the more difficult hills because I didn't train hard enough before setting out? So what if it takes an extra day or two to get back to Canmore – or, looking forward, an extra week to get to Jasper?

"SO WHAT! SO WHAT! SO WHAT!" I howl out, un-expectedly, at the moon and the mountains and the trees, startling myself and the wind and all the subtle forest sounds into total silence. Feeling self-conscious, I steal a look up and down the road to see if anyone is within ear-shot, before letting loose one final throaty burst. "WHO CARES?"

Apart from my ego, no one cares of course, yet a part of me is still focused on goals and distances, and remains caught up in a vicious swirl of judgment and expectation. Even though I've come out in search of balance and per-spective, this preoccupation continues to dominate. The outside world is always here, waiting to be explored, and it remains up to me to change, but after looking for too long through a muddled prism of debt-based capitalism and modern electronics, I remain largely blind to alterna-tive possibilities and linger in the maelstrom of my own distorted thinking.

I gather myself up enough to continue, and the road levels out just as the moon finally dips below the moun-tains to the west. From here to Canmore it's about 55 kilo-metres along a rolling and gently winding mountain road, but the distance hardly seems to matter anymore. Big sec-tions of loose gravel remain, similar to what from this day forward will be known as Meltdown Hill, but fortunately some stretches have already been driven off – the parallel tire ruts have cut down to the hard roadbed. A handful of the descents are surprisingly fast, and only occasionally do I get bogged down enough to require any serious cursing. To further distract from the idea of time and distance, all manner of hoof and paw prints are visible on the margin-ally softer clay of the shoulder, including three individual sets that belong, judging by their size, to black bears.

Sometime this summer, a yearling and two separate adults have all wandered sections of the road for a few hundred yards before disappearing again into the forest. It hasn't rained much recently, so the moulds marking their progress are probably all weeks or even months old, and the surface at the roadside is now so firm that an animal travelling this route within the last three weeks would probably have left no mark. It is yet another reminder that I am in bear country and should be diligent and aware. The trouble is, I've seen plenty of bears in the wild over the years and am not particularly frightened by them, which is not necessarily a good thing. At the Parry Sound dump in Ontario's cottage country, spotting a half dozen plump and habituated black bears was always a sure bet on a sultry summer evening, and Highway 37 in northern BC abounds with rumps rushing into the forest with the approach of any vehicle. For up close and personal, nothing beats a sea kayak and 20 metres of ocean separating you from a slightly confused bruin on BC's Pacific coast.

Closer to home, the CP Rail tracks at Kicking Horse Pass near Lake Louise are also a good place to spot both black and grizzly bears feeding on spilled grain, or simply using the comparatively level ground as a throughway. I've even come upon a black bear while cycling on the roadside between Jasper and Mount Robson, but the yearling was remarkably disinterested and simply peered curiously over the tall grass and 20-odd metres between us before returning peacefully to his lunch, a fish he had pulled from the nearby river. All were thrilling experiences, because a bear is without a doubt a fascinating animal, but none were what you would call an encounter. I've never been bluff charged or threatened in any way by a bear, or any other wild animal, come to think of it. But it only has to happen once.

I don't have a specific bear strategy and am not sure what I would do in a surprise meeting at close range. Fumble helplessly with my canister of bear spray; whimper; wet myself – these all come to mind as plausible options, but in the end I'd probably point my front wheel downhill and ride. Unfortunately, a grizzly is as fast as a horse over a short distance, and even on a bike it would be a close race that I would probably end up losing. So I take comfort in two small details: none of the tracks I've seen on the road look fresh, and more importantly, none of them are big enough to indicate grizzly.

After some pleasant riding with the thought of bears and coyotes bouncing around in my head, it isn't long before I find myself approaching the border between Peter Lougheed and Spray Lakes provincial parks, where there's a place I've been meaning to visit for years but have never got around to: Mount Engadine Lodge. A cozy six-room chalet-style hotel with two outlying cabins overlooking Moose Meadows, Mount Engadine Lodge is one of a handful private enterprises scattered throughout the Rockies that offer an oasis of luxury in an unspoiled natural setting. Swish accommodations have never really been my thing, but every once in a while it is nice to see how the other half lives.

Being weary of places like Mount Engadine, I approach the entrance with an unusual amount of caution. I'm tired, dusty and dressed like a guy who's been wandering around at the edge of the wilderness, which does nothing to relieve my sense of unease. Expense is the obvious deterrent to spending time in a place like this, but I also don't have much in common with people who can afford these pricey luxuries, so hanging around often makes me uncomfortable. Looking and smelling like a fur trader who's been out on the trapline for a week also doesn't help. Besides, what's the point in avoiding human interactions for a while, only to engage in an awkward set of forced conversations with strangers at first contact?

But I do need a coffee and some water and a few minutes to set out a plan for the afternoon, so I resist the urge to flee, and dust off my best sociable human persona before making for the main door.

Turns out innkeepers Chris and Shari-Lynn are extremely nice, and all the guests appear to be in full relaxation mode and don't seem desperate to talk about open heart surgery or hostile takeovers or massive real estate deals right off the bat, so I try to relax and enjoy the surroundings. Shari-Lynn shows me around the common areas of the lodge and casually offers tea or coffee out on the deck before going back to her paperwork in the small office. Chris eventually wanders over to introduce himself and assures me that beer can also be purchased from the bar and that if the last couple of days are any indication, the moose that frequent the meadow will be dropping by for a visit any time now. Intrigued by the unusual combination of alcohol, a comfortable deck chair, a couple of good books and large, photogenic wildlife, I settle in with my camera and notebook for an afternoon of leisure and contented relaxation, now confident that itinerary decisions can wait.

Contrary to my initial misgivings, Mount Engadine turns out to be charming in every way possible, and by the time I get halfway through my first beer, I am smitten. The magnetic sliding screen door that keeps small woodland creatures out and the resident cat, Nala, in; the mountain- and wildlife-inspired art; the antique skis and snowshoes on the wall; the mini-library, complete with magazine table; and the beginnings of the Spray River in the form of Smuts Creek meandering lazily by – all lend a rare combination of charm and casual style to the place. The rooms have no locks or keys or televisions, and there is no cell phone service in the area. House rules include tea and sweets from three to five in the afternoon, with dinner at seven and a two-stage breakfast – continental followed by hot – starting at eight a.m.

Mike, who works in the kitchen and comes out on the deck during his break, looks vaguely familiar, and we get to talking about the moose that come here to drink from the bog located below and to the right of the main deck. The water in the bog is laced with selenium, and the animals spend much of the summer and fall travelling to and from the mineral-rich oasis. Apparently, as many as eight to ten moose can be spotted at any one time, wallowing belly-deep in the slop or lingering in the meadow below – including the dominant male in the area, Whitestockings. So named for the graying fur of his lower legs, he is the alpha male and as such possesses the most impressive set of antlers, which if my calculations are correct should be nearly full grown at this point in the season.

The largest member of the deer family, moose are a bit ridiculous no matter which way you look at them. Exceedingly tall, with long, thin legs, they resemble cartoon-character horses drawn by a child artist with an eye for the absurd. Yet their impressive size helps project an indefinable strength that cannot be ignored. Behind only the bison, moose are the second-largest land animal in North America, and although they are nowhere near regal, a clumsy dignity prevails. A moose rarely hustles, preferring to amble through an average home range of 5 to 20 kilometres, where it lives for about 20 years. Unlike most other deer species, they do not usually form herds, preferring a solitary existence, except during the yearly rut. This makes the Mount Engadine bog gatherings something of an uncommon event in the moose world, and I'm willing to wait for it.

Unfortunately, it appears the local "swamp donkeys," as Mike affectionately refers to them, are feeling shy, as only a single cow, with this year's calf in tow, comes by for a drink in the time it takes me to sip on two Grasshopper Wheat Ales. The calf stays close to its mother and in the fashion of all young animals is both outlandish and cute. It's a thrill to creep slowly down the small path leading out to a viewing platform at the edge of the meadow, and after a few pictures I become habituated to the idea of having the awkward creatures around, as if the idea of moose dinner theatre was the most natural thing in the world.

I'm back on the main deck and well into my third beer when Whitestockings finally makes his much-anticipated appearance, but instead of beelining it for the bog, he decides instead to wander the meadow in the long late-afternoon shadows cast by Mount Shark and Shark Ridge. Coy or camera shy (I'm not sure which), he manages to stay just outside the effective maximum range of my long lens as Mike and I pass the time before dinner chatting about the people we know back in Canmore, a mere 35 kilometres away. Glancing across the meadow below, which is framed by the impressive silhouettes of Shark Ridge, Mount Smuts and the Fist, I realize that the distance to Canmore could easily be 1,000 miles – a whole other world that exists a world away.

By the time I get through that third beer, it's obvious that Whitestockings is not going to come any closer and that I'm not going anywhere, so I'm eventually led upstairs and down the hall, past rooms named Chickadee, Wolf and Elk, before being delivered to the aptly named Moose, a large suite with a queen bed, vaulted ceiling, two couches and a gas-burning stove in the corner. Shari-Lynn gives me a great deal on the room since it was going to be vacant tonight anyway, and after I strip off and shower, I quickly get lost in the decadence of crisp white sheets and a fluffy down comforter before drifting off for a late-afternoon nap to the sound of the other guests floating up from the deck below.

• • •

Waking up at Mount Engadine Lodge is as near a flawless experience as I've ever experienced in the hotel industry. That's a pretty big statement, I know, but the place really is great. It's not normally in my nature to gush – anyone who's read this far will notice I can complain about almost anything – yet the only thing I can find wrong with the lodge is that my salmon last night was just a touch dry, and that I would never be able to afford to stay for more than a couple of nights in any calendar year. But even with the steep rates, a short visit is time and money well spent. Last night I left my private patio door open and slept not to the soothing sounds of a meandering creek, as expected, but to the sloshing and snorting of moose wallowing in the bog. As it turns out, they simply needed the privacy of darkness for their daily visit, and that unusual experience alone made stopping over worthwhile. Now I feel like I don't ever want to leave.

After coffee on the deck in the growing sunshine, breakfast is served, but I've barely tucked into my elk sausages and eggs Benedict when I'm interrupted by the sudden appearance of Whitestockings out in the meadow. He's finally come out of the shadows, and I can't pass up the opportunity to finally get a good look at the old boy. Even though breakfast is delicious, it will have to go uneaten. I sprint back up to my room to collect my camera gear. By the time I make it back downstairs, however, my muse has already been put off by the crowd gathering on the deck and has begun to wander off across the meadow once again.

This is getting personal now, and I feel like Whitestockings is taunting me, appearing only in low light or when I don't have my equipment handy, but I have no intention of letting him slip away too easily. In an unusually proactive act, I've got spare batteries and extra lenses tucked in every pocket and am determined not to repeat the owl incident, in which I was fortunate enough to be in the right place at the right time but was completely unprepared when the best shot presented itself. One thing is for sure: Whitestockings will have dogged company this morning.

Stalking an animal is an undeniable thrill and a throwback to our hunter-gatherer days, when we wouldn't survive if we didn't go out and find food. There is something innate and compelling about the process, and the irresistible pull of hunter toward prey is not diminished by the fact that I'm not trying to kill my quarry; I'm merely hoping to take his picture. The same set of subtle interactions apply: he occasionally looks over his shoulder to see where I am and what I'm up to, while I attempt to get him within range of my long lens without instigating a confrontation or chasing him off into the surrounding forest.

Whitestockings does live in a protected area and in his lifetime has never had cause to fear humans, but that doesn't mean he's tame. Respect is warranted. One could even say it is recommended. If Whitestockings were so inclined, he could gore me with his formidable rack of full-sized fall antlers; or, standing better than six feet tall at the shoulder and weighing over 1,000 pounds at a guess, could stomp me to bits in about ten seconds flat. So I try to keep my distance despite the lure of the hunt.

Another guest at the lodge, a quiet German who doesn't speak much English, also appears to be a determined photographer, and before long we're both making our way along the gravel access road that leads to the cross-country ski trails and helipad at Mount Shark. Our prey is now almost all the way across the meadow, and at first we are both hesitant about leaving the comfort and relative safety of the road. We're now on the west side of Smuts creek, and a short, steep slope leads down to the flat of the valley bottom. A couple of female moose and one calf are also now just leaving the bog and slowly moving this way, which creates the uncomfortable circumstance of having moose on both sides of us should we venture too far from the road.

There is great debate growing around here about what exactly constitutes harassment of wild animals. It turns out that this part of the Rocky Mountains is one of the most easily accessible wilderness areas left anywhere on earth. Edmonton is about four hours away, Lethbridge is roughly three hours' drive, and Calgary is a good deal less than two, and within that range more than 2.5 million people make their homes. Calgary International Airport moves 12 million passengers a year, and although this provincial park lacks the infrastructure necessary for mass tourism, a growing number of people are finding their way here. While we may not have achieved the status of Africa's Serengeti plain or the reputation of Yellowstone, there are people who now travel to the Rocky Mountain Parks and the surrounding region specifically for the wildlife experience. I believe it comes as something of a surprise to them that so many animals live in such close proximity to such a large, permanent human population. Consequently, most are unprepared for the sudden appearance of large mammals at the roadside, and a good number are oblivious to proper etiquette.

The big issue is that a car, SUV or camper van is a remarkably unwieldy piece of equipment on narrow mountain roads, and it doesn't take many of them to create a hazardous situation for animal and human alike. Bear jams, goat jams, wolf jams and elk jams, among any number of other types of animal-inspired gridlock, are, like any traffic tie-up, stressful and dangerous – especially for the animals, which are now being struck by cars, trucks and trains at a rate that brings into question the sustainability of certain species in these parks. Although somewhat enlightened, even I can't say I've always been a model citizen of the wild world.

My first real experience in wildlife protocol came in the mid-'90s and was taught to me not by my parents or an experienced traveller, or even a park ranger. I didn't read it in a book, and I didn't extract the tip from a Parks info pamphlet. In this case it wasn't even a land animal who imparted the important lesson but 9,000 pounds of apex predator who was none too happy to be dealing with me. Before that day on the northeastern shore of Vancouver Island, I could be described as a wary yet persistent observer of wildlife and almost certainly as possessing poor manners. It was *Orcinus orca*, more commonly referred to as the killer whale, that began the long process of setting me straight.

I was travelling with my two brothers and my parents, and the day began with some casual paddling in our sea kayaks from a campsite on the shore, with the intent of crossing the dead-calm waters of Johnstone Strait and possibly moving up into Blackfish Sound before finding another campsite for the night. It was our third day on the water out of Telegraph Cove, and within 20 minutes a small pod of orcas announced its presence in the strait with the unmistakable pop and blow of a surfacing whale. It is a sound that can be heard nearly ten kilometres away and is sure to excite anyone with even a passing interest in wildlife. Sitting in a kayak no more than five metres long with your butt essentially at water level only magnifies the adrenalin rush, and the whales crossed the three or four kilometres of ocean with remarkable swiftness and were soon just a kilometre up the coast, travelling toward the campsite we had just abandoned.

Turning tail for a better look, we soon crossed their path, and seeing as the whales were now feeding on salmon in the waters below and not travelling from one place to another, we could paddle fast enough to get in for a closer look. One small motor boat, one small fishing boat, and our four kayaks (three singles and a double) accompanied the whales for breakfast, and soon enough an awkward little dance developed. The whales avoided the boats as best they could while training their focus on the fish below. Most of the time they surfaced 50 or 60 metres away on the ocean side and then circled back for a pass along the shoreline, but it was difficult to track all four whales at the same time, and inevitably one would surface in a spray of mist, without warning and much closer to the boats. Being young and dumb, I got it in my head that the best possible photo with my crummy little point-and-shoot would be of the big male – whose dorsal fin was easily two metres tall and twice as high as I was sitting in the kayak – shot from closer to the shoreline, with the other kayaks in the background.

This strategy proved effective at first; the whales passed often between my kayak and the other boats, but they never surfaced in quite the right place. Eventually, the big dorsal I was waiting for began to break the surface not 25 metres dead ahead, and it doesn't take a rocket scientist to figure out that an eight-metre-long whale is going to take a bit of space to surface and dive again. Fortunately, whereas I was paralyzed with fear, he was quick to action and swerved decisively to his right, comfortably avoiding a collision with the tip of my kayak. As he passed, I got a great view of his markings: smooth black skin contrasted with a pure white underbelly, a distinctive white eye patch and the grey saddle patch, unique to each individual animal, were all clearly visible from close range; and just ahead of the eye patch was a small black eye that, once catastrophe was averted, gave me one of the dirtiest looks I've ever got in my life.

The lesson was well received: don't crowd me!

Back out in the meadow with Whitestockings, the two females and the calf have passed us by and, being apathetic to our attentions, have moved on to the cover of the forest. Whitestockings obviously doesn't see us as a threat; having lain down five minutes ago, he continues to doze in the sunshine. But I am resolute in my efforts not to crowd him, much. The German and I are content to sit and wait to see what happens next. We both obviously want the same thing, and that is to capture a memorable image, but I also believe there is more to it than that. A good picture is one thing, but I also sense a deeper need. We want to interact with this moose in some important yet inexplicable way. We have some kind of unspoken desire to come into contact with a being that is not part of the usual set of human interactions; a deep-seeded wish to return to an uncomplicated way of being that is at once foreign yet natural.

Whatever the motivation, these experiences create indelible memories, and the common thread in these brief wildlife encounters, apart from wild animals being really cool, of course, is that I am always present and aware of my surroundings to a rare degree. My primal self has been activated at its core, and my base instincts are suddenly rejuvenated. I am keenly aware of the behaviour and subtle nuances coming from each individual animal (even as I occasionally act the oaf and the boor), and the surrounding environment stands out in sharp relief. The wind, the angle of the sun, how the light washes over the meadow – these mix with the subtle smells of fall's last, valiant stand. Or, in the case of the whales, the perfect mirror and warm, humid scent of a dead-calm ocean stirred my primitive being. In these moments I am vigilant. I am aware. I am awake. I am alive.

Sometimes, life is heaven.

• • •

GREAT GREY OWL

POLICEMAN'S CREEK BOARDWALK

LOADED UP AND READY TO GO

YAMNUSKA AND THE BOW RIVER

LATE EVENING ON THE BOW RIVER

195

MOUNT KIDD

THE EMPTY HIGHWAY SOUTH OF
KANANASKIS VILLAGE

HOME AWAY FROM HOME

A PERSISTENT CAMP COMPANION

KANANASKIS LAKES

MOODY SUNRISE OVER THE OPAL RANGE

LATE SUN ON THE OPAL RANGE

THE DECK AT MOUNT ENGADINE LODGE

MOTHER AND DAUGHTER CROSS THE MEADOW

A RAINBOW ON THE EAST END OF RUNDLE

A SURPRISING FOREST
DWELLER ALONG THE
BOW VALLEY PARKWAY

A QUIET MORNING ON BANFF AVE.

AN ACCIDENT WAITING TO HAPPEN

THE TRICKLE THAT STARTED IT ALL

WHICH WAY TO LAKE LOUISE?

ONE OF MANY SUPERLATIVE VIEWS FROM LARCH VALLEY

TAKING A BREAK NEAR THE COLUMBIA ICEFIELD

PREPARING FOR A COLD DESCENT

A CLIFF FACE ON THE ICEFIELD PARKWAY

THE BEGINNING OF ENDLESS CHAIN RIDGE

THE SUPPLY HELICOPTER
PREPARES FOR TAKEOFF AT
ABBOT PASS

INSTALLING AN
ANEMOMETER AT BOW HUT

BOOT KICKING MOUNT OLIVE –
PHOTO BY LAWRENCE WHITE

DESTINATION ST. NICHOLAS

THE WAPTA ICEFIELD

AN UNIDENTIFIED PARTY ON THE ATHABASCA GLACIER

Filled with excited energy after clomping around the meadow for about an hour, I finally come to realize with some regret that it really is time to go. As perfect as Mount Engadine may be, and as tempted as I may be to stay, I am on a larger mission, and there is no time to dilly-dally. Breakfast was interrupted by the impromptu photo shoot, but by the time I change into my cycling clothes and gather up my gear, a brown bag lunch has magically appeared on the dining room end table: cold-cut sandwiches, celery and carrot sticks and obscenely delicious home-made cookies.

The ride out from Engadine to my front door is only about 35 straightforward kilometres and proves uneventful. Working my way along the eastern shore of Spray Lakes Reservoir is easy going on what amounts to a gradual downhill grade, and surprisingly fast even with the freshly laid gravel. Sitting at the top of Whiteman's Gap with my sandwiches and my cookies I've now got a sweeping view of Canmore below, but I'm in no great rush to plunge back into my town, and by extension my old life. Plunging being an apt metaphor not only for the rapid descent into the Bow Valley from the Spray Lakes and Goat Creek valleys but also for the rapid return to that less charming version of myself who I know lives there. And so I linger.

The modern history of this gap is somewhat uncertain and is worth exploring, in the absence of the will to move. It is most likely named after Father Pierre-Jean De Smet, a Belgian priest who came here in 1845 from the same direction I have just travelled and who was surely the first European to cross the Divide in the southern Rockies from west to east. De Smet was on a peace mission with members of the Kootenay tribe, and upon crossing what is now known as White Man Pass, he erected a cross that he described as a "sign of salvation and peace to all the scattered and itinerant tribes east and west of these gigantic and lurid mountains." It stands to reason that if White Man Pass is named after De Smet, then Whiteman's Gap is probably named after him as well.

However, less than two months before De Smet passed through here, two British spies, Lieutenant Henry Warre and Lieutenant Mervin Vavasour, travelled past this very spot in the traditional east–west direction. Disguised as gentlemen adventurers, the pair led an entourage of nine Hudson's Bay employees to determine the US military capabilities in the Oregon territory. It is somewhat remarkable that between 1841 and 1845, only three parties used this route (Sinclair was the first, but his Métis heritage probably means the Gap was not named after him) and that two of them passed by in such rapid succession. Add spotty records for the time, and it's no wonder that the exact naming of this feature is in question.

While Warre, Vavasour and De Smet may have just missed crossing paths here, it does appear that they shared some common experiences. Both parties report that the mountains and valleys of the region were awe-inspiring, but both also found this part of the route physically demanding. Warre created the first known painting of the mountains in the Canmore Corridor in a work that depicts Mount Rundle and Cascade Mountain in a truly flattering light, and De Smet gushes in his journal about the grandeur of the Spray Valley. But he also relates a six-hour journey down the gap that left men and horses battered and bruised. His travelling companions, having now entered rival Blackfoot territory, also experienced nightmares while camping in the valley below.

Looking down on Canmore from high above, my fitful

sleep in this place appears to hinge on the conflict between setting down roots and abandoning that overworked path for the independence and uncertainty of the road. I don't really hate it here, I'm just uncomfortable trying to fit in; I can't seem to reconcile my place in this place. It doesn't help that the ocean of change altering the face of my community is the will of the many, and I am but one of the few who sees all this growth as fundamentally dangerous (or at the very least slightly distasteful). Still, I lack the courage to let it all go and pack up my bags and leave for good. So instead I bitch about one and escape out to the other and never really feel at peace with either.

I'm contemplating the whole predicament when one of the nice couples with whom I shared dinner last night stops and rolls down the car window to marvel openly at my progress. The trip didn't seem all that fast and certainly wasn't strenuous, but they are nevertheless impressed by the effort. In the casual atmosphere that accompanies vacation time, we share an easy laugh about our time together at the lodge and as a result share a fleeting moment of mutual understanding. He's a doctor and she's a lawyer, or maybe she's the doctor and he's the lawyer, but it doesn't matter much. Come to think of it, I can't even remember their names, but dinner was a surprisingly pleasant affair despite the differing lifestyles.

There were eight of us at the table, including myself and the picture-taking German, and after the initial discomfort of the company of strangers, the conversation was properly engaging and not one bit unpleasant. We did drift into some serious bullshit when the subject of international banking temporarily took centre stage, but mostly we talked about family and travel and aspirations and dreams, just like regular people.

It seems we all make choices that dictate the course of our lives, and there are times when our paths intersects with others' in unexpected ways, which lets us get a fresh perspective and an alternative view on the world at large. It is one of the gifts hidden in the challenges of travel. Matthiessen and the unexpected effect of his quest are again brought to mind unbidden. While in search of blue sheep and the ever-elusive Asian mountain cat *The Snow Leopard* is named after, he mused about the prospect of a "free life," and of "traveling light, without clinging or despising." Nepal remains a challenging travel destination to this day, and I can't fathom what it was like to spend time in a remote corner of the country over three decades ago, but somewhere in the struggles and the hardships of exploring an unknown land, Matthiessen came upon that version of himself that felt more natural and free.

If I understand the underlying message correctly, he becomes respectful and possibly even envious of the simple life of the Nepali people. Westerners often view the developing world as a place where there is nothing but hardship and struggle, equating as we so often do material wealth with happiness. In *The Snow Leopard*, Matthiessen observes a level of peace in simplicity where others might only see poverty and despair.

It's impossible to know if the feeling would have lasted indefinitely, of course – perhaps another few months of limited supplies, unreliable porters and the onset of a harsh Himalayan winter, and he would have been writing about settling down, burning his passport and anticipating the invention of the plasma TV. But it remains interesting to me that that kind of life of exploration and discovery is not as well received in our culture of babies and mortgages and retirement plans as settling down and punching the clock. Alternative approaches to living a life may make for good stories, but they're not exactly practical in our society. Living outside the box is hard, even for a short while.

I admit it, part of me envies the doctor and the lawyer and their stable, well-heeled lifestyle, and as they drive away I can't help but wonder if they also envy me and this window of freedom I've carved out for myself.

After finishing my last cookie, I execute a hair-raising and barely controlled descent on the freshly graded gravel to the pavement that starts near the Canmore Nordic Centre, perched just above town. Completing a loop begun a week ago, I return to the world of the responsible and civilized – whatever that means – at least for a day or two, and it will be interesting to see how smoothly that transition is going to go.

10.

THE AUBURN ROSE WEST COAST GRILL OR, JOEY AND PONCHO'S ALE HOUSE, POOL PUB & GOLF COURSE A.K.A. EVERY BAR I'VE EVER WORKED AT

Downtown there's a parade, but I don't think I wanna go.
>—The Tragically Hip

The lost horizons I can see, are filled with bars and factories
And in them all we fight to stay awake.
>—Gin Blossoms

"Come on, you dumb hillbilly bastard, quit pussyfooting around and hit him already."

For years I've been racking my brain trying to find the right sentence to encapsulate the experience of working in a bar, and the oratorical gem from above is as good as any I can come up with. I've worked in food and beverage off and on for as long as I care to remember, and when people ask me what I do for a living I am reluctant to admit what has become my everyday reality, which is that I'm a service industry lifer. Lately I am reminded of an old joke: father number one says, "My son is an actor in New York," and father number two says, "Oh really, what restaurant?" In my case you can substitute "writer" or "photographer" for "actor," and "pub" for "restaurant," but the sentiment is the same. I doubt there's anywhere else in the employment world where a vocation with so much opportunity still amounts to a dead end.

Not that it's such a bad life, on the face of it. Flexible hours have always been one of my favourite perks, and you are seldom confined to one place. If you don't like the way things are going, you can just walk down the street and get another job – often on the same day, during the summer months. In fact, after acquiring a few of the basic skills, you can work just about anywhere in the world as a waiter or bartender. If you happen to find the right niche, the money can be very good, and you have cash in hand every day. If you add the inherent social aspect of the job and the undeniable fun factor of working where everyone else goes to party, then I admit, sometimes it's the greatest job on earth.

Despite all these perks, however, working in a busy pub can also be a trying experience. The late nights, the long hours, and the inevitable drunken buffoons can slowly grind away at your will to live, creating an uneasy balance between the life you want and what you have to do to make a living. One night recently, this was my welcoming committee: a big, lumbering tradesman sitting at the bar with a friend, watching three-round amateur boxing on TV and spewing minor-league racial epithets, at considerable volume.

"Come on, you big Negro, knock that white boy the fuck out."

I notice that this guy is careful not to use the "other N-word," but he does take everything right to the jagged edge. You see, my redneck is not choosing sides in the televised fight playing out on multiple screens around the room; he just likes the sound of his own voice. Or more precisely, he likes it when other people can hear the sound of his voice. His nickname is a tribute to one of the Three Stooges, and my guess is that he christened himself in high school and never managed to advance past that adolescent stage of social development. I suspect a certain Mr. Howard is rolling in his grave.

I've noticed this Stooge wannabe just about every time I've been in the bar as a patron or an employee these last few months, because he's a big fella at six-three or six-four, and because he almost never stops talking, but mostly because he's got troublemaker written all over him. As I've said, the bar life is not all bad – there are plenty of nice people and good tippers out there to make it all worthwhile – but in the mix is a class of patron who inevitably gets into trouble at some point in the evening, and the amazing thing is that they are unflinching in their own defence no matter the circumstance. As you escort them out the door, they are adamant about having nothing to do with whatever dustup has occurred; they often have the gift of the gab and are always unsettlingly close to violent outbursts during their pleas of innocence. The remarkable thing is that it was always, without fail, the other guy who started it. Funny, that. But it isn't even the obvious knuckle-draggers who bother me the most; it's the people who don't look around the restaurant they're sitting in before offering unsolicited advice on any number of issues, or who assume that a job in serving is an easy thing.

My blood got to full boil after a string of letters appeared in the weeks following an opinion piece printed in one of the small town newspapers operating out of my little slice of heaven on earth, and coming as they did on the heels of one too many Stooge-esque experiences, I just couldn't let the complaints go without a fight. In my mind, being a long-time soldier in the service industry, as well as a frequent patron, put me in a certain position of authority on the subject of restaurant etiquette. The thinking was that since I've wasted half my life working in bars and restaurants, or eating and drinking in bars and restaurants, I could see both sides of the equation, and I responded to the various criticisms, both real and·imagined, with as much civility as I could muster. My rant went something like this:

> I wanted to stay out of the service debate because any transaction that involves the human element is going to have messy edges, but alas, the subject is just too tempting and I can't help myself.
>
> There will always be bad service. Period. And there are always going to be customers who are impossible to please, no matter how much training and due diligence an individual invests into their profession. To think that the question of quality, or lack thereof, in the restaurant world is a "Bow Valley thing" is both simplistic and narrow minded.
>
> Ninety-five per cent of all food and beverage transactions fall somewhere between the truly atrocious and the undeniably obnoxious, and A.W. Shier's letter to the editor on October 18th in the *Canmore Leader* inspires me to remind everyone that walking a mile in somebody else's shoes goes a long way to·understanding not only their actions in the moment, but who they are as well.
>
> In the 13 years that I have derived at least part of my income from the art of service I have, on occasion, been that guy any customer out there can find fault in. I've forgotten orders, served the

wrong item, delivered a drink without my tray, and served a meal with my thumb over the side of the plate, where it, gasp!, touched a French fry. I've also been tired, distracted, hung over, bored, drunk, frustrated, angry and grumpy. It's even possible that I've been and done all of these things on the same shift. To all aforementioned crimes I am forced to admit guilt, and do apologize for those moments when my actions have been detrimental to a paying customer's experience.

But, I've also been whistled at, shouted at, cursed at, and been asked to step outside to settle things like a man! I've seen people toss coins and cutlery roll-ups the length of three tables to get attention, and witnessed the theft of money right off the bar. I've watched customers completely rearrange seating plans uninvited only to block important service areas, and heard them modify items on the menu to the point where they are unrecognizable to the chef who orders, preps and cooks the meals. I've worked 10 hours straight without a coffee or meal break, knocked off 13 or 14 days in a row because my employer needed bodies, and never, in my professional life, have I ever taken a paid sick day (what's the euphemism used these days, a mental health day?), because they don't exist in the industry I work in. But that's the job, and I do my best to make the best of it, even when it isn't treating me the best. Just like everyone else who gets up and goes to work every day.

A.W. is correct to a degree. The paying public has every right to demand quality for their dollar, and if they don't get it they should take their dollars (including tip) elsewhere, and we, the employers and employees who benefit from those dollars, need to raise our game wherever and whenever humanly possible, but a quick peruse of Anthony Bourdain's *Kitchen Confidential* will reveal that the industry attracts those among us who are just a little off center, regardless of the training, accreditation, and health and safety monitoring A.W. mistakenly thinks is completely non-existent in the Valley.

Perhaps we should all try to remember that every food and beverage interaction is a two-way street, none of us are as charming and talented as we think we are, and oh yeah, just to put everyone at ease, all the good-time Charlies I know always manage to wash their hands.

—Jamey Glasnovic
Canmore, Alberta

It can feel like a war out there, with two sides working from opposing camps, trying to share an experience. There are bound to be issues. Add the significant financial component to the equation (food and beverage is a nine-billion-dollar business in Alberta alone, not including tips) and things can get positively confrontational. You want quality and value for your dollar, and we want to be treated like people who serve, not simple-minded beings who just fetch things for you. Our bosses are in it to make money. My entry into the public fray took two and half days to craft, at the expense of everything else in my life, because one full page in a Word document is hardly space enough to express what's truly on one's mind. And I really did have a difficult time trying to be civil.

. Now, just to put everyone's mind at ease, I do have to add that the kitchens and service areas in Canmore (and by extension Alberta and most everywhere else in Canada) are on the up and up. Everybody gets inspected often enough to stay diligent, and everyone has to pass inspection regularly in order to keep the doors open. That said, there is something everyone should know: *there are no perfect scenarios in life.* Hair gets in food, roll-ups fall on the floor, food goes off in dark corners of refrigerators, people sneeze and people cough. I've worked in eight different eating and drinking establishments over the years and have found that it happens in dingy taverns and swanky eateries in equal measure, but there's nothing going on that's likely to kill you, so get over it. If you don't fancy the idea that at least one meal at one time your life had an experience you don't want to know about before it reached your table, you better stay home and cook for yourself. I further challenge anyone who has a problem with service to get a job in the industry and be a part of the solution. Trust me, it's not always as easy or as fun as it may seem.

• • •

Surprisingly, rolling through Canmore after dropping down from the gap proves pleasurable in every way. The sun is shining, a gentle breeze is keeping the heat down, and everyone who is strolling around outside the shops and restaurants appears healthy and happy. Jocey is at work, so there's no rush to get home, and the Rose & Crown is on my route, so I see no reason why stopping in for a beer or two could be anything but a good idea. The 150-plus-seat patio is predictably chaotic but only three-quarters full, and it's easy enough to find a table of friends to join as the afternoon sun works its way across the sky. I am biased, of course, but do think we have one of the best patios in town, and as always, the views today are spectacular.

After a pint and a half, however, it becomes obvious that nothing has changed in the week I've been away. It's the same old people having the same old conversations while sitting in the same old seats, and suddenly I am reminded of why I was so desperate to get out of here. It's not that there's anything wrong with a friendly discussion over a couple of beers at a favourite watering hole, it's just this ground has been covered so many times before that my heart isn't in it anymore. After paying my bill, saying goodbye to my friends, and heading home to do some laundry, I find I'm more than ready to get out on the road again early the next day.

One of the obvious drawbacks to the route I've chosen for this journey is that I've got to go through Banff again in order to reach the Eastern Main Ranges, Lake Louise and eventually Jasper. Revisiting my neighbour to the west doesn't exactly inspire, because I've been here so many times and because I feel like I've spent too much time too close to home already, but I am determined to make another attempt. With a few solid days of riding under my belt, making it to Banff by bike the second time around is surprisingly easy. Even the short hill just inside the park gate, which seemed a stiff test two weeks ago, is now merely a simple and enjoyable task. The rest of the route is mostly flat, with a small, speedy downhill about midway along, where the road follows the right side of the valley just below a natural bench of ancient glacial till that runs nearly the entire length of this part of the corridor. If the wind is calm, as it is today, this whole section can be very fast on a bike, and is a popular training ride for local cyclists.

Turning left on Tunnel Mountain Road after coming off at the East Banff exit in order to access the campground, however, is a challenge, as the road climbs up the lower slopes of Tunnel Mountain for nearly three kilometres before levelling out near the Hoodoos Viewpoint, overlooking the Bow River. On the opposite side of the road from the viewpoint are over 1,100 campsites that make up the largest campground in the mountain parks. It is a cluster of three separate "villages" with differing amenities, including 320 full-service RV sites in the Trailer Court campground that can accommodate units up to 50 feet in length. The entire set-up barely approximates the experience of actual camping, except for the stunning views through just about any break in the trees and the resident elk wandering casually around the place. After quickly setting up my tent and stowing my gear, it's an easy ride down into town to see the sights.

Banff, for most of its modern existence, has been a destination. The area was extensively explored in the 1880s as a result of Canadian Pacific Railway development and soon became the flagship of the Canadian parks system, with the early designation "Banff Hot Springs Reservation." The townsite was originally called Siding 29 and was located at the foot of Cascade Mountain, and the idea of moving the town closer to the first spa at the mineral springs came about in 1886, when a proposed resort was beginning to take hold as part of the CPR's plan to bring tourists to the region. It was the completion of the Banff Springs Hotel in 1888 that made the move inevitable and made CPR vice president and general manager William Cornelius Van Horne's famous quote "Since we can't export the scenery, we'll have to import the tourists" not only a reality but a stunning success: The current population of Banff is roughly 8,500 people, but in high summer closer to 30,000 folks manage to crowd the streets, hotels and campgrounds.

On Banff Avenue today, the fall crowds are moderate, and instead of the usual bar and restaurant tour, I would like to spend a little time trying to educate myself about this place. Shunning my customary stops, I call in first at the Parks Canada information centre, and after a pleasant half-hour of map reading and gawking at photos, the next stop is the Banff Park Museum, at the opposite end of the main drag. Locally referred to as the dead-animal museum for its extensive collection of species native to the Rocky Mountains, stuffed and mounted in the style that was common in the early 20th century, this natural history museum also turns out to be a pleasant if somewhat morose diversion. Originally conceived in 1895, the collection at this national historic site has been at the current location since 1903, and the attendant zoo remained in operation until 1937, when the general attitude toward wildlife began to change, and animals began to be understood as important components of an ecosystem, not just as something to look at through the bars of a cage – a transition that was slow going in the early days.

With a respectful tour completed, the true goal for the afternoon is next on the itinerary: the Cave and Basin National Historic Site. I'm embarrassed to admit it, but in the decade and half since I first visited Banff, I've never been to the place where all of this began. The site is a bit out of the way compared to the other tourist attractions at the south end of town – it's down Cave Avenue in the opposite direction from Bow Falls, the Banff Springs Hotel, the Upper Hot Springs and the Sulphur Mountain gondola – but the short ride is pleasant and the weather is fine, so the detour is welcome.

The prevailing wisdom is that three CPR workers "discovered" what is now known as the Basin Spring in 1883, while searching for minerals at the end of the construction season, and stumbled upon the hole at the top of the cavern containing the Cave Spring shortly afterward, but there is evidence that at least one other party paid a visit prior to that. Two American prospectors even built a crude cabin in 1874 on the banks of the Bow River and overwintered here, but eventually all independent claims on the springs failed, the three railway workers were bought out by the federal government for a paltry sum, and our first national park was born.

Since that time, the Cave and Basin has undergone a number of changes. Early on, a bathhouse was built and a tunnel was blasted through the rock to facilitate access, eliminating the need to climb down a ladder to the Cave Spring through the hole in the ceiling. In the intervening century, pool facilities were added and then upgraded, only to prove too costly and difficult to maintain, and bathing is no longer permitted at the site. After I pay a fee and enter the cave, the strong smell of sulphur common to hot springs dominates my senses, and the pathway quickly becomes too low for a grown man to walk upright.

Opening up to a small, roughly circular chamber six or seven metres around in all directions, with a small, rough hole about a metre across in the ceiling, the cave is now off-limits to swimming and boasts an average temperature of 32.8 degrees Celsius. On the walls, mineral deposits have coalesced to form grotesque shapes, like something out of a science fiction movie, but after a few minutes the visit becomes a bit of an anticlimax, and I am tempted to peel off down to my skivvies for a swim, if only to liven up the place, but instead make a quick trip through the museum upstairs before heading to my final destination for the day.

At the other end of the spectrum from the Cave and Basin is the spa at the Fairmont Banff Springs Hotel. A goliath of stone, the Banff Springs is an iconic feature in the Canadian Rockies that can be seen from all over the surrounding valley at certain strategic viewpoints. It can host 1,700 guests in its 770 rooms. The main lobby is cavernous and well appointed, and for a brief moment the thought of checking in for a comfortable night's rest does cross my mind, but with the price of a standard room pushing $500 a night, there's little chance I'm ever going to stay here. It is, however, on my itinerary to sneak another peek at how the other half lives, and deep in the heart of the building is the Willow Stream Spa at Fairmont, which I access via key code surreptitiously obtained from a friend who works here but lives in Canmore. I half expect to get busted at the front door to the spa, but nobody gives me a second glance, and the code works like a charm.

In the men's change room, where you collect your robe and flip flops and stash your personal belongings in individual lockers assigned for that purpose, there is a decidedly country-club atmosphere. It feels like the kind of place where you should be whispering in a vaguely conspiratorial manner – although I don't have anyone to talk to – and in the men's lounge are tea, coffee, fruit, citrus water, cucumber water and insanely comfortable chairs with ottomans, set up in front of a medium-sized flat screen television. Deeper inside the men's quarters are a steam room at 60 degrees Celsius, a hot tub at 40 degrees, a dry sauna at 77 and an inhalation room at 38.

I can't say I understand the scientific process of relaxation, exactly, but there's no denying it feels good to casually move from one station to another, staying in each for just long enough to bleed away the aches and pains in my muscles and joints. But I do find the sauna far too dry and have a hard time taking a deep breath, so I only spend a minute or two in there. The best part is that only one other guy is using the men's-only facilities at the moment, so I have the whole place mostly to myself for nearly 20 minutes.

Out in the public area it's not exactly what you would call crowded either, and the clientele is mostly older ladies and fat, balding guys chilling out in lounge chairs poolside. Three small mineral-pool hot tubs are the highlight of this main atrium, with individual waterfalls plunging into them from a height of about five metres. At 40, 37 and 25 degrees Celsius respectively, I think the idea is to spend a bit of time in each in order to expand and contract blood vessels and improve circulation. A comparatively scrotum-scrunching large regular pool in the centre of the room is out of the question for soaking in, as far as I'm concerned, but is convenient for a refreshing dip and is in heavy use compared to the other options available. In the main pool, a lady is doing some kind of Zen floating deal with just her face and great big fake breasts breaking the surface of the water, and off at the far end, a handsome young couple are fooling around below the waterline in a manner that makes me think they think no one knows what they're up to.

Rounding out the impressive selection of soaking options are an outdoor pool and outdoor hot tub just beyond an extensive wall of glass, and of all the relaxation choices available, the 40-degree waterfall pool is my clear favourite. I do wonder if we really need four "Caution – Slippery When Wet" signs strewn about – don't most people already know that a pool deck is slippery when it gets wet? But there's soothing music throughout, and an air of opulence that stops just short of decadence, although someone feeding me peeled grapes would be nice. Presumably the whole experience is designed to rejuvenate the spirit and revitalize the body, and it does seem to work. The swirling, bubbling water of the tubs and the cascading sound of the faux falls conspire to drain away minor tension, and remarkably my left knee and right hip, which tend to ache much of the time these days, feel completely pain-free.

In all, it is pleasant and relaxing experience, as long as you remain unaware of (or unconcerned about) the price of luxury. Add-ons to the basic spa entry include all sorts of fancy indulgences. Of note, the Keep Your Shorts On one-hour $199 treatment is essentially a 60-minute sports massage with shorts and a T-shirt thrown in for good measure. But the options are nearly endless, and the prices reflect that boundless opportunity. My favourite is the four-hour Energy & Youth package, which includes a fitness training session, a soothing Thalasso or Herbal Kur (whatever that is): a customized traditional facial (Can those two words even be used together in the same sentence? If it's customized, doesn't that by definition negate the notion of traditional?); and a spa lunch, all for a mere $489, not including tip and taxes.

The way I see it is, if I'm going to blow three or four hundred bucks, it's going to be on a sleeping bag or a tent, not a rubdown and a bath, but that's just me. Still, these comforts would be easy to get used to. Wandering back to the men's lounge in my plush robe for another glass of cucumber water and a nap in front of *SportsCentre*, I realize that this book had better do well, because when my surgically repaired knee is nothing more than bone grinding on bone and my arthritic hip is begging for a replacement, I'm going to want to come for a soak in the pools every once in a while – say, two or three times a week, if they hire a grape peeler – and I understand they change the keypad combo regularly.

• • •

In my mellowed-out state of mind, I don't even remember the ride back through town, and I end up nearly as far as the Voyager once again before coming to my senses and realizing that I'm not staying there, and that I'm starving. I meant to stop in at the St. James's Gate, just off Banff Avenue on Wolf Street, for their famous mango bourbon chicken wings, but the Keg Steakhouse & Bar in the Caribou Lodge is an easy substitute in a pinch. Besides, I'm way too hungry to turn around and go back two or three blocks to the Gate. Entering through the lobby, I toy with the idea of a table off in some far corner of the restaurant, but instead gravitate to my comfort zone and take a seat at the far end of the bar. With playoff baseball on the big screen above a well-appointed back bar displaying over 60 different liquors and liqueurs as diversion, my bartender is quick with the menu and a pint, and I settle in with my notebook and my guidebooks for what I hope will be a fine meal.

Over the years, I've spent a lot of time thinking about the food and beverage experience. Admittedly, much of that energy lately has been used up taking subtle jabs at the average customer while I work, but I also can't help but critique most experiences when I'm on the other side of the bar or table. The irony, of course, is that despite all my bitching and moaning about the service industry, I genuinely like eating out. I would do it every meal if I could, and it doesn't even have to be in a restaurant. I like a good hot dog stand or takeout window, and convenience stores and gas stations have improved their prepackaged sandwich selections immeasurably in recent years. It might even be true that if it wasn't for the Fas Gas next door to my condo, I'd have wasted away to nothing by now, such is my interest in dabbling in the culinary arts. In a word, I'll eat just about anywhere, but preparing those meals in my own kitchen is a last resort.

Some more memorable repasts include barbequed squid on a stick off a hibachi at a harvest festival in Japan, greasy fried chicken out front of a hole-in-the-wall fast food counter in Fiji and a bratwurst on a street corner in New York City at 3 a.m. – something everyone should do at least once. While I may not be discerning (and very rarely am I demanding, for fear of something bad happening to my food between the kitchen and the table), I am prolific, and I believe that a big part of any adventure is the meals you eat along the way.

Dining out at the Keg this time around is disappointing, only in that it's very good, and so I have nothing to quietly complain about. In my experience there is something about a chain restaurant that is predictable almost to the point of being distasteful, but those same traits are exactly what makes them so appealing. Consistency of product, a high level of staff professionalism and a clean and organized room generally make for a pleasant evening, but the corporate blueprint can also lack creativity and, at times, enthusiasm. Still, my bartender is right on time with my second drink and practised enough to leave me alone as I doodle and flip absently through my books. You can tell he's been doing this for a while and is unconsciously running through a well-honed pattern of behaviour designed to get him to the end of the night with maximum tips intact – which, when I think about it, is the whole point.

I would venture to bet that the chances of having a more consistent restaurant experience increase in more expensive establishments, but the price of your entree does not always guarantee it. A more accurate indicator, and admittedly more difficult to figure out, is: How much does your server actually make? For many servers, service is an afterthought. Sure, most of us try our best, and most realize that our aggravation level usually decreases if the customer has a happy experience, but as with so many other menial jobs, money is the true motivator. Everything else, both good and bad, is a spinoff of that bottom line. Why else would anyone be insane enough to be a server? Hardly anybody goes to school for this; we just kind of fall into it. Hotel/motel management graduates generally work in chain hotels and motels, and everyone else you see usually gets on-the-job training after stumbling into the right place at the right time, which is usually when an employer is in a pinch. That's how it happened to me: I walked into the Shot Pool Pub in Kingston, Ontario, on a Thursday afternoon, in serious need of a job, and started the next day working the door (it was homecoming weekend and they needed an extra body). By the middle of the next week, someone had quit and I was on day bar. Welcome to the business, kid.

In the Bow Valley, the upside to this path in life is that we servers get to *live* here, whereas most everyone else just visits, but even the sweetest, kindest, most gentle soul will eventually be ground down. Not all turn bitter like me, but no one escapes the business unscathed, with their faith in humanity completely intact. It isn't even always the overtly distasteful experiences that wear you out; it's the banality of many of the everyday interactions. Plain old stupid rears its head far too often as well. Money mitigates the annoyance, at least for a while, and encourages good behaviour on our part, most of the time. Recently I did a poll of my fellow service drones to find out what their favourite stupid customer moments have been, and here's a sampling, with the question/comment first, followed by the polite server response, and the unspoken server thoughts in brackets:

– Do you have a washroom? *Yes sir, in the back corner by the pool table.* (What do you think? That everybody has to piss out by the dumpster? Of course we have a washroom.)

– Where's the rooftop patio? (Are you serious? Up the stairs on the roof maybe.)

– How's the weather on the patio? (Ummmm, you had to come *from* outside to get here; I've been working inside for the past three hours...)

Similar inane enquiries include:

– Are you open? *Yes, have a seat and a server will be with you in a moment.* (You got through the door didn't you?)

– It's my birthday; do I get a free drink? *I'm sorry, that's not company policy.* (Fuck off! If you were a regular customer, sure, I'd slide you a complimentary beverage. I'd even make it happen if

I'd seen you once or twice before tonight, *and* you were a good tipper. Otherwise, fuck off.)

But my all time personal favourite is:

– What's on special?

No hello, no how are you, just straight to the cheap drinks. It's even better when dingbat is on a date, because women looooovvve a cheapskate. My response to this one is always a very curt "Happy hour is from four to seven." End of conversation, and good luck getting my attention over the next couple of hours, because I already know it won't be worth my time.

As an aside, let me fill you in on a little quirk of the industry, a little of the game inside the game, if you will, because if you walk into an establishment that's smoking busy and want a refreshing beverage of the alcoholic variety, you ought to know the correct procedure. First and foremost, and where most people get it wrong, is that you want the drug and I control the drug. You have to be nice to me, not the other way around. Patience and pleasantness is the best approach on both of our parts, but it's best to let me begin the interaction. Don't wave your cash around like I'm a stripper, and don't tap the bar with keys or a coin. "Hey" and "Buddy" are not my name. Snapping your fingers might get you a punch in the mouth. Be ready with your order when I get to you and tip five bucks on the first round, and trust me, I'll find you in a crowd. "Excuse me" works great in a pinch, and if I really have taken longer than is reasonable and you don't act like an asshole about it, I'll probably even buy you a drink to make up for the fact I've just wasted your time.

If the place is deadsville, however, then the script is

flipped entirely. I have to be attentive and courteous, even if I don't feel like it. Fortunately I work somewhere that's busy most of the time, and when it's not, I have a core group of regulars who I am nice to, so you're shit out of luck, mister what's-on-special. Say hello before trying to get a dollar off your drink and leave a decent tip next time I get around to you, and maybe we'll become friends. And if not friends, then at least we'll have a pleasant and efficient professional relationship from here on out.

All that being said, I would be remiss in my bartender rant if I didn't tie up the affair with my Stooge wannabe, which I will do here. The dining room has died off completely, but the pub is busy and he's claiming to not have any money in his account to pay the rather substantial bill (like we've never heard that excuse before). After processing his debit card twice to no effect, the waitress serving his group comes to me to complain, seeing as she's got six or seven other tables that need attention and she doesn't have time to deal with this lunkhead anymore. The 20 seats around the bar are almost all taken, and a few people are also hovering within arm's length of their next drink, so I don't have time for this guy either, but I'm in charge when my boss is not around, so I have to sort it out.

After we've run his debit card through for a third time to the final conclusion of insufficient funds, dumb-dumb is feigning ignorance about any prior knowledge of the state of his bank account and by extension his ability to pay the tab. It's an obvious lie, and when I laugh out loud he quickly changes tack, claiming he gets paid Thursday at midnight and he'll be back Friday to square the tab. He swears! He even goes so far as to show me his empty wallet, and during the entire exchange I can hear the bar printer coughing up drink orders that are going unmade.

Not to be taken for a sucker, but desperate to get back to the duties of serving and away from babysitting a grown man, I remind him this was a going-away party and that all night long everyone within earshot has been listening to stories about how he was on the road tomorrow, heading for Calgary or Edmonton or Fort McMurray, where the real construction money is. It's all a bunch of bullshit, and I've heard it all before. I could probably stand here all night arguing and still get nowhere, so I snatch his driver's licence as collateral and agree to a Friday payback plan, before rushing back behind the bar to take care of my customers and the long-neglected service bar.

After a frantic game of catch-up, everything is finally back on track. Just as I'm thinking a serious crisis has been averted, a good regular customer comes in off the patio with some bad news. Apparently, my new favourite customer in the whole world has decided to drive home after all and is getting in his vehicle.

"What?"

"Yup, he's out there fiddling with his keys and trying to get in the truck."

I think about letting him go and maybe even calling the cops to have them look out for a beat-to-shit old white pickup. Remember early on, when I mentioned trains and rednecks? This is the kind of crap I was talking about, and for a split second I slip into silent prayer.

"Please, please, please, God, if you're really out there..."

But I have no idea which direction he's going or how long it will take for the police to respond. And amazingly, I would feel guilty if he were actually hurt after getting hit by a train. Not to mention how I would feel if he hurt someone else. Besides, I've given this idiot ten bucks for a cab because he was moaning about not being able to get home without his licence, and I don't want that donation wasted.

Out in the parking lot, it's showdown time. I don't much like fighting – it's dangerous and dumb, and the chances of injury are high even when you win – but every once in a while all other options are exhausted. After taking a deep breath to calm down, I slide up to the driver's-side window and rap on the glass. The window rolls down, and without even looking up from the dashboard, the clearly inebriated occupant barks, "What?"

"What the fuck do you think you're doing?"

"Going home."

"Not in that truck, you're not."

"Yeah," my Stooge says as he smirks and moves to turn the ignition key, "and who's going to stop me?" His dismissive tone pushes me over the edge, but instead of seeing red with rage, I feel a calm determination wash over me. I'm either going to bust him, beat him or take a beating.

"Listen, you idiot, if you drive away I'm going inside to call the cops. Don't forget, you're loaded, *and* I have your driver's licence. Getting to work for the next year or so is going to be bitch with a DUI suspension."

Remarkably, this information seems to get through his thick skull, and his body language changes abruptly from aggression and defiance to acceptance. The tension between us instantly drains away. As the cab pulls up, he agrees to get in, and even apologizes for being such a pain in the ass. I'm left scratching my head and wondering if I'm the unwitting victim in an episode of *Punk'd*. I half-expect Ashton Kutcher to come leaping out of the bushes, but when he doesn't in time for the punchline, I hustle back inside for another round of frantic catch-up behind the bar.

And people wonder why I so want to leave my old life behind.

PART THREE

THE HEART OF THE MOUNTAINS

11.

BOW VALLEY PARKWAY

It's time for a change, what else can I do?
With a clock ticking time, better make up my mind
Is it me, or is it you?

—Jim Cuddy, Greg Keelor (Blue Rodeo)

After a pleasing day and fantastic meal in Banff yesterday, my evening ended with just a hint of disappointment. Biking up the hill to Tunnel Mountain with a bellyful of surf-and-turf mixed with beer was noticeably uncomfortable, and once I was back at my site, the realities of camping in the largest campground in the mountain parks became abundantly clear. It was not crowded, exactly, this being the end of season, but it was also not private either. One thousand one hundred sites spread out across the mountain means there are enough people around to make you feel like you're in a campground, as opposed to being out camping, but even that was okay because everyone was behaving themselves. Most were quietly sitting around chatting or cooking a late dinner, and some were out for a leisurely stroll.

What was disappointing about the experience was the food storage shed with a half-finished jug of milk lying out, and the tarps and plastic and trash strewn everywhere or abandoned randomly in the large lockers. Also, something I didn't notice during set-up was the small pile of coffee grounds and completely unrecognizable bits of

241

food waste dumped just off the tent pad at the back of my site, and by the looks of it the mess had been there for quite some time. Not that I expected much, mind you – too many visitors and a worn-out summer staff looking to move on will always equate to an average experience, but I have woken up feeling better. I am outside, after all, and it turns out these places, these towns encroaching on my wilderness, are tolerable and even pleasant places to visit when I pretend I'm not actually living in them.

There certainly is a lot to do here, most of which I didn't get to in this short visit – the Banff Gondola, horseback riding at Warner Stables, the Whyte Museum of the Canadian Rockies, the Banff Centre and the Upper Hot Springs being the most obvious examples – and I could probably have spent a week getting to it all. But that's not the experience I've come searching for this time around, so without regret I put the town at my back and pedal out to the highway.

As I head west out of Banff, a strong, swirling headwind has kicked up, and an ominous storm cloud has materialized from out of nowhere and parked itself over the Massive and Bourgeau ranges. The storm cell is threatening to blot out the sun as it moves slowly across the sky, and to add to the challenge, a low cement retaining wall to my right also narrows the shoulder along this section of highway, creating a claustrophobic impression. It almost feels as if traffic is coming from over my left and right shoulder simultaneously as the sound of each speeding car is deflected in multiple directions in a confused mess of aggressive white noise. Within minutes, I'm sweaty from the effort of fighting the wind and chilly as a result of that same wind, not to mention a bit freaked out by the passing cars. Quickly I recognize this as a "put the head down and grind it out" kind of section. One that I won't look back on with any amount of fondness but still can't avoid. So I force myself to keep going.

On the bright side, these more challenging bits of road don't feel like insurmountable obstacles anymore; they've transformed into simple annoyances. What was once a seemingly unmanageable task is now a minor impediment on the journey from here to there, and so I put my head down and try to think about something else to pass the time. To further enforce my subtle shift in attitude, the cyclist who slips past with a casual hello doesn't cause much distress, because he is also working hard against the wind, clearly on a short training ride. I'm still able to draft for half a kilometre, even with all my stuff, before he's finally able to drop me, and it takes a long, long time for him to disappear from sight for good on the gently winding road ahead.

After about 20 or 30 minutes, turning up Bow Valley Parkway is a welcome relief from the stiff breeze, as the direction of travel changes by nearly 45 degrees and cuts through the protection offered by the surrounding forest. The parkway has no paved shoulder, but it is wide enough for a car and bike to pass safely side by side and has a fraction of the traffic of Highway 1. The trees here are predominantly even-aged stands of lodgepole pine that easily soak up the wind as the road hugs the right side of the valley, heading northwest under the dramatic silhouette of the Sawback Range. It is fall, so the occasional larch and a light scattering of deciduous trees are doing their annual fade, but it's not an explosion of colours like you would find in eastern North America. For the most part, the forest here remains a solid shade of green year-round, with only pockets of yellows and pale greens and the occasional whisper of red to mark the change of season. It is one of the things I do miss about living in the east: the annual riot of colour that is autumn.

But the nature of the parkway more than makes up for any perceived deficiencies in the surrounding trees. The original link between Banff and Lake Louise, it is as much a meandering trail as a modern road, and were it not paved it would be a pleasant, if slightly ambitious, stroll between the two mountain outposts. In two places the parkway even splits to allow eastbound and westbound travellers their own single track through the bush. This is a road for going somewhere, not for getting somewhere, and before long the underlying landscape in this area also begins to change in a subtle fashion, from the now-familiar overthrust formations common in the front ranges to the heftier, castellated mountains found in eastern main ranges (nearby Castle Mountain being the most obvious example).

Pedalling along, I begin to realize I am helplessly drawn to these kinds of places. Places I would never specifically seek out unless there was some kind of story to them, or places I might not otherwise notice. Suddenly, and with minimal provocation, there is an unknown out there that needs to be known, or at least witnessed, to be believed, and I am helpless to resist the urge to go and check it out. Then the experience is filed away in the personal-experience library with the hopes of someday being retrieved. At a dinner party maybe, or some other social gathering where it pays to appear worldly and experienced. "What's that? The Castle Boundary, oh I've been there, beautiful country, and did you know the mountains get higher starting at that point because the rocks are laid down in horizontal layers, making them less prone to erosion. It's true."

Personally, I've always like the idea of learning for learning's sake, and the truth is that this kind of information is more often than not simply forgotten. But it's still fun trying to search that knowledge out. Often the new goals are worth the effort, and sometimes circumstances conspire against the journey, but it's never a waste of time wondering what's out there.

Sometimes I think this hunger for active travel is all just giddy adolescence that doesn't want to die. There is a big part of me that doesn't want to grow up, not because I want to remain immature or irresponsible but because so far there has been very little in the *Being a Grown-Up* brochure that I find appealing, or even all that interesting. With so much of it apparently geared to the idea of indentured servitude and uninspired effort, I can't quite find the motivation to make a serious go of it, and so I wander out at the edges, hoping to find something interesting along the way. I can only hope that just being out here helps reconnect me to the land and to this place I've decided to call home.

On the ground near the Castle Boundary, there is actually nothing remarkable to see that would indicate a major change in topography – no great rift in the earth that would signify an obvious fault line. There's no sign erected here that I can find either. In fact, I wouldn't even realize I'm in the right place except that I read about it somewhere, but this is the nature of exploration; sometimes the discoveries made along the way don't amount to much. What does catch my eye in this area, however, is the commemorative internment camp statue and plaque set up rather inconspicuously by the side of the road.

When you think of the Canadian Rockies, the First World War does not immediately leap to mind. Canada sent troops overseas to help in the war effort, but the entire permanent population of the Bow Valley Corridor at the time was no more than a few thousand, so the number of souls directly connected to the conflict was minimal in terms of sheer numbers. But in terms of percentage of overall population, the war was very much a part of people's lives at the time, and the remoteness of the Bow Valley and the rugged landscape made it an ideal place for the government to house "enemy aliens," most of whom were Ukrainian immigrants who had left Europe to escape the conflict. Many were even Canadian citizens.

A total of 660 prisoners of war were held at the camp between 1915 and 1917, and the forced labour they provided helped expand the infrastructure of the young park. Much of that labour centred around the Banff Townsite, where the internees were transferred when winter became too severe for the simple tents at Castle Mountain. In summer they returned and worked on the new road linking Banff to Lake Louise.

My curiosity piqued, I wonder if there is anything left of the camp hidden somewhere in these woods, but 15 minutes of determined traipsing through the trees fails to turn up a single foundation, plank of wood or scrap of tent.

When I get back to my bike, two cyclists I saw earlier – they passed by heading west as I was taking a short break at the beginning of the parkway – are already returning from what I have to guess is Lake Louise, and I wonder, is that even possible? I was reading the information board at the start of the parkway and repacking an unbalanced pannier when they slipped past, and all I really noticed was how quiet their bikes were on the pavement and how quickly they were moving. From Banff (presumably where these speedsters started) to Lake Louise is roughly 110 kilometres round-trip, and these guys have covered two-thirds of that distance in the time it's taken me to get one-third of the way along the same route. My mind refuses to make the necessary calculations, but it is obvious they're hauling ass.

One of them asks, rather politely, "How's your day going so far?"

This guy doesn't even seem to be breathing hard, which is perplexing, and he looks like he's genuinely enjoying what must be a substantial effort. Guys like that drive me crazy. It's Highway 40 all over again, but despite my sudden exasperation at not being able to get my body to move like that, I manage a pleasant reply. "Great, thanks."

What I want to say is, "Piss off, nobody likes a hero. It's guys like you that make the rest of us look bad." I don't even really want to say it; I want to scream it at the top of my lungs. But of course I keep how I feel to myself, in part because they are moving at an impressive clip and there wouldn't be time to get it all out before they sped past. Besides, it's not their fault they've got the talent and the drive and the will to execute the effort, and yet I still quietly loathe them.

"Where you headed?" The same rider asks over a shoulder as they zip past.

"Jasper," I blurt out in an effort to explain away all the gear I'm hauling around, not to mention my slow pace.

"Sounds like a great ride. Good luck."

There's no time for a proper thanks, because they are already gone in a blur of competence and vigour, so I just wave and get back to my plodding ways. Glimpsing Castle

Mountain from along this stretch of road also confirms that I have indeed made the transition into the Eastern Main Ranges at some point, even if I never actually noticed the boundary as it passed beneath my wheels.

• • •

For the rest of the afternoon, the day-tripping cyclists keep popping into my thoughts, not because I aspire to their level of ability (it should be pretty clear by now that that ship has sailed), but because they really did appear to be having fun. To get out for a weekend, or a day, or even a few hours is a habit that has slipped from my regular routine, for some reason. A paddle down the Bow River; cross-country skiing or mountain biking on Goat Creek Trail; scrambling to the summit of some of the local peaks – these were more than simple diversions when I first moved out west; they were part of who I was. Yet the frequency of those small trips has been decreasing every year since.

Coming back outside for an extended tour through the region that I used to drop in on from time to time, I am only now beginning to appreciate what an important part of my life those short outings were. And although I have a habit of travelling alone, day trips are great to go on with friends. One of my fondest local travel memories actually occurred just across the valley from here, in winter, on one of those increasingly rare occasions where I forced myself off the couch and out of the house. This is how I remember it.

"Lunch!" Lawrence calls out as he slides to a stop in a small meadow just above where the heavy tree cover ends, and just below the small, flat expanse that must be our final destination for the day. Taylor Lake is almost directly opposite Castle Mountain, high up in a small valley and out of sight from the highway, and as far as I could tell we aren't quite there yet, but who am I to argue? After six kilometres of uphill travel in rental ski boots that don't quite fit properly, I was ready to stop half an hour ago. Frank has also already stopped just ahead, and Martin, whose brand new ski boots are already causing blisters, is two or three minutes behind me, just down the trail and out of sight. I was assured the lake was only 100 metres away 250 metres ago, but my philosophy is that you don't aggravate your guide with minor details before he even gets you into areas where his knowledge of avalanche procedures might prove valuable.

Besides, I'm hungry and thirsty, so I pull in behind Frank without a word, drop my pack and try to organize a place to sit where I won't sink up to my waist in the softening spring snow. A surprisingly challenging task when you factor in heavy legs from a long approach and low blood sugar. I nearly fall over twice.

"Where's Martin?" Lawrence asks casually once I've finally settled my rear on my pack, sandwich in one hand, water bottle in the other. I glance down the trail we have come up, hoping to see Martin's head bobbing along in stride just below the last little rise before the meadow. I could have sworn he was right behind me only a couple of minutes ago.

"I don't know," I answer between bites, "must have stopped to check his feet. He was complaining about his boots."

Satisfied with the answer and convinced that we don't need to go back to find him just yet, the three of us settle in to eat our lunches and wait.

As it turns out, summer and fall are not the only time

to visit the western mountains, although they are the more obvious choices. In many ways, winter and spring can be better. "It's too cold" and "it's too snowy" are common complaints, but I can't even begin to imagine living with the glum spectre of winter rain and low-lying cloud that persists for weeks on end, as is normal in much of the temperate world that manages to avoid a proper winter. Endless tropical sunshine and no discernible change in season are also a little too predictable for my taste. Here in the Rockies we enjoy a remarkable amount of sunshine in the colder months; not only that, there are fewer crowds, the ski hills on a long weekend or over the Christmas holidays notwithstanding. Snow is also decidedly easier to walk on in the backcountry, especially going downhill, and that's how backcountry skiing was added to my growing repertoire of outdoor pursuits.

The concept is fairly simple: adjustable bindings are attached to traditional downhill skis, allowing the free heel that a cross-country skier has. Skins are stretched over the underside of the ski to produce friction, and suddenly a downhiller can go uphill. Peel off the skin and lock the binding, and the reward for a long morning's slog is a ski run incomparable to anything a chairlift could access. The danger is that the technology opens up terrain prone to avalanche, and I'm not experienced enough to try to go into the backcountry on my own, which explains my company today.

Lawrence is the executive director of the Alpine Club of Canada and a good guy to know if you happen to be going into avalanche country, because his experience is extensive. Martin is a general contractor, and Frank paints houses for a living. We met while playing for the local men's soccer team, but our other common bond is a deep appreciation for this place. Not Canmore or Banff or Lake Louise per se, but this larger environment that we enjoy exploring together on occasion. Over the years, we've hiked Burstall Pass in summer and Peyto Glacier in fall; mountain biked and cross-country skied the Goat Creek Trail from Canmore to Banff; and canoed from Banff to Canmore. For a while we had a minor obsession with cross-country skiing by headlamp and the full moon, both at the Nordic Centre and Mount Shark, and backcountry skiing was probably an inevitable progression from that. It occurs to me, however, that Taylor Lake is the first destination we've all travelled to together as a complete group.

Taylor Lake is a tarn on the eastern slope of the Continental Divide that was left by a receding glacier when the Wisconsin Glaciation came to an end. In fact, all of these mountains were carved and scarred by those great glaciers in one way or another. In summer, these high mountain meadows are covered in western anemone, marsh marigold, buttercups and mountain laurel, but for now whiteness has buried everything but the trees and surrounding rock faces. Accessing this high country through a heavy cover of lodgepole pine and spruce that is short on views only made the approach seem longer than the aforementioned six kilometres, and as the climb progressed the joke became "So where's the lake again, just up ahead?" – repeated at every switchback and short rest stop after the first hour. Like kids on a long car trip asking, "Are we there yet?"

Now that we're actually here (or at least 25 metres from here), I'm tempted to prod Lawrence once again but think better of it in the end and take another long swig from my water bottle.

Within a few minutes, Martin reaches the meadow,

and although the weather is unsettled and threatening snow, it is warm enough to linger as we discuss the plan for the afternoon. Martin breaks out his lunch and, after careful consideration, decides against carrying on because of his feet. Having come this far, three of us decide to make a quick dash up Panorama Ridge while Martin stays behind. It shouldn't take more than an hour to gain the ridge, ski down to a frozen-over Taylor Lake and pick him up on the way out to the car. Heading up the lower reaches of the ridge, we stop for pictures only once and make good time.

One of the technical details of a backcountry ski set-up that makes it different from regular cross-country skis is that you can adjust the height at which your heel strikes the footplate beneath your feet – the idea is to remove unnecessary strain on the calf muscles and Achilles tendons by shortening the distance they have to travel with each step. You set the binding flat for flat ground, raise it slightly for a gentle incline and pop it up as high as possible for a steep slope. It's a simple adjustment and works remarkably well but can take a bit of getting used to.

"Hey," I eventually call out to Frank and Lawrence, who have already manoeuvred a switchback and are almost directly above, "this is really awkward, like being on a pair of high heels." Realizing what kind of ammunition I've just given them, I quickly add, "Not that I know what that feels like, of course."

"Of course," Frank says dryly, and then laughs.

As we continue to chug upward in a tight zigzag pattern, a vague sensation of being followed begins to nag at me, and as we approach the last of the scattering of trees and gain access to views along both sides of the ridge, the feeling intensifies. The idea that we are being stalked by an animal does come to mind (remember those cougar stories), but I'm getting tired, and it's hard to concentrate on any-thing other than keeping both skis under me on the steep slope, so I let the feeling fade. After a few more strides it dawns on me the impression of something out there in the forest might also be another skier coming up from be-hind, but that doesn't make sense either. How could any-one possibly catch us? We've been making steady progress all day. Eventually I realize it has to be Martin, who prob-ably sat in the snow for all of ten minutes before realizing it was going to be a long, cold wait.

We're all surprised to see him, and he's been skiing dou-ble time to make up ground, so we stop to let him catch his breath. Before anyone has a chance to mention the sudden change in plans, he deadpans, "So where the fuck is the lake?"

The lake is just up the drainage from our lunchtime meadow and is at least a couple of hundred vertical me-tres below us and to our left now, not along this ridge that ultimately keeps the water from draining directly east and into the Bow River. Martin knows that. We all know that, and it's precisely what makes the statement so funny, and I almost fall over laughing right there in the snow. Reunited, we clear the treeline and trudge up the final me-tres to a flat spot on the ridge before taking a break to en-joy the view, which despite the deteriorating conditions is still spectacular.

Skiing through knee-deep powder back down into the bowl containing Taylor Lake is a thrill. The grade is steep but the snow soft and forgiving, which almost makes up for the fact that my first downhill of the season has come on what would be classified a black diamond run, in April no less, and somehow I manage not to fall ass over teaket-tle. But, as hard on the thighs as the pitch is, and as much as we laboured on the uphill to get here, it's the ski out that proves to be the true test. Hard-packed and fast, it's a six-kilometre bobsled run with the added bonus of millions of trees encroaching on the edge of the track, ready to punish any deviation from the route. There are some hairy moments, but fortunately we all make it back to the car in one piece, though the last two kilometres are skied on wobbly sticks of Jell-O.

While packing up the gear and sipping hot chocolate from a Thermos, I come to realize one of the true beauties of this place, which I so often overlook: it's chock full of these little out-of-the-way adventures. There are guidebooks and trail guides and scramble guides filled with day trips and weekend excursions for the sedate and ambitious alike. In fact, there's so much to do and so much to see in this pocket of protected landscape – much of it requiring little more than force of will and a bit of effort – that it would be impossible to see it all. I think that's wonderful.

12.

INTO THE ALPINE

Don't it always seem to go, that you don't know what you've got
'til it's gone,
They paved paradise, put up a parking lot.

—Joni Mitchell

Great things are done when men and mountains meet;
This is not done by jostling in the street.

—William Blake

There's frost on the pumpkin and lead in the legs this morning, but I am determined. I'm now firmly in the Eastern Main Ranges and very much want to get up off the valley floor and into the alpine. Yesterday afternoon consisted of little more than a leisurely afternoon pedal to Lake Louise Village from the Castle Boundary, followed by a bracing uphill bike ride after dropping off all my gear at the hostel to look in on the famous lake, another tarn that sits four kilometres up the western valley wall. I had hoped to catch a glimpse of some wildlife along Bow Valley Parkway before getting to Lake Louise – various ungulates, bears, coyotes and wolves frequent the area – but in the end nothing bigger than a squirrel or a bird presented itself. The lakefront however, was the predictable zoo of tourists milling about and taking pictures, so I didn't stay long.

While Banff may have been the birthplace of modern tourism in national parks, Lake Louise is where exploration gained a foothold and the fledgling sport of mountaineering became an important part of the local culture. In the 1890s, adventurous souls from the United States and Great Britain came here to test themselves on the unclimbed peaks surrounding the lake, and outfitters began to travel north into the valleys leading to the Columbia Icefield. By the turn of the century, the CPR had correctly deduced that mountaineering was here to stay and that the presence of mountain guides made the endeavour far safer, so they began importing accomplished Swiss guides to complement their hotel interests.

The most famous of these early guides was undoubtedly the Feuz family. Between them, Edward and sons Edward Jr., Ernest and Walter, along with nephew Gottfried, led 130 first ascents in the Rockies, Purcells and Selkirks. For $5 a day, they would also lead clients up traditional routes on any number of established peaks, and remarkably, in nearly half a century of guiding, not a single client was seriously injured. It's unlikely I will climb anything significant while I'm here, guide or no guide, and I doubt there are any reasonable first ascents left to be had anywhere in these mountains anyway, but a hike similar to the Kananaskis fire lookout outing could be in order. Moraine Lake is roughly 15 kilometres away from the Lake Louise Village and will be the staging point for a foray to Larch Valley, a popular day hike that is among the "must see" destinations in Banff National Park. The trouble is, as with most things to do around here, the end goal is decidedly uphill, and what should simply be a long, mindless grunt upward is exacerbated by an obnoxious amount of traffic and a curiously unfriendly road.

Lake Louise Drive is narrow with no shoulder and is disproportionately occupied by heavy vehicles, including full-sized 56-seat tour buses and delivery trucks servicing the Chateau Lake Louise and surrounding hotel properties. As I pedal up the valley wall, the sun is still low in the sky and casts long shadows through the trees and across the road. It's colder this morning than I had at first anticipated, so I find myself in the curious position of having my hands and shins frozen by the elements while at the same time I sweat like a madman from the exertion. It is not a pleasant experience, and the only hope is that things will settle down after the junction with Moraine Lake Road, where the route levels out somewhat as it makes its way around the lower reaches of Fairview Mountain and Mount Temple.

But veering left onto Moraine Lake Road proves even worse. The road is narrower by 10 to 15 per cent, and getting tucked deeper into the trees makes things even colder. Although the delivery trucks that service this road appear to be smaller on average, they make up for it by insisting on navigating the route as quickly as humanly possible. As if it was a race. The individual cars travelling up to Moraine Lake also can't seem to resist the call to action and speed along just as recklessly. It is without a doubt dangerous, but I've ridden enough road miles in my life to accept dangerous as part of the equation. Right now I'm irritated, and it isn't long before I'm actually yelling at vehicles as they pass.

To the 20-something kid in the Mustang with his trophy girlfriend sitting dutifully by his side I shout, "Hey dickhead, do me a favour, don't pass when a tour bus or supply truck is coming in the opposite direction."

For the aging cougar in the Mercedes who I meet on a hairpin turn rated at 30 kilometres an hour, "Yo, crazy lady, when did 70 become the new 30?" seems in order.

And to the vacuum truck travelling downhill at break-neck speed, presumably with hundreds of gallons of raw sewage on board, I say, "Please sir, after you. And have a nice day."

As most of these slightly out-of-the-way destinations are, Moraine Lake is well worth the effort, and maybe even the agro of making my way here in the company of all these cars. It's yet another tarn lodged in a different hanging valley left by retreating ice, though there is still some debate about how Moraine Lake was formed, among those who take the time to think about these things. At the eastern end of the lake is a significant rubble heap appropriately named the Rockpile. Explorer Walter Wilcox assumed that this was a glacial moraine left behind by retreating ice, and so the lake was named.

Further inspection has led some to believe that the Rockpile is actually rock slide debris from the cliffs to the south, and still others think the rock slide fell on the last big glacier to fill the valley and was then transported forward until the time of retreat, making it both rock slide and moraine. Whatever the case, Rock Slide–Moraine Lake would be an awkward appellation that few would consider seriously, and so Moraine Lake remains Moraine Lake no matter how it ultimately came to be.

On this fine fall day the lakefront is not nearly the mess of people that Lake Louise often hosts but is still busy, and after a quick sprint up the Rockpile for my "20-dollar view" (the back of the Canadian 20-dollar bill displayed the image of this valley up until 1989), I want nothing more than to get away from the crowds, a decidedly difficult task on this hike at this time of year. Technically, I am contravening Parks Canada rules by attempting this route in the fall by myself (there has never been a recorded case where a grizzly has attacked a group of four or more, apparently) but have also heard rumours that the minimum four-person group regulation is simply a way of deterring people from the very popular destination even if the local bears have already left the area for the season.

After only a few minutes, it becomes clear that I need not have worried too much about travelling by myself. The first part of the hike is up a steep slope littered with switchbacks through a stately forest of Engelmann spruce and alpine fir, and although there are not many folks about, there are enough for me not to feel isolated or vulnerable. At no point am I completely out of contact with other hikers for more than a minute or two, and if a warden happens to ask, the plan is to say, "I'm with them," and point to the nearest group. Along the route there are some great views down through the trees to Moraine Lake that help distract from the effort, and from this height the colour of the water is otherworldly – it has to be seen to be believed.

Most of these high alpine lakes have something in common that at once links them together and marks them as individual entities: their unique colours. Ranging from turquoise to emerald with all shades of blue/green between, the unusual hues are the result of active glaciers further upstream grinding away at the bedrock below. After the fine particles get washed into a lake, they remain suspended in the frigid waters, where sunlight is absorbed through all colours of the spectrum except green and blue. The exact colour of each lake depends on the amount of rock flour being deposited at any given time and can change noticeably in the space of only a few hours.

Farther up the trail, Moraine Lake eventually disappears from view altogether, and the trees that give this valley its name come front and centre. The Lyell's larch, or subalpine larch, is a rare tree in Canada and grows only in scattered areas of southwestern Alberta and southeastern BC. These trees are unique in that they are deciduous conifers – evergreens that change colour and drop their needles – but it is not the rare nature of these trees or the unusual habits they engage in that draws people here, it's the stunning display of colour that is absent in much of the forest in the mountain parks, dominated as it is by lodgepole pine, Engelmann spruce and Douglas fir. Larches are a brightish shade of green in summer compared to other evergreens and are often covered in a black, woolly down that drapes over their branches like so many funeral veils, but in the fall their needles grow pale and for a short time turn a dramatic yellow and gold before falling to the forest floor.

It is a spectacular sight, even to someone accustomed to these wonders, and on this glorious fall day there are somewhere between 100 and 200 hikers scattered along the valley and up the lower reaches of Sentinel Pass, taking it all in. Turns out the bigger crowds were largely absent from Moraine Lake not because it's a little more out of the way but because the people are all up here – plus there are at least ten dogs. It's not exactly the first place I would think to walk the dog, yet here they are in abundance, and most surprising is that all kinds of dogs are represented. There are big dogs, fat dogs and short dogs. There are also guard dogs and pocket dogs and dogs made to run. Scattered among the smart dogs are a distressing number of dumb dogs, as well as cute dogs and a handful of truly ugly dogs, which I didn't think was possible to this degree.

Of particular note in this doggie parade, which resembles a kennel club show crossed with *Jack Hanna's Animal*

Adventures, is the older foursome I meet midway up the pass, walking a skittish young Irish setter on a leash, who likes to chase pebbles that are kicked loose on the trail. At this point in the hike we're on a narrow trail full of switchbacks on a steep scree slope. If you were to fall here you wouldn't be any more certain to die than if you fell down a flight of stairs at home, but you would remove an uncomfortable amount of skin and possibly bash your head on any of the larger rocks on the way down. A broken arm or leg is also a strong possibility, but for the group of septuagenarians being led downhill by an overexcited *Canis lupus familiaris*, a fractured hip is practically guaranteed. Feeling tired and a little off balance from the altitude, I step off the trail at a tight corner and let them pass, and scratch my head at the wonder of it.

A little farther on, I pass one kid of about 12 screaming bloody blue murder while his parents hustle the obviously exhausted little bastard down, which is exactly the experience you want to have while attempting to commune with nature. He's completely off his head and in desperate need of a time out. His parents are mortified but powerless to calm him down. The thought crosses my mind that I might as well be in a McDonald's Playzone instead of on a high alpine pass in one of the world's premier national parks, but such is the cost of promoting your treasures too effectively. Sometimes too many people drop by to have a look.

It seems appropriate to mention here that the future of these mountain parks is likely to become a hot topic for debate over the coming decades. Parks Canada, a government organization responsible for overseeing and maintaining all of our national parks, national historic sites and national marine conservation areas, is at a critical time in the administration of these resources. In all, there are 215 properties in the three designations that fall under the Parks Canada banner, and one of the stated principles of the organization is as follows, and I'm quoting the official Parks Canada website here, "National Parks are a country-wide system of representative natural areas of Canadian significance. By law, they are protected for public understanding, appreciation and enjoyment, while being maintained in an unimpaired state for future generations."

Protecting our natural heritage is a noble and lofty goal, worthy of our attention, our time and whatever resources we can find to uphold those ideals. But the plan might be impossible to execute in real life, at least here in Banff National Park. Four million visitors enter the park every year, not including any number of people who don't buy a park pass and are not officially counted. The number grows even further when vehicles simply travelling on the main national highway, the Trans-Canada, are factored in. Through-traffic is not required to register and pay upon entering the park system between Banff and Kootenay or Yoho, and what those numbers would add up to is anyone's guess.

On a different page on the Parks website, the organization takes responsibility for, and again I'm quoting, "protecting these magnificent natural areas and managing them for visitors to understand, appreciate, and enjoy in a way that doesn't compromise their integrity."

And therein lies the rub.

Four to six million people visiting, living in and travelling through any confined space is bound to disrupt the natural process. It is inevitable and unavoidable. I am the definition of pessimistic optimist. I want to believe it's possible to love this land en masse and not love it to death. I want to subscribe to the Parks Canada idea that natural areas can be commercially viable and ecologically sound at the same time. I even believe the grand plan may actually work in other national parks, where visitation is somewhat less vigorous. I want it all to be doable and true but wonder if that wish is practicable here and now, let alone a decade or two in the future, when human pressures will no doubt have increased.

At the top of Sentinel Pass, the crowds are draining away downslope. Having eschewed the convenience of motorized transportation for a good half of the trip up here, I have arrived late, and the majority of the people I've encountered today have been on the way down. A few hungover or clueless day hikers, hearty souls and photographers with an understanding of how late twilight comes in this part of the world are still moving upward, but in the space of 45 minutes Larch Valley has essentially emptied out. Still, a human presence remains in my consciousness long after it disappears from view, and the experience of today only reinforces a vague sense of despair that creeps in beside the powerful sense of wonder I get whenever I'm out in the natural world. I can't help but think that there are simply too many of us around. Granted, I live in a sparsely populated province (just over 3.5 million people now call Alberta home) that has followed the modern trend of moving to urban centres (2.1 million people live in the five biggest cities), but it is still possible to feel overwhelmed in an uninhabited valley if you come at the wrong time of year.

Deep down, these feelings about encroaching humanity are not malicious (although there are moments) or critical (again, sometimes). But from the indifferent observational view point that's available when you're too tired to get upset, it appears we've exploded and expanded in a way we can't keep up with. It's true that we've chosen to congregate in increasingly large numbers (for the first time in human history there are now more people living in urban as opposed to rural environments) and I should have got out way before I ever did, but when the predicament spills out to these kinds of places, I can't help but feel we're gradually overrunning everything.

That, I suppose, will teach me to come up here on a warm and sunny Sunday afternoon in the fall.

Enjoying the last of my water and a snack at the top of the pass while taking in the incredible view down Larch Valley on one side and Paradise Valley on the other, I am struck by the notion that what this place really needs are a couple of big grizzlies roaming around, if only to discourage the masses.

• • •

Today being Monday, I'm keen to take advantage of the post-weekend thinning of the crowd. Riding up to the Chateau Lake Louise in surprisingly good form after yesterday's efforts, with the added bonus of a remarkable drop in vehicular traffic, leads me to imagine stomping up Fairview Mountain in the company of no one but myself and the occasional woodland creature. The lakeside in front of the Chateau does not contain the crush of humanity you'll see on a midsummer or weekend day, but it is still a mess of people scurrying to and fro, taking pictures and talking excitedly – so, having locked up my bike to a no-parking sign in one of the parking lots, I try and find the trailhead quickly and barely even glance at the famous lake as I pass.

A few hundred yards up the trail, a remarkable transformation occurs. A dark, forbidding forest comes to the forefront, and the people prattling about below disappear from consciousness. It calms the senses. A great cocoon of green envelops me, absorbing all sound and swallowing me up in its mysteries. The forest here is mature and thick and more suited to small mammals and birds than to larger wildlife, yet the trail information board near the start of the hike does have a rather enlightening photograph of a mother grizzly and two cubs wandering off down a trail that looks remarkably like this one. For a moment I have a twinge of worry about doing this hike on my own, but a reassuring tap on my bear spray canister brings with it a measure of acceptance – *c'est la vie*, what will be will be, and after only a few steps the woods consume me completely.

A little farther along, on the eastern aspect of Fairview, avalanche chutes emptied of snow are visible as debris fields scattered with dwarf trees, which struggle valiantly in the difficult growing conditions (namely a shadowy, rocky slope), only to get clobbered intermittently by avalanche in winter and rockfall in summer. It's a miracle they survive at all, yet here they are, bent and broken and clinging to life, and I choose to see their struggle as a testament to perseverance and hope. Eventually, as the trail winds ever upward, the forest thins out completely and I am deposited in an incredible high alpine meadow with a scattering of larches and, more importantly, no people to distract from the experiencing of it. There are no dogs and no overstimulated children to be seen, and that is no small relief.

If I want to carry on from here, the effort turns into a scramble, which is what a hike becomes when the destination is on top of a mountain. What I find intriguing about scrambling, as opposed to regular hiking, is the obvious change in perspective in a relatively short amount of time. That change is subtle and slow to develop as one foot moves in front of the other on a narrow path that doesn't vary significantly from step to step. Look up occasionally, and it's only more trail, with slightly different details. It isn't until you turn around at a strategic viewpoint that the full extent of your effort become apparent, which never fails to produce a brief moment of pure joy. The experience is more pronounced with vertical travel, as opposed to a long day of walking or biking in the foothills or on the prairies, and is why I expect so many people are drawn to high places. There is a sense of accomplishment that is tangible and abrupt, even if you don't actually reach the top.

I'm not a proper climber, but I do like the idea of it. The principles, ethos and self-reliance necessary for extended time outdoors; the simple beauty of the outdoors; the effort required once you convince your mind and body to stop complaining – these are all compelling in a way that defies definition. I'm no longer a thrill-for-thrill's-sake kind of guy, so the inherent danger of lofty peaks is not enough to drive me, and yet these more meagre heights continue to lure me. I've been to Everest Base Camp, at roughly 5300 metres, and have scrambled to a half a dozen local summits in the 3000-metre range, but I have never climbed a significant peak. I've also strapped on the harness a couple of times for some indoor wall work but have never scaled a difficult face out in the elements. Yet here I am, clinging on the margins of a sport that is defined by extremes, drawn by the challenges of pushing my feet upward and forward. I suppose it could be said I'm hanging on to a belief in the process of perseverance and hope, just like the dwarf trees.

Making the final push from the col is sweaty work along the south-facing slope. The sun is moving toward its peak, and the bare rock is absorbing and radiating heat much like a parking lot in a suburban subdivision would. Fairview is nothing more than a walk up, and at no point do your hands need to physically touch the rock, but it is most definitely up. The interminable climb – on what amounts to a rock pile that has been shattered over the years by the elements, to be dispersed on a downhill vector by gravity – produces a cool view: a riot of browns and greys scattered all over the hillside, with specks of black and green moss, all set up against an impossibly blue autumn sky. Shimmering heat waves radiate off the bare slope.

If I fix my gaze and don't shift it to the left or the right, and then tilt the landscape forward to a flat plane, I could easily be lost in the desert somewhere, with visions of camels and water-filled oases dancing across my field of vision before disappearing back into the recesses of a heat-tortured mind. As is, it's the top of the mountain that defies the senses, shimmering in the heat and drifting in and out of reach, always just beyond the next little rise.

• • •

I admit it, I was hoping to be the first one up Fairview Mountain today, but I did see a group of three hikers skating down the scree slope to my right while I was having my heat-induced hallucinations, and disappointingly, there was already a couple at the top when I finally got there. Fortunately, they seem as uninterested in me as I am in them, and we respectfully ignore one another in order to maintain the illusion of solitude. Being first, even on a day hike, has a way of making you feel special, like a proper explorer, and I do take solace in the fact I'm probably the first to bike up from the village before starting my scramble.

As far as peaks go, Fairview is positively spacious, and it's another gorgeous day, so I stake my claim on a slab of rock that's just the perfect height to have a seat on while I take in the views, which are understandably spectacular, justifying the name Fairview. This vantage point offers a bird's-eye view of the Bow Valley, and it doesn't take much imagination to trace my route along the ribbon of road cutting through the trees on the valley bottom back toward Canmore. Across the valley, the Lake Louise ski area is clearly visible, its lower runs dwarfed by the sheer mass of mountain above them. To the north, the individual strata lines on Mounts Whyte, Niblock and St. Piran are also clearly visible, indicating untold centuries' worth of sedimentary deposits laid down when this whole area was still a shallow sea, 1.5 billion years ago. And to the west, Mount Victoria and the Victoria Glacier are seemingly close enough to touch. Even this late in the season, the volume of snow and ice remaining on the face of Victoria is impressive. As it turns out, Canadian mountaineering history was made not far from here.

In August 1896, a group from the Appalachian Mountain Club made an attempt on Mount Lefroy (to the left of Mount Victoria and currently obscured by the peak of Mount Aberdeen), where Philip Stanley Abbot became the first fatality of North American mountaineering. The accident called into question the wisdom of climbing as sport, but club member Charles Fay organized a talented and experienced group and came back to the mountain the next year to the day and summited

Lefroy without incident. Straddling both the Continental Divide and the Alberta–British Columbia border, Abbot Pass Hut – named for Philip – sits on the windswept col between Mount Lefroy and Mount Victoria and at just a hair under 2930 metres is the second-highest permanent habitable structure in Canada, falling short of the height of Neil Colgan Hut, in the nearby Valley of the Ten Peaks, by a little over 30 metres. Abbot Hut was built in 1922 by the Swiss guides in an attempt to promote mountaineering in the area.

The Alpine Club of Canada currently oversees the operation of 23 backcountry huts in the mountainous regions of Alberta and British Columbia. The purpose of the structures is to provide outdoor enthusiasts with shelter and facilities from which they can pursue their activity of choice, mountaineering being the obvious example, and many are strategically located in regions where long approaches make a day trip impossible. Some are recommended only for the most ardent of alpinists (especially in winter), and almost all require a level of preparation and an understanding of the wilderness environment to be enjoyed properly.

But these backcountry huts are also a fantastic national resource and are not the exclusive domain of the hard-core athlete. A few, like the Elizabeth Parker Hut at Lake O'Hara and the A.O. Wheeler Hut at Rogers Pass, are easily accessible and surrounded by walking, hiking or cross-country ski routes ranging from easy to strenuous, making them an oasis of tranquility after a casual day's hike or ski. Elk Lakes Cabin and the Wates–Gibson Hut are three- to six-hour hikes along relatively easy trails, and these shelters can simply be used as places to unwind for the weekend – no activity required beyond getting there.

Preparing these facilities for use each spring is a tremendous undertaking. Wood must be transported, latrine and propane tanks swapped out and general repairs after a harsh winter executed. Because of the remote nature of many of the shelters and the fact that some are snowbound until late June or early July, the ACC is forced to use helicopters for the job – and let me tell you, Abbot Pass Hut is an incredible place to go via helicopter. As it turns out, my friend Lawrence is a good guy to know not only if you happen to be travelling in avalanche country in winter but also when there's some grunt work to be done in exchange for an unusual experience in the mountains – and I was standing in the right place at the right time when one of the calls for volunteers went out.

Visiting the col over 100 years after Mr. Abbot's untimely demise, it's hard to imagine much has changed. Even in late June, the temperature hovered around three degrees Celsius and was easily below zero with the wind chill, and once our chartered Bell 407 helicopter buzzed back down to the staging area at Lake O'Hara for supplies, all that could be heard was the wind. Whipping and swirling through the pass and ensuring it will never be an easy place to visit, even by air. Abbot Pass is a rocky, barren, hard place, forever exposed to the elements, and is not for the faint of heart. The wind is nearly perpetual, with rain or snow a regular companion. As in many places at high elevations, conditions are often tenuous at best, even when the valley bottoms remain pleasant. The circumstances of our trip inspired the strange sense of vertigo that comes from being dumped unceremoniously in unfamiliar territory.

On the flanks of Mount Victoria, the decidedly handsome stone hut is only about 15 vertical metres above the landing site. The snow was hard-packed and stable, but the walk up was challenging because the same couldn't be said of my legs. The flight itself was remarkably smooth, with little turbulence, but disembarking from a helicopter that has landed on a high mountain pass and has yet to power down is another matter altogether. We were instructed in the pre-flight briefing to – and I quote – "Never, never, never pass around the back end of the machine because of the proximity of the tail rotor."

"Fair enough," I thought. I've seen the fight scene near the end of *Raiders of the Lost Ark* and have equated rotors and propellers with spinning blades of death ever since. But then the pilot mentioned that while passing around the front, we should be mindful of the instrumentation package that protrudes six inches from the nose of the bird at waist height, because breaking it off is an expensive faux pas.

Gotcha.

He then carried on with a few more helpful tips, like "Keep your head down until well clear of the landing site."

Obviously.

"And oh yeah, we'll be setting down within ten feet of the edge of the col, and it's one hell of a drop to Lake Oesa, so don't drift too far off the front either."

Suddenly, volunteering to haul some wood around and to help to dislodge an empty propane tank frozen solid into the ground didn't seem like such a great idea, even with a free helicopter ride thrown in as incentive – until I put things in perspective.

In 1922, the work crew responsible for the hut rafted supplies across Lake Louise, hauled them on pack horses up the Victoria Glacier and then organized a series of winches and ladders in order to lug everything on their own backs up the final section through the notorious "Death Trap" (a perilous section of the route prone to rock and ice fall), no doubt covering the most dangerous ground multiple times in a single day. All of this executed before even beginning to actually build a hut on a narrow strip of inhospitable ground in the stiff breeze that was surely a regular companion. The result of that heroic (if slightly insane) effort is a surprisingly large and attractive stone structure now recognized as a national historic site, situated where no building has any right to be.

Since those early days, thousands more have visited the old-fashioned way (on foot) and enjoyed the basic comforts facilitated by the Alpine Club of Canada, who took over management of the hut in 1985.

And now, sitting on top of Fairview, I make a mental note to make the trek up to the historic hut one of these days. As I'm daydreaming about future adventures, the summit of Fairview begins to slowly fill up. Another solo hiker appears not long after I settle in on my perch, and after that another couple shows up and we exchange quick hellos and everyone tries to find their own space at the top. It isn't until a Korean couple comes up and we reach an unspoken critical density that it becomes clear a private experience with nature is not to be had after all. We've reached some kind of mountaintop equation where an unspecific number of people per square metre transforms the landscape under our feet, and it's impossible to ignore each other's presence any longer. I'm suddenly inspired to try and be pleasant, if only to reinforce the Canadian reputation of friendliness.

"Hello," I say, not entirely sure the greeting will be understood, but when I get an enthusiastic hello in return, I am encouraged.

"How are you?" seems the likely progression in the conversation, and what I want to impress upon them is the importance of following the same route down from Fairview Mountain as they have come up. There's a helpful plaque bolted to the naked stone at the summit, reminding people that although tempting – the lake, far below, is visible from here – descending via the northern aspect of the mountain is extremely hazardous and not recommended under any circumstances, due to difficult route-finding and a dangerous cliff band. The problem is that the warning is written in English and French, which is no help whatsoever to these international guests. Especially considering that "Thank you" was their answer to "How are you?"

Flustered but not deterred, I try miming the importance of going back the way they came but that only looks a bizarre pantomime, so I eventually go back to my perch and my sandwich to find a brave and remarkably rotund chipmunk sniffing around the rest of my lunch.

Eventually, Martin and Shumin, a couple of older gentlemen out on a day trip, make the top and ask to share part of my perch. Turns out they're both smart guys, and remarkably eloquent. Despite the growing social anxiety that has overtaken me in recent years (not to mention the failed attempt at international diplomacy with the Koreans), I find these guys easy to talk to. We get on to having a good chat about the environment, alternative energy for the future and good climbs and hikes in the area, while casually eating our bag lunches. They even mention a few local destinations I've never even heard of, let alone tried, and I make a mental note to check my guidebooks when I get back to the hostel, to see if any of these locations will fit into my itinerary.

So it appears that among the masses there are people who make the effort to come to places like this and still have a healthy sense of wonder, and suddenly I can relate once again to my fellow man. My passions are not misplaced, and my beliefs are worthy of consideration. It has always been my conviction that you can't visit Lake Louise or the Grand Canyon or the Khumbu Valley without being moved. These vistas – along with hundreds of other natural wonders around the world – are simply too awesome for the soul to take lightly. They are humbling in their grandeur and powerful beyond human measure, but when we make them too accessible we cheapen them, and by extension cheapen our experience of them.

Make no mistake, they are still powerful and wonderful, but it is decidedly more difficult to experience those emotions in a crowd, from behind a bus window, or while standing on a slab of pavement. It is my growing belief that you need to experience at least a modicum of discomfort from either the weather or the effort in order to properly engage them. Ideally both should factor into the process. Otherwise the experience is less valued and our vision dulled. Our interaction with the natural world reduced to a picture or a postcard. You have to sweat, you have to get dirty, and I contend that if it's too hot or too cold or too windy or too wet, then it's probably just right, because that discomfort is your all-access backstage pass. Whereas the ticket you bought by taking the easy way is akin to rush seating or upper bowl. Or possibly even side-stage, partially obstructed. There will be a moment in the experience that is remarkable, but it is not the same as real understanding, felt at your core. It's not like earning your way up to the front row.

Bidding adieu to my new friends, I bound down off

Fairview Mountain as only a man who feels on top of the world can bound. My emotions are at the surface once again, but they are overwhelmingly positive now, and I exist here in the heart of the mountains, hopeful for change. My bitterness has been tempered by optimism brought on by my conversations on the mountaintop, and my negativity has been scraped away by honest effort. Sure, the descent is hard on the quads and the knees, but gravity propels me forward, and I can't help but wear out the superlatives on the way down. This place is simultaneously breathtaking, gorgeous, stunning and dazzling, and under the circumstances I can't begin to imagine why anyone would ever want to live in a big city, with all its concrete, glass and steel, when all this beauty is out here.

At the moment I don't know how they manage it, to be honest.

• • •

Clomping down the last of my back trail with leg-weary footfalls, I eventually make my way from the silence and the peace of the forest and return to the shit-show that is the lakefront on a sunny afternoon. It has got much busier since this morning, with the late-season tours making their mid-afternoon stops, and the transition is both dramatic and jarring. I admit it's an interesting human tableau, but what you overhear too often in this situation is, unfortunately, spoiled rich people complaining about insignificant details: "The service at dinner last night was terrible, I specifically asked for no croutons in my Caesar salad." "Why is the parking lot so far from the lakeshore?" "Are there no boat tours? There should be boat tours." And on and on it goes.

Mixed in with the idle moaners, however, are plenty of

languages I don't understand and accents I can't put my finger on, as well as the inevitable ski bums and burnouts who are mainstays in mountain culture. These bit players hang around at the fringes of most mountain towns, washing dishes or tending bar or cleaning guest rooms while waiting for epic snow dumps. I, for one, like the spirit in them, choosing as they do a lifestyle over a steady job and financial gain. Unfortunately, their great contribution in the here and now is to announce, at full volume, how baked or blasted they plan to get later on tonight. The fact that there has been no big snow in five months seems not to matter one bit, as they give the impression of being content to wait out their own particular version of an "off-season" as long as the dope is good and the booze is cheap.

The experience at the lake edge is nearly enough to cloud an otherwise spectacular day, and I'm more than a bit aggravated that my reflective afternoon has been infringed upon yet again. Taking a deep breath and plunging into the crowd, I walk by a young, slim, sharply dressed Japanese woman with an umbrella in her hand – I know, I know, its pronounced "parasol" when there's not a cloud in the sky – and whisper, "It's not raining," before returning to my bike for the trip down the narrow but smooth roadway to the HI–Lake Louise Alpine Centre Hostel. It took nearly 40 minutes to bike up to Lake Louise this morning but takes only five and a half minutes to get back down. That speedy rush alone has managed to blow away with pure thrill any negative thoughts that were brewing.

13.

LAGGAN STATION

No reason to get excited, the thief he kindly spoke
There are many here among us who feel that life is but a joke
But you and I, we've been through that, and this is not our fate
So let us not talk falsely now, the hour is getting late.

—Bob Dylan

After a shower and a bit of light stretching, I find I'm up for a little exploring, as long as it remains at ground level. I'm tired and more than a little sore, and there's no way I can face the idea of going up anywhere today. Sentinel Pass, at 2605 metres above sea level, and Fairview Mountain, at 2744 metres above the same base marker, are a combined 2277 vertical metres of ascent above Lake Louise Village, which sits at approximately 1536 metres. As a result, even the stairs to the guest lounge at the Alpine Centre are mild torture as my body rebels against the heavy labours of the last few days. My calf muscles are as tight as guitar strings, and my hamstrings fairly hum with a background ache that no amount of Advil can seem to nullify. My thighs are just heavy blocks of unresponsive flesh.

After a standard restaurant breakfast of eggs, sausage, hash browns and toast at Bill Peyto's Café, the plan is to explore Lake Louise Village, such as it is. I've been here at least a dozen times before, but often I've just been passing through, and I've never spent more than a single night at a time in a campground or hotel. I'm determined to try and get to know it better. Out the back of the Alpine Centre are some easy walking trails that eventually lead to the banks of the Bow River – a good opportunity to meander without much effort. Instead, I'm inexplicably drawn to the economic centre of things and so follow a gravel trail that veers left, amble purposefully through the Post Hotel parking lot, and find myself on the banks of the Pipestone River, just above where it joins up with the Bow, in no time at all.

I love a rushing river because it drowns out the outside world, but it also calms my overactive mind, like a natural version of the Banff Springs waterfalls. I am instantly soothed and take the time to sit at a picnic table in a treed park on the south bank to let the sound of the water wash over me, although it's unlikely I'll be inspired to venture into this tributary anytime soon. The river here is fast and looks cold, even after a summer of solar radiation beating into its meagre depths. Like all the watercourses originating in these mountains – with the singular exception of the Miette River up in Jasper – the Pipestone is glacier-fed and stubbornly refuses to warm up in any season. So I take a pass on a late-morning swim.

At Laggan's Mountain Bakery & Delicatessen, a jar on the counter has a cartoon taped to it that depicts a coffee house scene remarkably like the one I'm standing in. The caption says, "God knows when you don't tip." Of course I love the cartoon, because it's a bit of an inside joke I'm privy to, and because it gives me something to read while I wait to place my order. I also end up catch myself laughing out loud with a little too much enthusiasm when neither of the two customers ahead of me gets the joke. At least I don't think they get the joke, because they don't drop any coins in the jar.

It's impossible to really get away from the service industry once you've worked in it for a while, because everywhere you go there's service in one form or another that you either provide or receive. Even if you eventually get out, service becomes part of your internal makeup and you notice things that might otherwise be missed. It is an often overlooked fact that most service staff could not survive without the extra coins and occasional bills left behind in billfolds and tips jars, and no owner wants to pay a proper living wage to said service staff because it would make his product unmanageably expensive. This quirk in the food and beverage system can be difficult to explain to regular folks, let alone foreigners who are unfamiliar with the process, without sounding entitled or greedy, and the misreading of the practice creates an uneasy balance between service, appropriate compensation and the overall customer experience.

It might surprise most foreigners, and possibly even some North Americans, to know the average server makes *below* minimum wage in Canada and the United States, and as a result has to rely on tips to make up the difference, which makes tipping a necessary economic process, as important as actually paying for the original goods. Without it, no matter how insignificant a few coins may appear, there very well could be nobody behind that counter or bar top tomorrow. In such an obvious tourist destination, some important customs continue to go unheeded, however, and I see no harm in poking fun at the gratuity-challenged. It's certainly a more socially acceptable way of dealing with it than my less-than-delicate approach, which is to whisper, "You cheap prick" under my breath as I turn to ring something in or clear away glassware.

Good for you, I think as I wait patiently after placing my order and reread the cartoon a half-dozen times, giggling a little each time. I can see how the occasional ignoramus who's never worked a service job in his life could be offended by the blatant appeal for funds, and have actually heard people make comments to this effect, but I see it as a subtle reminder to those who might otherwise slip their change into their pocket when no one is looking that people around here work for a living, and it's not always an easy thing to get by. But then my large mocha comes to $4.87, and from my 20-dollar bill I get three fives and 13 cents, and I can't help wondering what God thinks of that.

All you can do in this world is try, and too many times in my life I've had to ask to break down a fiver. If she had simply given me a loonie and two toonies, she would have earned an extra couple of bucks. I just hope Saint Grat will excuse the meagre offering under the circumstances.

I take my coffee back outside, to a parking lot designed for about 100 cars, with a special section reserved for tour buses and RVs. Lake Louise is less a village than a hamlet, and even then it's a stretch. "Way station" seems most appropriate. Originally named Holt City when it was a CPR construction camp, it was later renamed Laggan Station and then, in 1914, Lake Louise Station. It is still not much more than a handful of shops and some outlying hotels. At 1536 metres it is the highest permanent community in Canada, with a population of around 1,600 people, 750 of whom are Chateau Lake Louise staff who live up the hill in designated staff accommodation. In point of fact, almost all private accommodation is staff accommodation of one form or another in this town. There are no leafy neighbourhoods and no single-family homes with broad front yards, just condo-style lodging near each of the bigger hotels.

In addition to Laggan's Deli, Samson Mall has the usual services available in a town of this size. Bow River Trading and the Trailhead Café cater to the tourist crowd, and I'm always amazed that every single main street in every single mountain town has a store dedicated exclusively to candy, in this case the Olde Tyme Candy Shoppe. Less surprising is the liquor store at the end of the row, which is pretty much standard issue everywhere, except this one has no brand attached to it, it's just "Liquor Store." After popping in to the Viewpoint for a dose of inspiration from its mountain books, photos and posters, and picking up some last-minute supplies for tomorrow at Wilson Mountain Sports, I finally make my way over to the Parks info centre to purchase a backcountry camping permit.

You've got to hand it to the people at Parks Canada; for all their bureaucratic two-stepping, they certainly do know how to put together an information centre. I might not have been too impressed with the state of Tunnel Mountain campground back in Banff, or with the overall direction Parks management is taking at the moment, for that matter, but there is no denying their info centres are well done. On Banff Avenue, right here in front of me, and up in Jasper, the three primary info centres servicing the parks are all well thought out, informative and full of pictures and displays designed to enlighten and entertain. I would even go so far as to say they inspire.

Of particular note today is the tectonostratigraphic flow chart, a rather complicated set of diagrams that tries to explain the geology of these mountains and how they formed. Despite the technical nature of the display, my inner nerd is stimulated. There is also a classic glacier shot spread across an entire wall that channels my inner photographer almost enough to send me back outside with my camera, and near the entrance is a simple diorama of mountains that compares the mighty Himalayas, the now trendy Andes, the venerable Alps, BC's Coastal Mountains, my Rocky Mountains and the ancient Appalachians of eastern North America.

The display is remarkably uncomplicated yet effective, with six-inch-thick pieces of Plexiglas carved out in the vague shape of a mountain chain thrusting up and out of a flat base, the tallest one reaching three or four inches to the sky. The clear glass is lit from below and is a simple yet effective way to compare the height of each range. In terms of pure stature, the mountains outside, which seem so lofty and substantial in person, are only fifth on the list of height from sea level. But believe me, they look high from up close.

The highlight of the self-guided tour of the Lake Louise Information Centre, however, is undoubtedly the Parks Canada movie on the giant screen in a tiny theatre. *Welcome to Banff National Park* reminds me of the nature programs and wildlife shorts from my childhood. It is filled with breathtaking fly-by and wildlife footage and is nothing if not a tug on the heartstrings, containing as it does all the best natural highlights of the parks, in the best light. My cynical eye now sees it all as propaganda, of course, designed to distract from what appears to be the current mission of maximum visitorship and tourist dollars spent, but this mountain and wildlife porn is still good enough to choke me up.

I remain mesmerized by the images passing before me in quick succession and can't help but sit and watch the short film three times before wandering off to find a place to have lunch.

• • •

After lunch at the Station Restaurant, located in the historic Laggan train station, and a quick nap back at the Alpine Centre, I grab a coffee from Bill Peyto's Café and retire to the deck to enjoy the last of the afternoon sunshine with my new book, *Hooker & Brown*, by local writer Jerry Auld. Set here in the Rockies, the novel follows the exploits of two young mountaineers as they attempt to unravel the mystery and myth surrounding two fabled peaks said to exist somewhere along this chain of mountains. Mount Hooker and Mount Brown were thought to be monsters hidden deep in an impenetrable wilderness.

David Thompson was the first European to cross Athabasca Pass in 1811, and an uncharacteristic error for the usually meticulous explorer led to his estimating the pass's elevation at 3353 metres. In turn, Ross Cox and Thomas Drummond calculated the surrounding peaks to be approximately 4877 and 5486 metres respectively in 1814, most likely taking their baseline from Thompson's measurements. David Douglas muddied the waters further in 1827 by climbing one of the peaks and proclaiming it to be "the highest yet known in the North Continent of America," despite evidence to the contrary found in his later journal notes. A botanist by trade, Douglas named the mountains after colleagues William Hooker and Robert Brown, and the comedy of errors surrounding the early estimation of the peaks has created a legend in local mountaineering lore that survives to this day.

On the deck at the Alpine Centre, it's a busy time of day, with groups checking in while others return from day trips in the mountains or short visits to the village or the lake. All types of people are milling about, and the scene is similar to what you would find in just about any major travel destination in the world. A mildly confused chaos prevails as foreigners try to navigate the subtle intricacies of unfamiliar check-in procedures.

There are also young kids (the 18- to 25-year-old crowd) wandering around looking vaguely lost (or at least decidedly directionless) as they search for something without even really knowing what they're looking for, and on some level I find I still relate. Mixed in with those lost souls are the experienced travellers, moving in ones and twos, hip to where the deals are and obviously on individual missions of discovery. Then there are the fours and sixes, groups that tend to be older and coupled off – today most of these appear to be ardent hikers in their 50s and 60s, and they remind me of my parents.

Like most teenagers, I held a certain amount of disdain for my parents back in the day. I liked them well enough, but as is custom I tended to focus on their shortcomings, which at the time included a tendency toward cut-rate travel. Camping, a cottage with no electricity, and low-end motels dominated our summer outings, and I saw that as an affront to my God-given right to a bed I didn't have to share with my brother, and to cable television. In my ignorance, I failed to realize it was the travel, not the accommodation, that mattered. And now I find I want to be more like these aging adventurers before me today. Where once I saw them as poor schmucks who wouldn't spring for proper hotels, they now come across as comfortable and curious travellers. It's even possible they've seen "the better side," but choose this instead. A path in life I've only begun to contemplate recently. Most importantly, they seem happy to be alive, and happy to be here, and I find I envy their easy manner. I am even willing to concede that my parents might have been much wiser than they appeared at first glance all those years ago – but don't tell them I said so.

And finally there are the hard-core alpinists and serious backcountry enthusiasts. Decked out with full complements of gear and heavy packs, they radiate a sober purpose. They are doing what I had, in the back of my mind, thought I might do a little of on this trip, and that is climb mountains. There is a part of me that is inspired to greater heights and more difficult tasks by their mere presence here, and a part that tries to be indifferent to it all but fails. The truth is, I resent their talent, their force of will and their physical gifts. So I pretend I don't see these guys with their ripped physiques, battered gear and sunburned faces; instead, I quietly drink my coffee and read.

After I finish a couple of chapters, the sunlight begins to sift through the trees and edge the tops of the mountains to the west, and the temperature drops accordingly. It is now too chilly to sit out on the deck comfortably, so I make my way inside with the idea of maybe reading some emails and reconnecting with my old life – a desire I've managed to resist up to now, with no great hardship. In fact, I've almost been afraid of opening my inbox for fear of being absorbed back into a life of inane detail through the artificial conduit of cyberspace, but being around all these people compels me to check in. It's what you do when you're in Rome, I guess – you act like a Roman – and I'm lured to the computers in the second-floor guest lounge.

The lounge itself is comfortable and spacious, with high ceilings, a stone fireplace and the requisite woodwork throughout. There's a pool table, a number of couches and chairs, a foosball table and an oversized wooden chess set from which some idiot has decided to steal the black king and queen. And of course there are four computers beckoning from one corner. Logging on requires the user to buy minutes from the front desk. After purchasing a code that costs a few bucks for every 20 minutes, I figure I might as might as well get a beer while I'm at it, and pop in once again to Peyto's Café.

After I finally get online, the actual contents of the latest emails are unremarkable. There are a few new Facebook requests and a fair amount of junk mail and company newsletters I haven't yet figured out how to block. Apart from a check-in with Jocey about further plans for the trip, there's nothing special in the correspondence, and I am strangely disappointed.

On the one hand, I've been trying to cut most ties to my life in Canmore, yet on the other there is still a piece of me that wants to be involved. *Please, please, please let me be a part. I know I'm shunning you now, but I don't want to be left out.* It feels weird and desperate. Of course I want to care about my old life, or at least I feel like I should care, but then I find that deep down I don't. The screen is a portal to a world I'm not particularly interested in anymore, and it feels intrusive yet strangely compelling at the same time.

But I am going to need to go back at some point, and I will have to find a job. The unshakable spectre of looming debt is no small factor in my life and weighs heavily on my psyche. My bank account is dipping hard into negative digits, and recently my credit limit was graciously adjusted upward to a number I dare not think about – without my consent, by the way. I just opened up a letter and there is was, an extra five grand. Those legalized loan sharks have me in their sights, and like every other dummy with poor self-control I continue to buy in at 11.99 per cent. My only solace is that although they may eventually ruin me, it's unlikely they'll come around and break my legs. I hope.

After sending a couple of quick, if uninspired, responses, I head back downstairs to the toilet, and to get another beer. Having left my papers and notebook on the keyboard, I come back up to the lounge, only to find a young blond woman working at my station. Stopping mid-stride, with a clearly audible "hmmm" escaping my lips, I'm sort of at a loss of what to do under the circumstances. The woman using up my computer minutes is not unattractive, yet possesses a hardness about her and is clearly a big-city girl. Eventually she notices me hovering.

"Oh, I'll be off in a minute," she says with a thick German accent, almost dismissively.

"Oh, okay. I didn't realize I was finished."

I don't actually say that, obviously, but boy do I want to, with as much sarcasm as I can muster. Instead I pick up my stuff from around her and move to the monitor one chair over. A woman was sitting in this same spot not five minutes before I went downstairs, and she couldn't manage to get the machine to boot up. My computer hijacker also took a crack at it before I went on my refuelling mission, but obviously she decided it would be easier, or cheaper, to jump on my machine when I wasn't looking. It doesn't take much of an effort to fire it up, and now I'm beyond agitated and none too charitable to boot.

Missy can type like the wind, I'll give her that, but I'm seething now and can't concentrate on my screen or think about anything else except the obnoxious piece of work to my right. Maybe she's a secretary back in Munich, or a court stenographer, but then again a secretary would have been able to start up the computer I'm on. Maybe she's just accustomed to batting her eyelashes and getting whatever she wants, and her less-than-thoughtful behaviour brings to mind some of the other less charming details I've noticed around here, empty potato chip packages and leftover food littering the common areas being the most egregious.

Whatever her particular malfunction, and whether this was an intentional act or not, I can't help but realize that this is why I try to avoid other people, and why people should probably try a little harder to avoid me. There's no telling when I'm going to finally snap, and in the words of comedian Russell Peters when describing his less than patient father (insert East Indian accent here, which Russell uses in his act whenever he imitates his dad): "Somebody gonna get-a hurt real bad."

The mental image of Peters imitating his father almost makes me laugh out loud, and after a couple of minutes more, Miss Munich logs off, says thanks in a most pleasant manner and disappears down the stairs. All I can manage is a confused and slightly exasperated "No problem."

• • •

Still achy and in need of sleep after dinner at Peyto's Café, I head back to my dorm room the long way, through the bowels of the facility. I'm hoping for some inspiration en route but find none. The common kitchen downstairs is still half-filled with small groups talking and laughing over dinner, and the ski-storage room is completely deserted. In the opposite wing, the laundry room and sauna are also temporarily abandoned, and after 15 minutes of watching *Top Gun* in the TV room with a dozen other guests, I get to my appointed room only to find a new roommate already off in la-la land.

A quick downward flick of the light switch and a hushed "sorry" is followed by an awkward scramble into a vacant top bunk, and I am reminded of the challenges of shared accommodation. The awkwardness of being around strangers in this situation is worse than a crowded elevator ride, not to mention longer and much more intimate. The measured breathing and the overly self-conscious movements make for an uncomfortable process. But in the end the dude just snorts, rolls over, snores briefly and then is as silent as mouse. By the time I finally nod off, I'm seriously thinking of checking for vitals.

Twenty minutes later, a new guy comes in for the night, and he's not loud but is not exactly quiet either. Settling into his bunk, he reads for God knows how long, and every time I turn, rustle or roll over, I hope the action somehow projects the idea that some of us are trying to sleep. After a time I begin reciting the mantra "read in the common room – read in the common room – read in the common room" over and over in my head, to no avail. Buddy continues to read, clearly unaware of the late hour, and this time I'm thinking about homicide when I finally nod off again.

Fifteen minutes after that, the last of my bunkmates comes in, and we go through the whole process once again. He reads for even longer, and I don't know if it's my overactive imagination, but his bed light seems brighter than any other.

Secretly, I hope I snore.

14.

THE BACKCOUNTRY

I've spent my life watching sky and sea change colour
Hypnotized by the beauty of it all,
and you ask me why I'm singing
Well, it is good for me; it can be good for you.

—Hothouse Flowers

At precisely seven thirty a.m., my watch alarm goes off somewhere down at the bottom of the bed. The sound is muffled by the clothes and equipment stuffed in the bag containing the watch, but it's still a foreign sound, loud enough to drag a person from the deepest of sleep no matter how badly the body wants just a few hours more. By the time I swim up to a level of consciousness that can actually figure out what the offending noise is, the damn thing has already been chiming for 12 or 13 seconds, so I just leave it. I didn't sleep well and can barely imagine getting up before noon today, let alone right now. Besides, the watch is too far away to stop before it reaches the automatic 20-second shut off, and I'm way too sluggish to bother getting there before then. It's programmed to go off a second time five minutes after the first alarm, before falling silent until the same time tomorrow morning, but instead of taking care of it and getting on with my day, I let my passive-aggressive tendencies get the better of me and drift off for a short catnap. Four minutes and 40 seconds later, we go through the whole noisy process again.

After finally making my way out of bed a few minutes later, and before gathering up my gear as recklessly as possible, I am faced with today's reality: travelling to the Skoki wilderness and Baker Lake will mean going uphill once again, if I can manage it. Stopping for coffee and a simple takeaway breakfast at Laggan's is an act of procrastination as much as anything, but once the caffeine hits my system I am finally able to properly assess the situation.

Standing outside Wilson Mountain Sports, flexing a few of the muscles that were giving me grief yesterday, I find that I ache but am not overly sore. My mochaccino is not contributing to my energy levels in the way that I had hoped, and I remain lethargic. On the plus side, I will be headed up the other side of the valley this time, in the direction of the Lake Louise Ski Resort and away from the last of the summer crowds. In winter, it will be the more popular destination because of the ski hill, but until the snow arrives the eastern side of the valley can be largely overlooked, which is more than fine by me.

The bike up toward the ski hill is bracing and difficult to warm to but is mercifully vehicle-free. I make a right on Temple Road, where a stretch of gravel leads to the Fish Creek parking area and a gate that restricts access to Temple Lodge. This is tough to navigate at any speed, due to its abundance of washboard ruts. It's a stretch of rattle-crash-bang riding that threatens to throw my saddlebags and jar a few internal organs free but in the end is short-lived.

I lock my bike to a small tree hidden away in the woods. This might seem ridiculous given the long odds of someone actually stumbling upon the random location, but my big-city instincts prohibit me from just leaving it lying around for a couple of days. Rearranging my gear into my daypack proves a challenging task that deteriorates into a slipshod job, with bits and pieces of clothing and camera gear jammed into every nook and cranny. Had I actually bothered to give this a proper try before setting out this morning, I wouldn't have to leave a quarter of my supplies hidden in my saddlebags next to my bike. But thankfully I did bring plenty of bungee cords, so two or three days' worth of equipment and food will still be coming with me. I just hope it doesn't rain much, because the poncho I picked up at Wilson's an hour ago didn't make the final cut.

The beginning of the hike into Skoki is long and without much encouragement, following as it does the access road up to Temple Lodge. Unfortunately, this part of the route offers no extensive views or stimulating visuals. It's all just gravel at my feet and trees on both sides, and in the absence of anything else to think about, I wonder: Does trudging up this uninspired pathway qualify as an adventure? In monotonous moments like this, I've spent a considerable amount of time thinking about the subject, and wonder what *adventure* means exactly. In the *Oxford Paperback Dictionary & Thesaurus*, the first two definitions are 1) an unusual and exciting experience; and 2) a hazardous activity. The book goes on to define an *adventurer* as someone who seeks adventure for personal gain or pleasure. Perhaps a bit less helpful is the definition of *adventurous* as "adventuresome or enterprising," and not un-noteworthy is the fact that *daring* and *foolhardy* sit right next to each other in the list of synonyms.

I hate to admit it, but there have been times in the last few years when I have passed up perfectly good opportunities to get out into this wilderness – for a hike, for a bike ride, for a cross-country ski, for a paddle – simply because it didn't seem adventurous enough. Not enough days out of the house, not enough distance to cover, not enough suffering predicted. If it's not a monumental struggle, then it's not an adventure, at least in the sense that I have come to understand the word, but I'm beginning to think I might be missing the point. J. Monroe Thorington, in his book *The Glittering Mountains of Canada*, wrote, "We were not pioneers ourselves, but we journeyed over old trails that were new to us, and with hearts open. Who shall distinguish?" Interesting thought, especially in these modern times, dominated as they are by the idea of accomplishment as a benchmark of success.

If we mark our lives through stories and we gauge our progress through human interaction and how we compare to those around us, then to some people just biking to Banff from Canmore would be considered an extreme activity outside their usual routine, and would by definition be an adventure to them. On the other hand, I live in one of the adventure capitals of the country. The 24 Hours of Adrenalin mountain bike race, the TransRockies Challenge and the Rocky Mountain Half Marathon all take place in whole or in part in my town, and those are just the sanctioned events. There are also the Alpine Club huts and the outings its members embark on, not to mention the independent climbers and hikers and skiers. But I have come to a time in my life where I have to accept that my physical abilities put me right smack in the middle of the lower end of the curve in terms of local adventure personalities. Chic Scott and Will Gadd live in my hometown among any number of other notable outdoorsy types, and there are at least three current or former residents I've heard of who have reached the summit of Mount Everest.

So while I may be physically able compared to many, and even adventurous to some, out in these wilds I am normal at best and perhaps even below average. If I truly am unremarkable in my quest, the question is: In this world of extremes, can I live with that? Or does my ego keep me from accepting my place as the happy wanderer bringing up the rear, tramping across well-travelled ground in the hopes of finding nothing more and nothing less than a new experience? It is a question worthy of further thought, and it appears that this morning I have nothing but time for it.

So, despite my lingering fatigue, the thought of finding some hint into the meaning of all this walking is in the end energizing, and that's probably a good thing. After three kilometres, the trail here is still just an old and worn gravel road that climbs relentlessly with only the occasional view, because I am still well below treeline. It is a journey without charm or excitement, where the alluring and compelling nature of a narrow path snaking off into the quiet distance is conspicuously absent, replaced by small potholes and loose stones. But this may still be an adventure, simply because I've never been here before and it has been an effort to get here. And that will have to do for now.

• • •

Eventually the monotony of the hike is broken by an unexpected meeting with three pretty brown horses who seem as surprised to see me as I them. The corral that houses the trio is something I would expect out on the prairie, not perched on the side of a mountain, but it is a welcome spot for a break after a long start to the morning. After dropping my pack and sipping some water, I try to interact with the shy beasts but ultimately fail to make a connection. I try moving up and down the fence line while making that ridiculous "come here, boy" click-clicking noise out the side of my mouth, but they don't seem to want to have anything to do with me. In fact they spend most of my effort actually moving away. I would have thought that with so little foot traffic up this way they'd be keen on a little company, but that just goes to show what I know about horses. Maybe living in the heart of grizzly bear territory has made them wary. Then again, maybe they're just disagreeable.

To be fair, I've never really understood horses, and they probably sense my ineptitude where their species is concerned. They are certainly more attractive than their cousins the moose, after all. A moose is nothing if not ridiculous. A horse, on the other hand, is graceful – beautiful, even. But I've always found them to be skittish and unpredictable as well, which is probably why I've always preferred a bike saddle to a saddle of the more traditional variety. It's not that I dislike horses; I just don't understand their behaviour, and my relationship could best be described as a mild fascination mixed with a healthy dose of mistrust. In the end, these horses want nothing to do with me and avoid any attempt at a deeper understanding.

The route continues to be quite steep in places, with little reward for the effort. There are still no stunning vistas, and after finally arriving at the Ptarmigan Chairlift at the southern end of the ski area, I'm greeted by the less-than-comforting sound of heavy machinery droning away in the forest; resort improvements are underway in the only season possible. With the first of November less than a month away, the boys doing the grunt work up here are probably on a tight deadline and are banging and crashing in a rush to get the job done before the coming snow buries the opportunity to finish.

A little farther along, a small information kiosk has the usual maps and bear warnings posted on the wall, as well as a small bench on which to rest my weary legs, but after a quick sip of water and a couple of blissful minutes unburdened by my pack, I decide against lingering. With my lack of sleep last night, I'm not exactly feeling spry, but it's too early for lunch, and if I sit for too long I run the risk of never getting up again. Shortly afterward, in my obsession to put the hum of industrious humanity behind me, I somehow miss the trail marker directing hikers to Boulder Pass, and I end up a couple of hundred yards up a steep ski run before it dawns on me that hiking trails are rarely 40 metres wide.

I descend in a flurry of cursing and self-recrimination – a not uncommon overreaction on my part – but everything gets better once I locate the proper route. It's an old fire road that has deteriorated – or improved, depending on your point of view – and doesn't look like it has seen vehicular traffic of any kind for a very long time, and the trail slowly transforms into a pleasant wooded stroll with a more gradual incline that encourages a brisk pace.

All good forest trails are the same, in my experience, no matter where you are in the world: hard-packed earth littered with stones and boulders of various sizes, with slippery roots and the occasional muddy bog or downed tree to navigate. This little stretch is similar to ones I encountered on short trips with my parents on the Appalachian Trail in New England, or bits of the West Coast Trail on Vancouver Island, and I find this strangely comforting. Walking here is familiar and natural, and the going is effortless. Before long, the easy trail spits me out into a mountain meadow littered with larches and bisected by what is undoubtedly a very cold stream. Standing on a small footbridge and looking down into the water, I can see that even the stones making up the streambed look chilly as they glisten in the late-morning sun, and I find I have been looking forward to this part of the journey since I first made the decision to step away from my habits all those months ago.

Pushing on with renewed vigour, I eventually make it up and over the aptly named Boulder Pass, which is strewn with rocks of all shapes and sizes that have come tumbling down off of Redoubt Mountain over the past millennium, and the world transforms right before my very eyes. Crossing the pass is like stepping into a new world, or a lost world, one that has remained largely untouched by the hand of man. There is blue sky off in one direction, and high, wispy clouds stretch out in the other. Mount Temple is back over my shoulder, looking appropriately regal in the distance on the far side of the Bow Valley, and I can't be sure, but in the near distance it appears I'm now higher than all the peaks that make up the ski resort, which from the Samson parking lot this morning seemed impossibly high and distant.

Up ahead, the trail streaking its way along the left side of Ptarmigan Lake is wide and littered with evidence of hikers and horse parties in the form of dried-up muddy footprints, and mirror-image reflections of Mount Douglas and Mount St. Bride are coming up off the dead-calm waters of the lake. There isn't a single airplane contrail to be seen across the entire sweep of sky, and it's easy to imagine this path as an overworked game trail or ancient trade route through the mountains.

Off to my right are stubborn north-facing snowbanks,

about the size of Olympic swimming pools, hanging on the edge of the lake for dear life, as if afraid of sliding in and getting wet. Although I'm now above treeline, the subtle smells of the forest linger. Making my way toward the trail junction with Deception Pass gradually takes me up and away from the water's edge, and strangely this lake appears flatter than other lakes. I don't know whether it's the naked shoreline or the stark contrast with the surrounding mountains that causes the optical illusion, but it's undeniable: from a slightly raised viewpoint, it's hard to imagine how Ptarmigan keeps its banks. It looks as if it should just spill off in all directions.

Despite the increasingly remote feel of the Ptarmigan Valley, it turns out I haven't been completely alone over the last couple of hours. Another solo hiker with what appears to be a similar plan has been travelling up toward the pass today as well, and I've been trying to avoid him since somewhere around the horse corral. He's been slowly gaining on me, but we've taking different rest stops, so I haven't actually come in contact with him until now, even though I have been aware of him for a good part of the morning. At some point, he got past me while I was having a pee in the woods, and at the trail junction that takes hikers up over Deception Pass or down to Baker Lake, we finally cross paths and compare travel plans.

"How's it going?" I ask when I reach the junction.

"Well, thanks, and you?"

"Good, good, it's a beautiful day for it." And after a short pause to sip from my water bottle and take in the stunning scenery: "Where you headed?"

"Just over the pass, I'll probably camp in Merlin Meadows. Are you going to Baker Lake?"

"Yeah, I think so, and then around the mountain tomorrow."

"I'll be doing the same from the opposite direction. I'll probably see you at some point," he says after shouldering his pack.

"Probably," I say as I drop mine for a moment and find a place to sit.

Beyond that, the conversation doesn't amount to much, but this fellow traveller seems like a decent sort, out for a rejuvenating and life-affirming stroll, just like me. The thought of bumping into him again tomorrow is not an altogether unpleasant idea either, as this is prime grizzly bear terrain. As I finish my snack, I watch his bright red backpack work its way up the pass, but I am in no hurry to continue. I can see my campsite from here, and it's an easy downhill amble, so I'm willing to linger. As I wait for the red dot to disappear, the high cirrus clouds to the east drift over Fossil Mountain, creating some remarkable patterns in the sky. With no obvious intent, they shift as they dance across the horizon, much like an aurora borealis would, before parking atop the mountain like a crown.

Moving on down the trail, I eventually find myself lying down to shoot some pictures from a low angle with the alpine meadow in the foreground, and I am soon covered in fine dust from chest to toe as all my attention gets sucked up the viewfinder. It's only after a few minutes of concentrated shooting that I sense a presence somewhere nearby and realize that lying on the ground in bear country with a limited field of view is not exactly predator-aware behaviour. A part of my primitive brain has been tweaked, and suddenly my senses are on high alert. I'm immediately aware that without a weapon I'm just another animal out here, one that is decidedly not at the top of the food chain.

A glance at the bear spray holstered on my pack a few feet away is calming, as is a quick scan of the landscape below for any freakishly large and hairy clumps of bushes that also happen to be moving. Nothing presents itself, but I can't shake the sensation that something is near, or that I'm being watched.

Realizing a smart predator would circle around behind and try and catch me unaware, I spin about abruptly and find no threat, but I do notice that my new friend is now almost out of sight, near the top of Deception Pass. Not that he'd be any help in a crisis at this point. So despite this little foray into the backcountry, it appears I still don't belong to the wild world. I may be closer than most because I make the effort to get out from time to time, but I'm still insulated from a real life lived outside, thanks to the time I've spent in my cocoon of concrete, plaster and steel; I'm coated with a rime of years spent in a civilized existence. Part of my being may still be instinctually aware, but my calibration remains a bit off. I get another chill and glance in every direction across the open ground before chanting a few choruses of "hey bears, ho bears" just for good measure. Finally I pack up and continue down to Baker Lake.

I recall the park staff at the information centre in Lake Louise assuring me that the bears have moved out of this valley for the time being, but I can't help but wonder to where. The wardens were never clear on that point. With my luck, I would get Bert and Ted, the absent-minded buffoons of the bear world. You see, Bert and Ted are not ambitious bears and have only drifted off in an unspecific direction, as opposed to purposely moving to more appropriate fall ranges. With my luck, they're just one valley over, sitting around, talking bear talk, when Ted realizes he's misplaced his wallet.

"Hey, Bert, have you seen my wallet? I think I forgot it in that last valley. I can't find it anywhere."

"Bummer, man. Haven't seen it," Bert replies in the relaxed tone of someone who doesn't much care.

"Damn," Ted says dejectedly, then looks to the sky and decides an afternoon stroll might not be a bad idea. "But it's a nice enough day. I'm going to go find it. I'll be back in a couple of hours."

In this scenario, Bert remains unmoved by his companion's predicament and simply lies back in a bed of mountain wildflowers, content to waste away the rest of the afternoon snacking on the last of the season's buffalo berries. After Ted has moved 50 metres back in the direction they've just come from, Bert shouts, "Bring back dinner."

Ted just grunts and gives an absent-minded wave as he goes.

When it eventually happens that I meet up with a bear in the backcountry, when I am unfortunate enough to come face to face with *Ursus arctos horribilis* on a narrow trail, I bet that's the bear I will get.

• • •

There's no immediate threat to explain my minor freak-out in the high meadow, and as I amble down to the campsite at Baker Lake, the gentle pace of mid-afternoon soothes away all worries. It's warm and sunny, and after nearly ten kilometres of uphill walking, gravity is now my friend. Fossil Mountain eventually transforms from a symmetrical ovoid, which looks remarkably like Australia's Uluru, into an enormous genie lamp with an oversized spout.

The campsite is a slightly raised area in a collection of trees at the eastern end of the lake. Dropping my gear in the lee of the trees, which will shield any gathering wind,

I wonder if I've ever felt so good in my life. Even though I was dead tired to start the day and it has been a long slog up here, I feel great. My legs and my back no longer ache, and my knee feels strong and stable. Even my hip is causing no issues at present. I realize, with a rush of self-satisfaction, that this is the reason I came to the Skoki wilderness in the first place: to challenge myself, to enjoy the simplicity of the outdoors, and to experiment with a quieter and less complicated life. For a long time now, I have needed to get away from the avalanche of background noise that has become my everyday existence, and I'm ready to just be here, which feels remarkably natural. When I bought my backcountry camping permit, there was mention that not many people registered to spend time in the area, so I wonder if I'll have the entire campground to myself. Once again, as at the beginning of the Fairview Mountain hike, the possibility of pure solitude seems a fabulous notion. I only hope it comes true this time around.

Then, just as I start to pull the gear from my pack in order to set up camp, I hear faint voices. I stop dead in my tracks, bitterly disappointed that I might have to share this little corner of Eden. The voices are hard to pinpoint but seem to be coming from somewhere back in the direction I have just come from. I haven't yet explored the whole site, so I leave my gear in a heap and backtrack up the trail, hoping not to be seen. Moving cautiously and quietly, I spy three horses tethered at the outside edge of the trees that protect the campsite; somehow I didn't notice them when I first passed. I wonder if they're the same ones from the corral earlier today, although I can't figure out how they could have possibly got around me along the way. It's clear the owners are at the lakeside, just out of sight.

I circle back the way I came and scooch my gear toward the bushes to make it less conspicuous, and then make my way down to the water's edge to investigate further. As I crouch slightly, careful to keep any bushes and short trees between me and the interlopers, one thing becomes clear: I am not built for covert operations. Even a moose would look graceful compared to me. Peering around a particularly large evergreen toward the water's edge, I eventually spy three 20-something women 50 metres up the shoreline, standing around and talking. To my relief, it's obvious that they're on a break and not planning to camp overnight, and they don't seem to notice me as I slink back out of sight. But as they're getting prepared to return to their horses, they do cast a glance in my direction, and inexplicably I jump deeper into the woods, as if I was committing a crime by watching them from the cover of the trees. For some reason I keep a suspicious eye on them as they mount up and make their way slowly up valley.

Human contact successfully avoided, I take a moment to relax and inspect my surroundings. If there's a prettier campsite on earth, I don't know where it is, and standing at the edge of the earthen platform on the opposite side of the valley is a mix of evergreen peppered with a healthy dose of yellowing Lyell larches at the peak of their seasonal change of colour. Down at the shore of Baker Lake, the water is held back by ribs of solid rock that create a series of bays and minnow-filled pools that eventually spill out over a short waterfall before turning into Baker Creek.

As the afternoon sunshine continues to beat down into the bowl created by the lake, it is collected and focused by Fossil Mountain at my back. As a result, the temperature has spiked to well over 20 degrees Celsius, and after a brisk uphill walk with a heavy pack, I am tempted to have a swim, even though I know the water will most likely be freezing. But then again, it might be the only chance I'll ever get to swim in a lake at over 2300 metres in October. Impulsively, for there is no sane reason to attempt this act, I peel off for the skinniest of skinny dips.

Freezing doesn't even come close to describing the water temperature as I dip a toe tentatively into my own private mountain pool. *Bitter* and *vicious* come close but are too aggressive, so eventually I settle on *glacial* as an apt descriptor. I carefully wade to mid-thigh, and my knees and feet go numb in seconds. It goes without saying that I have no interest in getting my private parts involved in the equation. Standing like a fool in my birthday suit, I can't help but think about abandoning the idea of getting all the way wet. After another two minutes of wavering, my lower extremities disappear from consciousness altogether, and before I get the chance to chicken out, I dive below the surface and into the abyss, where the water muffles my girlish screams.

The water is crystal clear and just deep enough for me to stay completely submerged. I manage half a dozen underwater breaststrokes before I'm forced to grab a shocked breath. Dolphin-diving back underwater, I make a mad scramble toward shore, and after shaking uncontrollably on a large rock warmed by the sun, I do manage a second short dive. But a long swim here is completely out of the question without a wetsuit.

Back on my rock for the second time, naked as the day I was born, I am now a shivering mass of goosebumps as I wait for the sun to dry me. Having had no plan for this foolishness, I don't have a towel handy, and glancing down, I can't help but notice a steady stream of blood snaking its way down my left shin from a gash on my kneecap. With my lower extremities flash-frozen, I never noticed scraping my knee on a rock on the lake bottom. The cut is not at all serious and the water is clearly accelerating the bleeding process, but there is a concern. If I thought I was a mobile meat market when I lay down in the middle of a meadow taking pictures, I'm surely worse off as a stuck pig bleeding out by a mountain stream, and once again I've thoughtfully left my bear spray safely back up at the site.

After I've pulled on my underwear and retrieved the first-aid kit and bear spray, triage by the stream is easy work. I do have to extract a small stone from under my skin, and the blood mixed with water creates a remarkable mess, which I splash into the start of the creek, where it will quickly dilute and wash downstream. Bandaged up, and with the shock of the water largely passed, I feel no great need to get dressed again, and setting up camp in just my underwear feels great. With the sun beating down and a warm, gentle breeze now swirling through the valley, I am as ancient as the rocks making up the mountains that surround me, and as fresh as the plants and trees that have taken hold on the lower slopes and in the valleys. Looking out to the south at a storm gathering there, I have more than enough time to take a few deep, relaxing breaths.

It also doesn't appear that anyone is going to join me in my hideaway by the lake, so it could be that I have finally achieved one of the goals of this trip: to spend some time alone out in the elements. In becoming autonomous and independent in this manner, I am a mountain man – for today, at least.

15.

MERLIN MEADOWS

Now I'm trying to get back, what I know that I should be
Hoping to God I was just a temporary absentee.

—Gerard McHugh

The next day's weather is not nearly as glorious as it has
been in the previous few weeks. A muted grey overcast prevails, with threat of rain, and by the time I make it down to
Cotton Grass Pass (yes, it appears I've just walked downhill to cross a mountain pass – not the usual way of doing these things), a light mist has developed. There's not
enough moisture in the air to warrant putting on a jacket
straight away, but there is enough to get you wet without
one after only a few minutes. Since I sweat like a fiend at
the best of times, I opt to go without, preferring to be cool
and damp as opposed to hot and clammy. It's not a hardship, exactly, but is not an entirely pleasant experience
either.

It isn't a long way around Fossil Mountain, maybe ten
kilometres from Baker Lake to the trail junction near
Skoki Lodge, so I expect to bump into my travel buddy
from yesterday at some point. But that never happens, and
the only humans I encounter all day are two young hippie
types early on in my trek, heading in the opposite direction. After a brief chat to compare notes on the trail ahead,
and in the absence of any long views, I am left to contemplate the trail and the valley bottom, and my walk.

There is something about being outside like this that is liberating in a way I cannot describe, but living outside for any length of time would indeed be hard. I've got my modern gear and easily transported prepackaged food to simplify the journey, leaving me to worry about little more than the effort and the weather, which can lead to a false sense of security.

Yesterday, in between dips in my mountain pool, I slipped on the rock I was using to sun myself. My feet came out from under me as easily as if I was in a soap-slicked bathtub at home, and for a moment I was airborne, completely detached from terra firma. In that split second of surprise, there was no thought of recovery, or even of the calamity of crashing back down on hard stone – there was only reaction. Without conscious effort, I managed to splay three limbs out in all directions while simultaneously planting the fourth, which happened to be a leg, firmly in the middle of the rock, where by some miracle it found purchase and I remained upright and unhurt.

In an act of dumb luck and quick reflexes, I was spared any number of serious injuries, including but not limited to a broken wrist, dislocated elbow, head trauma or ligament damage to my knee. In a worst-case scenario, I could easily have found myself lying there with a compound fracture of the leg, with no way to call for help.

I wonder what I would do in those circumstances. Would I have the strength and determination to drag myself back up to the campsite after such a catastrophic mishap? Do I have what it takes to improvise a splint and some makeshift crutches in order to get back to civilization? Would I be able to drag myself over to the main trail, or even back to the junction with the Deception Pass Trail, leg dangling uselessly all the while, in order to wait for help? Or, would I simply lie down in the campsite, perhaps for days, in the hope someone might happen along? I shudder to think about the consequences of just one misstep or lapse in concentration. But that's the point, I guess: out here, actions have real and immediate consequences, and sometimes those consequences are dire.

Calamity averted, and despite the various shortcomings in my wilderness acumen, I can survive out in the natural world for a time. I can bundle myself against the cold, shade myself from the heat and take shelter from the rain. I can draw and filter water from the rivers and streams to slake my thirst, and I can pack in a conscientious way that allows me to eat for three or four days, or maybe even a week. But without some intensive study and what would surely be a few lean months and fair bit of suffering, I would never be able to sustain myself out here for long.

The truth is, I wouldn't know a poisonous mushroom from a magic mushroom if it jumped up and bit me on the ass, and I wouldn't be able to pick out too many palatable berries. Nor would I be able to identify any poisonous plants. I like steak and I like chicken, and don't even get me started about bacon. I'm an omnivore who leans toward carnivore, but could I kill to get my dinner? I doubt I could. In fact, I'm more inclined to pet the animals I've seen over the course of this trip than to try and turn them into a meal, and besides, except for the horses, I haven't come across anything bigger than a squirrel in days.

Waiting out the heaviest of the rain under a particularly robust Engelmann spruce not far from Skoki Lodge and the campsite at Merlin Meadows, I begin to wonder whether this outdoor life would really suit me if I was forced to live it every single day. Am I truly interested in simpler goals and dreams, or am I being nostalgic for days past and overly romantic in my visions of a rugged Old West kind of life, or perhaps of the hunter-gatherer existence of our more primitive ancestors? Am I just playing at being a mountain man? Or should I get on board already with the current tides of time – plug in and tune out and leave all these simple dreams behind as I waste away the hours in front of the TV?

I'm already most of the way there anyway. These days there's nothing unusual about a burnt-out North American whose work doesn't keep up with the debt accumulated in pursuit of the good life, or a person so bored with the everyday that they would do just about anything to shake the monotony (yet so overstimulated that they have no energy left to effect change). I've always fancied myself an outsider, hopelessly trapped in an ocean of fools, a devotee to the belief that it is actually all these people that are making us so stressed out, confused and lonely. Yet five minutes after setting up camp in Merlin Meadows, while picking my way down the path to the creek to filter some water, there is still a part of me that hopes someone will appear on the trail and bring with them a little distraction and some company. I'd probably even welcome Bert and Ted, as long as they didn't overstay their welcome. Or eat me, of course.

• • •

For the moment, the rain has stopped, and I take the window of opportunity to cook dinner, even though it's only five o'clock. Tonight it's not Santa Fe-style rice with chicken but Kathmandu curry with rice, eaten straight from the bag, with tiramisu for dessert, all from Backpacker's Pantry. I have to admit, this stuff has come a long way from the days when eating freeze-dried fare was like choking down warmed and only mildly flavoured cardboard. Granted, the chicken from last night's Santa Fe did remind me of the box my pair of Salomon boots came in, but that's because I was so hungry as to be too impatient with the steeping process. It improved dramatically as the meal went on and more moisture was absorbed.

Today's curry is shockingly good hearty, mildly spicy and perfectly prepared using my new Jetboil, which up until last night was just taking up space in my pack. Sure, the bag containing the meal is annoyingly tall, too tall to eat with a regular-sized spoon without getting sloppy knuckles, but the plastic is sturdy enough to tip up and drink out of without getting food all over the place.

Where the curry is a pleasant surprise, the Jetboil is a revelation. It took no time at all to get a rolling boil going – it actually took longer to read the instructions than to force the water to 100 degrees – and I didn't even have the knob set to high. The thing is an engineering marvel that cools off fast and stores easily. It's rare that I am 100 per cent impressed with anything – though the rating does dip to 95 per cent a few days later, when I realize it's next to impossible to tell how much fuel is left in the canister until it's too late. But still, for short trips it's a gem.

After dinner, I notice that there's fresh snow out on Richardson Glacier and the western horizon remains dark and ominous. The sky is not angry, not threatening a big storm, but it is ponderous and bruised, heavy with the anticipation of a change in season. A short rain squall chases me back to the tent temporarily, and after it passes I spend a little time working on getting a fire going, unwilling to be confined by the weather to my small tent. A fire can be warm and comforting, but can also be difficult to maintain in a damp environment. All the deadfall in the immediate area is wet, and I can't keep the flames stoked for long. There have been periods of light rain most of the day, so getting it going is not so much the trouble as keeping it going, and at no point in the evening could it be considered a warm fire.

Eventually, I decide the effort is not worth the reward and let it begin to die away. In the gathering gloom, I can just barely make out another cloudburst slowly making its way down valley, and after ten minutes the rain kicks up again with something between persistence and fury. So I put my fire out of its misery by peeing on it, before retiring to my warm, dry cocoon and my books. Checking my watch before drifting off to sleep a half-hour later, I find it's only 7:43 p.m., but I can't manage to keep my eyes open any longer and am out cold by eight.

•••

By morning, the previous night's rain has frozen in a tiny pool in a small dip in the fabric of my tent above the air vent near my feet, and a layer of frost covers all the tent poles. The season was bound to change eventually, but somehow I feel the transformation has now begun in earnest. Surprisingly, considering the temperature is not yet above zero, I've woken up chipper and ready to go, which I admit is more than a little unusual for me. In this light-hearted mood, packing up and getting ready to walk back out to Lake Louise is a joy, not a job, and if I could actually whistle I'm sure I would be doing it while I work. My sleeping bag stuffs easily into its bag, and my tent collapses and stows away in no time at all. Even my porridge tastes unusually inspired this morning. For once, striking camp proves effortless and fun. I'm not sure what I should attribute this remarkable change in attitude to, but I am getting a glimpse of what all those "morning people" have been going on about for all these years.

As I walk back up past Skoki Lodge, which is boarded up for the shoulder season while awaiting winter's cross-country skiers, it starts to rain again. It's a light, drizzly kind of rain that is barely noticeable, almost like a mist, and the farther up the pass I get, the more persistent that mist becomes. Climbing ever higher, I can actually see a delicate snow falling on some of the surrounding peaks, including Fossil to my left and Ptarmigan to my right, and the flat overcast gives way to a howling wind by the time I make it to the top of Deception Pass. There, the experience is much like standing in a cloud with rain in it, and the sun is nothing more than a sickly weak orb in the southern sky. The amazing thing is, I'm not much bothered by the inclement weather.

In my cold-weather training top, I'm soaking wet but remarkably warm from the uphill effort, and I feel strong and happy. There is a moment in every long outing when a threshold is crossed and everything becomes a downhill ride, metaphorically speaking. The psychological crux of this trip is now done, just like that, without my ever realizing an important crossroads was coming today. I can walk and I can ride, it's what I do, and I am comfortable with that. It's a simple existence, and all of a sudden I feel like I can go home anytime I want, with no regrets. Sure, there are more challenges ahead, as surely as there are other places to go and see beyond this mountain chain, but I escaped the prison that had been building up in my mind, and did it my way, and it has been great. I fed myself, navigated the wilderness and, most importantly, didn't have a psychotic break just because I hadn't had any significant human contact for a couple of days.

It can be easy to forget what you're capable of, and my everyday life is full of negative self-talk – "you're just a bum," "you're lazy," and "you're directionless" being persistent themes – but none of that matters anymore. The stigma of being unwilling or unable to function in modern-day society holds no sway out here. Eat when you're hungry, rest when you're tired, drink when you're thirsty; everything else is just details. Sure, being the social animals that we are, there were some heebie-jeebie moments alone in the campgrounds at Baker Lake and Merlin Meadows, where I thought I might come apart at the seams, but the sensation always passed quickly enough, with no lasting effects.

With the promise of cold beer and a warm bed waiting in Lake Louise, I am propelled down Deception Pass, over Boulder Pass, and out of the backcountry in a fraction of the time it took to plod up to this forgotten world, but this rugged place will always remain in my heart.

16.

THE WONDERTRAIL

Let the beauty we love be what we do.

—Rumi

What a profound difference 24 hours can make.

Yesterday's rain has persisted in the valley bottoms, and a significant amount of snow is caught in the trees, starting at about 1800 metres, so it appears I got down out of the Skoki wilderness just in time. But with a low cloud ceiling and temperatures hovering barely above freezing, the idea of riding my bike up toward a high mountain pass is not an altogether welcoming one. It has been a quiet morning in Bill Peyto's Café, and I've spent most of it sitting around drinking coffee and trying to decide what to do. The long-range weather forecast is not promising for either Lake Louise or Jasper, but it's not exactly demoralizing either: it's a mixed bag of possibilities, including snow, sleet, rain and the chance of sunny breaks scattered throughout. Peering deep into my nearly empty coffee cup, I am distressed to find I still want to make it to Jasper more than I want to go home, so eventually I gather up my gear and make my way outside once again.

Pedalling out of Lake Louise can only be described as a shock to the system after the peace and quiet of the last few days. To be on a busy road again is one thing, but the state of affairs at the junction with Highway 93 makes the transition that much worse. The highway here is hectic and undeniably dangerous as it chokes down to the intersection where Highway 1 veers west over the Continental Divide via Kicking Horse Pass and the Icefields Parkway continues north toward Saskatchewan River Crossing and Jasper. This is where tandem cyclists Husband and Stoltenberg met their fate in 2003, and it is distressingly easy to imagine something bad happening again at any time. The ongoing construction at the junction does make travel slower than normal, but it is also more confused in its passing, which adds another level of risk. Even with the reduced speeds, traffic noise and construction commotion dominate. Once the work here is finished, the interchange will be safer than it was originally, but for the moment it's a gauntlet of chaos and danger that is no fun to pedal through.

Up Highway 93, things quiet down significantly, as I expected they might. Through-traffic and commercial transports have veered left over Kicking Horse Pass on the way to the coast, and the gatekeeper at the Parks Canada checkpoint kindly gives me a pass on my lack of a park pass and simply waves me through, even though technically I qualify as a vehicle. The long, slow climb toward Bow Pass is cold work at first, but I soon fall into a rhythm and the discomfort fades. From the base of the hill, it's 40 kilometres up an average 4 to 6 per cent grade to the summit of the pass. Interestingly, this route was not the first choice of many of the original explorers in the region. Swampy sections and deadfall deterred most of them, and the Pipestone Valley was the preferred travel route. Those early challenges have been solved thanks to the advent of pavement, and in 1920 surveyor and explorer A.O. Wheeler wrote:

Through dense primeval forests, muskeg, burnt and fallen timber and along rough and steeply sloping hillsides, a constant flow of travel will demand a broad, well-ballasted motor road ... this wondertrail will be world renowned.

Absolutely true, and for fear of actually encouraging people to come here in numbers exceeding the current summer flood, I have to concede that Wheeler's vision has proven to be nothing short of spot-on. This could be the most scenic mountain road in the world. And if it's not number one, then the Icefields Parkway certainly rates in the top five. Along this route, it is said, 600 glaciers can be seen from the road; upon its opening in the spring of 1940, *The Banff Crag and Canyon* declared that the landscape it travelled through was like "20 Switzerlands in one." I don't know about that, but from experience I can say it is remarkable.

Despite my familiarity with this road, it has been long enough since my last visit that it almost seems brand new. In better conditions, it provides impressive views from near Herbert Lake back toward the mountains around Lake Louise, but today these are largely obscured by the weather and by the fact that I've got my head down against the wind and the grade. Inching ever upward to the fresh snowline, the road levels out somewhat around five kilometres from the junction with Highway 1, and at the 15-kilometre mark I skirt two significant storm cells: one that consumes Pulpit Peak and most of Hector Lake with barely a second thought, and a second that blows through 20 minutes later and seems intent on adding volume to Crowfoot Glacier, just to the other side of the considerable mass that is Bow Peak.

The first brought with it a light drizzle and a few hard snowflakes that bounced comically up off the blacktop, but the second was carried on a glacial wind that indicated Mother Nature could put an end to this little adventure at any moment. As I pedal along, hoping to avoid the worst of the impending weather, all the oncoming cars have their headlights on, even though it is not yet noon, and I can detect concern on some of the occupants' faces. Judging by the amount of snow clinging to their cars, it's clear that heavier weather awaits up ahead, and I can almost hear them chatting to one another in my head:

"Hey, honey, take a look at this nut job, he's going the wrong way."

"That poor boy, he's going to freeze to death."

At the Crowfoot Glacier viewpoint, the snow begins to fall for real, and it's a cold snow, made up of tight little flakes. The barrage has not deteriorated to the point where it could be called pellets, but they are also not the gentle, fluffy, drifting flakes that one would associate with Christmas cards and sleigh rides. For its part, the wind, which is not vicious so much as bitter, has also picked up and is blowing in hard across Bow Lake. Within minutes, the squall stuck on Bow Peak blows over, leaving only that hard wind in its wake, and then restarts, only to shift its focus again, this time toward the south. This snow betrays a harsh environment that is sometimes reluctant to accept visitors. Crowfoot Glacier may have receded over the last century (to the point where it no longer really looks like a crow's foot – one of the toes broke off in the 1920s), but it is still formidable, weathered and prehistoric, and there was a time not all that long ago when this whole valley must surely have been filled with ice, which is a chilling thought.

At the pullout, the occasional car stops to take in the sights, now largely muted by the storm, but no one sticks around for long. Since the snow started, I've noticed, nobody really wants to get out of their vehicles. They just take a quick peek at the deteriorating views through the windshield and then speed off. The only thing keeping me from moving on is that I don't have far to go to reach today's destination of Num-Ti-Jah Lodge and so don't mind hanging around. Already prepared for the season in an overcoat of new puffy winter feathers, a lone Clark's nutcracker hops to the top of a snowbank plowed up after a September blizzard, and I wander over for a photo. He's figured out that meagre winter pickings can sometimes be enhanced by what humans carelessly leave behind, and is patiently waiting for something to fall out of my pocket. As tempted as I am by his nearly irresistible charm, I don't oblige.

Just as I'm stowing my camera gear for the short push on to the lodge, a car pulls up and a handsome young man jumps out with his point-and-shoot camera. He's clearly disappointed that the weather is not co-operating, but still wants to make the best of it. I like his enthusiasm. His equally attractive travelling companion, however, clearly wants nothing to do with the whole scene. She fidgets noticeably in the passenger seat, obviously put out by this delay in getting to the next hotel on their itinerary, and when she finally notices me standing next to my bike not three metres away, she gives me cursory glance that still manages to convey a belief that I must be completely and totally insane. Not unlike her boyfriend. A gesture that makes me feel immeasurably better about the day even though the entire effort will only add up to about 40 kilometres of travel.

The snow picks up once again and begins to fall in heavy, wet flakes. To the left, Bow Lake is a dark, ominous mass of water. Wind-whipped, impenetrable and forbidding, it appears angry that it will soon be frozen over and buried in white until spring. As the road nears the shore, I pass three touring cyclists coming from the opposite direction who are in for a long, cold downhill into Lake Louise, and after five more minutes the storm renews its fury, just as I pull up to the front doors of the lodge.

The weather doesn't exactly clear up during the afternoon, but it does stop snowing, creating the perfect opportunity for lounging around in luxury after a few hours of battling the elements. Like Mount Engadine Lodge, Num-Ti-Jah is a privately owned operation within the park system that caters to those whose idea of mountain travel does not include camping or the primitive appointments of a backcountry hut. In 1900, legendary outfitter and hunter Jimmy Simpson established a camp here on the shores of Bow Lake, and in 1920 he obtained a lease to build a cabin. After work began on the parkway in the early '30s, the lodge was expanded to accommodate increased local traffic, and "the red roof at the blue lake" became a destination for those looking to explore the upper Bow Valley.

The lodge has a huge dining room and great mountain art throughout, including some truly fantastic archival panoramas in the pool room (as in table, not tub), and I am especially taken by the log construction in the common areas, with the inherent twists and bends and warps in all the beams and supports. The guest lounge on the opposite side of the building from the main dining room is especially attractive, with old wood and antique furnishings and a map desk filled with more maps than you can shake a stick at. There are laminated copies of Natural Resources Canada topographic maps of Bow Lakes, Banff and Jasper, as well as Kootenay and Mount Assiniboine, and the tried-and-true Gem Trek Publishing renditions of the Columbia Icefields, Bow Lake and Saskatchewan Crossing, among many others. I could spend hours and maybe even days in a room like this, poring over them all and imagining going to all the places I have not yet visited.

Upstairs, things are a touch more basic. In my room, the floorboards creak and groan when I walk, and the layout is nothing less than haphazard. If you can imagine a map of Indiana with a tapered spit of land reaching to the shores of Lake Erie, then you can get an idea of where my small window sits – at the end of that spit. The most remarkable thing about the room, which costs upwards of $150 a night, is that you can actually hear other guests carrying on conversations in other rooms but can't really pin down where the sound is coming from. It could be below, above or next door. The upper two floors don't look as if they've been renovated much since old Jimmy Simpson ran the place all those years ago. Which, upon reflection, is decidedly cool, since the last thing the Rockies need, in my humble opinion, is another Fairmont-style chateau.

• • •

What to do, what to do, what to do?

The snow has stopped falling and the sun has come out temporarily, but the improving conditions are not much comfort this morning. It's still cold, and the parking lot, driveway and highway remain covered in a thin layer of white. Wandering back to the lodge for breakfast after pondering the state of the highway for a good ten minutes, I realize there are now some difficult decisions to make. My penance for taking this trip so late in the season is the inevitability of winter conditions, which are now finally upon me in force. I suppose I could call Jocey and she could come up from Canmore to get me later this afternoon, or I can push on and hope the situation doesn't deteriorate to the point where it would take a couple of days before I could be rescued. It's not unusual for this highway to be snowed in during the winter, and up here it wouldn't take long for the weather to turn in that direction very quickly. It fact, it has been trying to do so for a few days now.

Two days ago, Lawrence drove up from Canmore, and although the weather eased off after I made it to the lodge, it never really cleared completely. He had business to attend to for the Alpine Club – specifically, overseeing the installation of an anemometer (a device that measures and records wind activity) at Bow Hut, to gauge the feasibility of using wind power at the facility, and once again I was tagging along. Unfortunately, there was no helicopter ride worked into the deal this time, so we had to hike up to the hut from Num-Ti-Jah.

Skirting the northern edge of the lake, the trail is well-worn and straightforward, and after 45 minutes of walking we were in the backcountry. Bow Hut sits just below the Wapta Icefield and is a popular destination from which mountaineers and ski-touring enthusiasts launch their attempts at any number of local peaks and classic ski routes. Originally built in 1968, the hut is the largest and one of the most popular in the ACC inventory, and was upgraded to its current size in 1989.

It took about three and a half hours to cover the eight kilometres from the lakeshore to the barren rocky platform on which Bow Hut is perched, and a light dusting of snow up high helped contribute to the raw, almost lunar feel of the landscape. Once there, I was nothing short of useless on the install – all I could manage were a few snapshots with my camera and a respectful interest expressed from an appropriate distance, and coming back down later that same day proved no great hardship. After a decadent meal and another cushy night in the lodge, I made a deal with myself to carry on bicycling first thing in the morning.

Pulling everything together quickly in an attempt to get a head start on what would undoubtedly be a long day of riding, I once again found myself inexplicably excited to go – only to look outside and into the teeth of a blizzard. Unlike the sporadic cloudbursts up to this point, this was persistent snow, coming down in measurable amounts. I wandered the five minutes up to the highway to assess the situation, only to find an accumulation developing. It wasn't much, just three or four centimetres, but the road was definitely white-top and not black. Even though the tire paths of the occasional passing car had cut sloppy wet melt paths down the main part of the road, things did not look promising.

If it had been another walking day, there would have been no problem: just slap on a heavy toque and go. But lots of things can go wrong on two narrow tires with too much gear haphazardly strapped around them. A drop in temperature of even one or two degrees could turn the moisture under the snow and on the road to black ice, or another heavy bout of the white stuff could make me virtually invisible to approaching motorists. A best-case scenario would be an icy and sloppy left-side shower of slush endured with every passing car or tour bus. Yesterday I decided to give it 24 hours, and now I'm standing in exactly the same place, thinking exactly the same thing: Should I stay or should I go?

On the one hand, I am feeling pretty good. Coming off three weeks of accumulated effort and five straight days of solid pushing means my legs are strong and my back is sturdy. My lips are chapped, my clothes are filthy and I've got a bit of colour in my skin, so I must be doing something right. Tack on yesterday's leisurely day off, and I am positively powerful. In fact, it's been years since I've felt this fit. On the other hand, the lodge is exceedingly warm and welcoming, and apart from the paper-thin walls upstairs, I could scarcely be more content than I would be repeating yesterday's program of sitting around drinking coffee and reading all morning, having a quick nap, then sitting around drinking beer and reading all afternoon as the snow gently blew around outside the window.

In these times of indecision, it is amazing what sometimes comes to mind to get you moving. For example, back in the spring I was standing in the parking lot outside work, staring off into space, and much like today it was one of those decisive moments that come unbidden. I was just about to start my shift, and it was a day just like any other day, but instead of getting prepared for the inevitable yet predictable string of events that make up my nights on the job, I was wondering what would happen if I just kept walking instead of pulling open the door and clocking in for what felt like the two millionth time in my life. What if, instead of agreeing to do my part in another day that was going to be exactly like so many that had come before, I didn't? What if I just stopped doing what I was doing that second and stepped off in a direction that never again intersected with what had become habit? What would happen to me in that scenario? Would I be happier? Would I be better off? Would it even make a difference? I didn't know, but I wanted to find out.

It turns out I didn't have the courage to just walk away at that moment, but the thought did get me moving on a different course. I began planning for this trip into the heart of these mountains, and as the weather begins to break apart, there is no denying this is anything but habit. So I make my way back to the lodge with renewed enthusiasm. I'm going, no matter what.

After paying my rather hefty bill and executing two trips up to my room to retrieve all my gear, I am immediately slapped in the face for the bold decision. A cold wind is again coming down from Bow Glacier, and as it sweeps across Bow Lake and slams into the lodge, I do my best to ignore it and continue strapping my gear to my bike as spindrift snow is blown every which way. When I'm just about done and getting ready to push off, Scott, one of the waiters I've become friendly with over the last few days, wanders over from the staff accommodations behind the lodge.

"Heading home?" he asks innocently enough.

"Nope," I say, with a mischievous tilt of the head and what I am sure is a perverse twinkle in my eye. Scott gives me a sideways look like I've gone off the deep end and then grins the "you're a crazy bastard" grin, indicating that he gets it.

"So you're going to carry on to Jasper then?"

"Well, not all in one go," I say. "But I'll get there."

Scott shifts his gaze out to the surrounding environment, with its strong winter overtones, and grins again. For a moment I think he's thinking about joining me.

"I'll tell you what," he says finally. "If you don't turn up in Canmore in about a week, I'll send out a search party."

"I'd appreciate that," I say as I reach out to shake hands. "But give it ten days, in case the weather gets bad and I have to hole up at one of the campgrounds near the Icefields."

Scott laughs and takes my hand with a solid grip, then wishes me luck as I wobble out toward the main road, gently zigzagging for stability on the slick driveway and crunching through muddy, ice-covered puddles as I go. I wave once without even looking back.

Riding on a snow-covered road is not as difficult as it might appear at first glance, as long as the conditions are right. Deep snow is an unholy pain in the ass and not worth the effort, in my opinion, but any accumulation less than ten centimetres is manageable as long as the underlying surface is not hard-packed or covered in ice. It's a bit unnerving at first, I admit, as all snow conditions are slippery to some degree, but I'm finding that if I stick to the shoulder and avoid the compacted tracks left by the handful of cars that have already passed this morning, my tires are gripping nicely enough. The sun is suddenly pounding down from over my right shoulder through a break in the clouds, and the early-winter wind is plowing into me from up ahead and to the left, but the incline is gentle leading up to the final crest of Bow Pass. Pulling the brakes produces a momentary squeak as friction dries the brake pads and wheel rims, but I find I can stop more or less on command without locking up and going into a skid.

Travel here is through a comely subalpine meadow made up primarily of willows and sedges, prime mule deer and moose habitat. Unfortunately, there are no wild animals out and about this morning, just snow snakes whipping across the highway and dancing through my spokes. It occurs to me that I should probably break out the point-and-shoot camera and try to get a picture of this rather unusual phenomenon, but in the end I decide not to push my luck and instead concentrate on the task at hand.

Reaching the top of the pass turns out to be much easier work than anticipated. At 2069 metres, Bow Pass is the highest point on the Icefield Parkway, beating out Sunwapta Pass a little farther up the road by a mere 46 metres, but coming from this direction it doesn't feel as steep or as difficult to climb, especially when you start the day three-quarters of the way there, as I have done today. At the top I do stop for the requisite photos, because the whole thing seems a little absurd, in the best possible way. Biking in the snow in the Rocky Mountains certainly qualifies as an adventure experience to remember, and I want to take it all in. The weather continues to break apart, and there is now more sunshine in the sky than dark and ominous storm clouds, which have been the dominant feature for a few days.

Adding to the meteorological intrigue, it turns out Bow Pass is also a fairly significant hydrological apex. Flowing from here are the North and South Saskatchewan River systems. The water that sets out in two opposite directions in these mountains eventually reconnects in – you guessed it – Saskatchewan, before eventually flowing into Lake Winnipeg, more than 3000 kilometres to the east of this spot. From there, a drop of water that first fell here has the chance of making its way to the Atlantic Ocean via Hudson Bay, which is by any measure a remarkable journey.

I find I'm fond of a good hydrological apex not because I have a scientific interest in these things, but because I can imagine that journey. A waterway is nature's explorer: starting innocently enough as a single drop of rain or tiny glimmer of meltwater, it travels overland with only an inkling of what it will find, moving through a diversity of landscapes before returning to the water cycle to begin the trip all over again in a different location. I may be inspired by mountains, but it occurs to me that I'm more like a river in my wandering.

• • •

Down the far side of Bow Summit, the conditions are somewhat less agreeable, and as if to reinforce how precarious riding around in the snow can sometimes be, my body tenses up unconsciously with the subtle change in circumstances, even before I'm fully aware of the shift. Whereas on the way up the pass the going was snowy but sure, the far side feels slick under my wheels due to the low angle of the sun and the fact that the road is just now coming out of the shadow cast by the pass itself. This produces a slight change in the melt/freeze cycle and makes the surface slippery and dangerous, but my bike desperately wants to roll with gravity. It's a steep drop toward Waterfowl Lakes – 270 metres in under six kilometres – and pulling the brakes for another test of my stopping power is now a shaky proposition. One wrong move, and my guess is that everything will slip right out from under me before I have time to react.

As if to confirm that assessment, I come upon a young Japanese couple in a rented Ford Mustang at the first bend in the road. At this particular curve, there is a slight angle toward the inside of the corner, and it appears the car has simply slid off sideways and is now hung up on the lip of the ditch. I contemplate just pedalling by and maybe giving them a casual wave (wouldn't that be a story to tell their folks back home in Tokyo) but instead put a foot down and clamp the brakes hard, executing an exhilarating if not exactly graceful three-point skid that goes on for three metres before finally coming to a stop. I'm not sure why I've stopped – they don't speak any English, and my Japanese is limited to "*moshi moshi*," "*arigato*," and "*biiru*," which translates to "hello," "thank you," and "beer." But through a laboured series of gestures and some awkward Japanglish, it soon becomes clear they've got a tow truck on the way, and so I press on.

A few hundred metres down the hill, the abrupt drop in elevation equates to a minor increase in temperature, and the snow and ice instantly transform to slush and water. A delicate balancing act is no longer necessary to stay upright, and a speedy descent is no longer dangerous, but the ground is incredibly sloppy. Then, as if that wasn't enough, the road soon drifts into the shade on the eastern side of the valley and the temperature drops precipitously again. Fortunately, it doesn't appear to have rained or snowed much on this section of road overnight, so the pavement is dry, but the combination of shade and speed and temperature is decidedly uncomfortable. It's easily minus-20 with the wind chill, but there's no point in stopping until I can find a block of sunshine to warm myself, so I pull up my face mask, secure my sunglasses so I don't freeze my eyeballs, and alternate my hands on the handle bars and under my jacket while trying to ignore the fact that I can't feel my feet. And so the rest of the early morning goes: cold, mostly downhill riding in the shadow of the long string of mountains to my right.

After stomping my feet back to consciousness by the shores of Lower Waterfowl Lake and continuing with my descent to Saskatchewan River Crossing, I find the day has been passing too quickly. It's still way too early to stop riding, but it's also a long way to the next available campsite, located on the rocky slopes opposite the Athabasca Glacier, 48 kilometres farther up the road. Having blown my hotel/motel budget to smithereens at Num-Ti-Jah, I can't stay in the chalets here either, and it's not the distance ahead that concerns me so much as the considerable climb in between. I'm also not entirely confident the campsite will still be open when I get there.

So I try not to think about it, preferring instead to soak up the sunshine in this relatively broad valley and gaze out at one of my favourite vistas along the whole Rocky Mountain chain. Across the valley to the south, Mount Murchison soars nearly two kilometres above the valley floor, and to the west the Continental Divide stands tall in the form of the Waputik and Churchill ranges, which are separated by the determined meandering of the Howse River. It is in this valley that the North Saskatchewan, Howse and Mistaya rivers converge and cut across the north-south orientation of the mountains to flow out onto the foothills and prairies beyond.

Comparatively little snow falls here in the rain shadow of the Divide, which makes it an ideal winter range for wild animals and for the men who once tracked them. While Banff and Jasper are now recognized as the primary entry points to the Canadian Rockies, it was here that the early fur traders and explorers first penetrated the mountains, including David Thompson. His presence left such a mark on the history of the area that Highway 11, which starts here and leads out to Rocky Mountain House, is called the David Thompson Highway.

After I eat a shockingly expensive lunch at the Crossing Resort and navigate the surprising number of cars and tour buses in the parking lot, the afternoon gets off to a spectacular start as I wind gradually back up into the high country. The temperature has warmed considerably, at least compared to the last few days, as the sun radiates off the towering ramparts of Mount Wilson to the right. Fall colours abound in pockets of deciduous trees lining the side of the road. This stretch of road encourages one of the most diverse mixes of trees anywhere in the parks due to the abundance of gravel laid down by seasonal and underground stream beds. A mixed montane forest has taken a stand against the dominant evergreen species, creating a veritable riot of colour as trembling aspen, balsam poplar and white spruce battle for space amongst the lodgepole pine and Douglas fir, and for miles there is very little traffic to speak of.

Despite the warmth of early afternoon, a fall crispness remains in the background, and by the time I make it to the Graveyard Flats, an extensive gravel outwash plain where early hunting parties often camped, I realize I'm beginning to get tired. It turns out that the mistake in the plan for the afternoon was not exactly the upcoming climb (having done it once before, I am fully prepared to suffer through it) but the access to it, which is much longer than I remember. The flats between Saskatchewan River Crossing and the foot of the Sunwapta Pass climb seem to carry on forever. And then, without warning, the weather changes again, from beautiful fall to dingy winter, in what seems like a minute.

A big system is caught up on the Continental Divide here, and this new weather in the valleys is brought on by a change in wind patterns that pick up momentum as they come barrelling down out of the drainages. Passing under the popular winter ice-climbing destination called Weeping Wall, the temperature remains above freezing, but just barely, and a very light and wispy snow begins to get batted around the valley bottom. By the time I reach the Big Bend (a mercifully flat section of road that breaks up the climb and evens out the grade), the snow is pelting down, full-blizzard style, and the big fat, wet, wind-driven flakes soak me instantly. Thankfully, turning uphill puts the wind at my back, which actually helps push me up the steep slope, but the pavement is just saturated enough to kick up water from my wheels, and I am quickly soaked from head to toe.

As I'm contemplating this charming turn of events and cursing the little voice that whispered *go for it* outside Num-Ti-Jah Lodge this morning, the green Jeep flies by and one of the young guys inside thrusts an enthusiastic thumbs up out the passenger side window and shouts, "Hey! You're the mmmaaaannnnnnnn!"

Great. I may have to dig a hole in a snowbank to keep from freezing to death before the day is out, and dinner will end up being trail mix and half-frozen beef jerky, but at least I'm the man.

Fortunately, it doesn't end up coming to that. Up around the corner from the North Saskatchewan Valley Viewpoint, the snow lets up as quickly as it appeared, and by the time I make it to the junction with Nigel Pass Trail, the clouds have broken apart enough to let random shafts of sunlight reach the ground once again. It's still cold riding in the long shadow of Parker Ridge, but the views are appropriately superb on the eastern side of the valley, where the shattered cloud allows a low sun to penetrate.

It's still a worry to be tired and wet so late in the day, so despite the grinding ascent that marks the second half of the climb, I refuse to take a break until the parking lot at Parker Ridge, a few kilometres up the road. When I finally get there, some very cool light is scattered across the new snow on the ridge, but more storm clouds are gathering in behind Mount Athabasca, and a group of young backcountry skiers packing their van after an afternoon of carving early-season turns is reason enough not to hang around for long.

• • •

A glacier is a remarkable thing, complex and cold and yet alive in a way that takes a little imagination to understand. Snow falls in Arctic and temperate climates, as well as at higher elevations farther south, and if the accumulation exceeds what melts away in the warmer months, then what remains becomes compacted as season after season builds up above. Eventually, that volume creates enough weight to crush the snow into ice, and in turn that ice develops a mass that cannot resist gravity, and a glacier is born. Bring enough ancient ice together in the proper location (i.e., where the yearly snowpack is deep and glaciers have an opportunity to flow out in more than one direction), and the gigantic frozen heap becomes an icefield.

The Columbia Icefield is the largest icefield south of the Arctic Circle and – thanks to Athabasca Glacier, which tumbles down between Mount Andromeda and Snow Dome – is also the best known in the Canadian Rockies. Athabasca Glacier is one of eight of what they call outlet valley glaciers, and with minimal effort you can actually park your car and walk out on the ice. Like most glaciers and ice caps around the globe, Athabasca is in serious recession, but even in retreat it is still plenty impressive – one kilometre wide, six kilometres long and over 300 metres thick, with a volume of roughly 640 million cubic metres. Yet, it only accounts for 2 per cent of the total Columbia Icefield area.

Higher up, the icefield proper is nothing short of mind-boggling. At roughly 325 square kilometres, it represents 30 per cent of the glaciated area in Jasper National Park and is three times as big as the surface area of the city of Toronto. Over six metres of snow fall at the roadside here every year, and in the main accumulation zone, more than ten metres of snow piles up every season. It is a winter landscape, even in summer, thanks to the geography of the region and the katabatic winds that routinely tumble off the glacier and drive the surrounding air temperature down by as much as ten degrees Celsius. If there was any doubt about what season dominates here, it is put to rest by a mean annual temperature that is a teeth-chattering *minus*-8.8 degrees Celsius.

But here's the thing about an icefield and its glaciers: for all the moaning and cracking and groaning that goes on during the slow-motion flow downhill, not to mention the crushing weight that easily scars and scours rock, and the ability to alter local weather, for all of that it's still just water. In fact, glaciers and icefields are the world's primary storehouse of fresh water. The world's oceans store 97 per cent of all the water on earth, but that is decidedly undrinkable because of the salt content. All the freshwater rivers, lakes, ponds, and reservoirs make up a scant 0.036 per cent of the world's total supply. Moisture in the atmosphere in the form of clouds and rain contributes a measly 0.001 per cent.

Permanent ice and snow is where all the fresh water is – it accounts for 70 per cent of what is palatable for most terrestrial plants and animals, including us. This is an amazing number. Part of what makes glaciers so important is that they hold that water and then release it at remarkably opportune times for use by all organisms that live downstream. This is crucial not only to local ecosystems but to so many farther-flung ecosystems that find themselves somewhere downhill. In warm climates, deforestation is a dangerous practice because the forest acts as a sponge, holding water in the wet season so that it can be released slowly in the dry. In colder climates, a glacier works in much the same way, accumulating snow in winter, freezing it solid and then letting it go when flow rates are at their lowest, providing for such minor downstream trifles as crop irrigation and drinking water.

Granted, most of this icy stockpile is bound at the poles and in Greenland, where its major contribution is to keep its own water from inundating half the planet (if all the ice in the world was to spontaneously melt, sea levels would rise by anywhere between 200 and 400 feet!), but the role glaciers play in regulating the availability of this life-sustaining fluid is often overlooked. What appears to be a harsh and unwelcoming landscape here is in fact life-giving in ways we have only begun to appreciate. Unfortunately, the storehouse is rapidly depleting just about everywhere.

It must be noted that the earth does go through natural cycles of long-term freeze and thaw, but global warming through human action (specifically the enthusiastic burning of fossil fuels) is now thought by many to be *the* contributing factor in the recent decline in permanent snow and ice. The Himalayas in particular may be vulnerable in this shifting climate model. The mighty peaks and deep valleys that make up that mountain chain are the birthplace of no fewer than nine major river systems, including the Yellow, the Yangtze, the Mekong, Salween, Irrawaddy, Brahmaputra, Ganges, Sutlej and Indus. Well over three billion people live downstream of the source of these rivers and rely in one fashion or another on the water they provide, which means that glaciers and annual snowfalls in this area serve close to 50 per cent of the world's population, many of whom are already subject to poverty, famine, drought and floods. The ecological, geopolitical and social implications of a large portion of that ice and snow disappearing in the next 50 to 100 years are almost too staggering to think about.

In this immediate vicinity, the state of the permanent ice of the Canadian Rockies is also a growing concern. The Athabasca Glacier has retreated 1.6 kilometres since 1870, but that gradual withdrawal has slowed recently to one to three metres a year, down from the overall average of 13 metres per year since the late 1800s. But new research, conducted by Christina Tennant in a thesis project for a doctoral degree, indicates that as of 2005 the Columbia Icefield as a whole may actually cover only 223 square kilometres, a third less area than most of the conventional literature would indicate. It's a development that only reinforces the idea that large climate systems are difficult to measure and understand, and are even harder to predict.

What is clear, however, is that most of the water that pours south out of these mountains in the course of a year has already been allotted for use. Flow rates can be argued, and how much a melting glacier actually contributes to the overall water supply is still being studied, but contracts have been signed, and the Bow River (supplied in part by the Wapta Icefield, just a couple of valleys over from here) and its tributaries are spoken for. What that means is that if the population of southern Alberta grows or the water supply diminishes, or both, well, then we're going to have a set of complicated problems on our hands right here at home.

Apparently, the English word *rivalry* comes from a Latin term for "one who uses the same stream as another." While we are a rich province, and so the struggle for water rights might not mean chaos and anarchy right off the bat, you can't un-ring a bell. While it may be true that we have managed to figure out how to turn sand into oil up in Fort McMurray, techniques for creating massive volumes of water out of thin air still elude us. If the climate scientists are right and the temperatures continue to rise globally, then the geopolitical hot topic in the Western World will shift rather rapidly from hydrocarbons to plain old H_2O. It does not bode well for a peaceful and harmonious future.

• • •

After quickly setting up my tent and unpacking my sleeping bag and insulated pad, I realize I'm starting to get cold now that I've stopped moving. My shirt is still wet with sweat, and alarming amounts of heat are quickly being whisked away in the form of steam rising up off my body. I dig out my backup toque and another set of clothes and go through the always enjoyable process of stripping off in temperatures dipping fast into the negative digits in order to put on a dry under-layer. That done, I head back down to the site entrance to pay my camping fee and gather some wood for a fire. The self-registration process here is an act of good faith on the campers' part, but for the life of me I can't figure out why Parks Canada doesn't just use whole numbers in its price structure. Twenty-four fifty is still going to be 25 dollars when you're in the middle of nowhere and don't have any change. Just make it 25 dollars already.

After dropping my fee in the safe box provided and

picking through the pile for the driest logs, I start back up to my site and bump into a young, fit Australian on a wood run of his own.

"Hey, you the guy on the bike, mate?" He asks in a friendly tone, as if we've been mates for years.

"Yeah," I answer, a bit distractedly. I'm happy to have made it to the campsite before the sun finally sets, but there's still a huge cloud hovering over Snow Dome and Mount Kitchener, and if it moves over to this side of the valley, it could get dark and cold and snowy very quickly. But my new mate is obviously curious about the journey I'm on, so I indulge him.

"Just pulled in a few minutes ago," I say, while trying not to appear too preoccupied.

"You're making decent time. We passed you about three-quarters of the way up the pass and we're not even finished setting up camp."

This comes as a bit of surprise to me. "Oh, man, it didn't feel like I was making good time. The sun has been sitting so low on the horizon all afternoon I didn't think I would make it before dark."

"Job well done, then," he says as he cradles a pile of wood and starts back to the cabins.

"Thanks."

The Aussie stops short after taking a few steps and turns slightly.

"Say, if you want to warm up, drop by the cooking cabin. We've got a fire going and it's plenty warm inside."

"Are you part of an organized group?"

"Yamnuska Mountain Adventures," he says with an air of both authority and pride. "I'm one of the guides, and we're going out on the glacier tomorrow."

"Tempting," I say in reply. Sometimes opportunities

arise that are hard to resist. "I'm going to finish setting up first, but maybe after dinner."

"No worries, mate, you're welcome anytime."

It is a generous offer, and a shrewd individual might even be able to wrangle an invitation up onto the glacier, but I know almost immediately that I won't go. First of all, I'm pretty tired and realize I won't be good company, but more importantly I need to absorb and process what has just happened. Biking up here is not some great accomplishment on the big stage, like paddling across an ocean or summiting Mount Everest, but after all the worry and doubt surrounding the idea of lighting off on a month-long mountain adventure when I probably should be doing something productive like working, it has proven extremely important to me. It is a second crux I have just come through without fully realizing it. The first one, experienced on the way up Deception Pass, was psychological, a confirmation that I do fit in and am comfortable out in the natural world. This one was physical: close to 100 kilometres of mountain travel in challenging conditions in a single day. I find I want to sit with it, absorb the implications of it, and revel in the simple yet challenging deed without going through the effort of polite social interaction.

Back at the site, the sun has disappeared behind the mountains on the far side of the valley and the temperature continues to drop. I stoke up a great fire and enjoy another Kathmandu curry with rice, followed once again by tiramisu for dessert. My meal is hearty and delicious, and as I absorb the beauty of a wild day, a hard day and a good day, the emotions behind the effort continue to bubble to the surface as my fire burns and crackles at my feet. A single month away is hardly enough time to change the course of a life, and it won't be long before I exist once again in a day-to-day far removed from these uncomplicated and challenging pleasures. But for now, this bit of rugged wrapped up in an embarrassment of beauty will do. Walking back down to the woodpile for a couple more logs, I am once again tempted by the smell of wood smoke and the faint sound of voices coming from over in the cabin, but I'm still not inspired enough to join them. Even out here in the middle of nowhere, with minimal human contact over the last ten days, it appears I'm still peopled out, although the genuine hospitality from the leader of the Yamnuska group does give me a measure of hope for us all.

17.

Look at all the plans I made, falling down like scraps of paper.
I will leave them where they lie to remind me.

—Neil Finn (Crowded House)

I woke before dawn with snow falling *inside* my tent. The mini-blizzard would come down in concentrated bursts whenever I rolled over and happened to touch the side of the shelter with a knee or a foot, and in my groggy pre-waking state it took a few seconds to figure out I wasn't actually in the open air. Condensation from my breathing had accumulated overnight, and because the temperature outside had dropped to minus-15 degrees Celsius, the entire curved roof of my shelter was a riot of ice crystals that would fall at the slightest provocation. I did spend the night snug as a bug in my cocoon of down and nylon, but winter was nipping at every opening, trying to get in. If any part of my body happened to drift off the insulated pad, a determined chill would inevitably find its way through my defences.

This kind of weather is why man invented fibreglass insulation and central heating.

Outside the tent, the weather is clear and very cold, and as the last stars drain from the sky, I have to clap my hands together vigorously and jump up and down a couple of times to get the blood flowing. The point of getting up before dawn on the coldest night of the trip so far was

341

to try and get a few sunrise pictures of the glacier and surrounding mountains, but now that the time for that kind of foolishness is at hand, I can't help but question the decision. The batteries in my headlamp are weak and can only cast a pale yellow glow, and my hands are unresponsive to the neural impulses that are usually automatic. My internal fluids feel like sludge. Of particular note: my pen and the shallow stream that was flowing freely through the campsite last night are both frozen solid.

After a brief stop at the Columbia Icefield Discovery Centre (a large, rather charmless edifice designed to inform – and more importantly feed and water – up to 8,000 summer visitors a day) to get warm, my morning starts with a big downhill section right off the bat, followed by some rather unexpected uphill riding near Tangle Creek. It's an exercise in freeze-and-thaw punctuated by another chilly downhill just after the Sunwapta Canyon Viewpoint, which after four steep kilometres spits a rider out onto the floor of the Sunwapta Valley.

The valley here is a broad, meandering outwash plain with long views that provide something of a change from the confined valleys of the high country nearer the Columbia Icefield. The riding is easy and the points of interest come and go in quick succession: Beauty Creek and the backwaters of the Sunwapta River, which attract moose and waterfowl; the Jonas Slide, whose pink-tinted boulders mark a truly monumental collapse from up on the adjoining hillside, four kilometres to the east; Bubbling Springs, a *cold* water spring that is something of an oddity in this landscape peppered with thermal features; and to the right, just north of Poboktan Creek, the seemingly ever-present Endless Chain Ridge, 20 kilometres of continuous overthrust mountain that indicates a transition back into the Front Ranges and is my companion for a couple of hours.

It is my last day on the road, and despite what should be a pleasant morning, I never really warm to the task. Maybe it's the stubborn cool temperatures or yesterday's big climb, but today I feel unusually tired and for the first time on this trip, genuinely homesick. It's as if all of a sudden the battle is no longer in me, and nearly 50 kilometres after lighting out from the campground on what should be a triumphant finale, I find myself limping in to Sunwapta Falls with low blood sugar and a decidedly cranky disposition.

Lunch doesn't help much, and I make my way back outside quickly. It's while I'm packing up for the final 50 kilometres that a middle-aged French couple (from France, as opposed to Quebec) approach me on their way to the restaurant from their car. I assume they're going to ask directions to Banff or Jasper, or where the toilets are, so when it becomes clear they're interested in where I've come from and where I'm headed, it's a bit of a surprise. Granted, the conversation doesn't exactly flow, as neither of us is comfortable in the other's mother tongue, but eventually I get it across that I've just come from camping at the Icefield.

The gentleman especially seems astonished by this feat, which to me now feels like not such a big deal. Ride through the snow; freeze your balls off on a long, shadowy descent; climb a huge mountain pass; hibernate for eight hours in subzero temperatures; freeze your balls off all over again the next day – piece of cake, or perhaps more appropriately, *c'est du gâteau*.

But in retrospect, his look is how I looked at the hardcore alpinists back in Lake Louise. Back there, peering over the top of my book, I felt what amounted to a sort of amazed curiosity mixed with a healthy dose of hope and possibility and maybe even a touch of envy – even if I was never going to undertake that particular challenge, it was still comforting to know the option was out there. It was inspiring to think an escape to something different was possible, regardless of whether I was able to take advantage of it.

Perhaps it is the same for this couple: they've come to the other side of the world and seen something unexpected that made them think about travel and adventure. Even if they never hike a single step or pedal a single kilometre, the spirit of it has been stirred in them, and maybe they'll try something they've been meaning to do for a long time but have never got around to. If nothing else, the encounter energizes me for the final push on to Jasper Townsite.

$$\bullet \; \bullet \; \bullet$$

By mid-afternoon, the weather has finally warmed up and most of the southbound traffic has gone, timed to arrive in Banff or Calgary before dinner, for those headed south. Similarly, northbound travellers are already safely at home or checked into their hotels, so it is nice to have the road mostly to myself. Unfortunately, the surge in energy from my lunchtime conversation doesn't last, and before long I begin to get mildly annoyed by the seemingly endless undulations in the road. Obviously it's downhill from the Columbia Icefield Centre, at 1900 metres, to Jasper Townsite, at just over 1000 metres, but it is not as straightforward or easygoing as one would expect, and after about 20 kilometres, I began to lag noticeably once again.

So it appears I don't have the strength or the stamina

to be that go-getter-at-all-costs type of person anymore. It used to be I could knock off 150-kilometre days back to back to back with minimal fuss, and now I find a single 100-kilometre day to be more than challenging enough. I may still have the instinct and desire to shun society and strike out on my own for weeks at a time, but I now lack the physical strength and endurance the effort requires. I like to think I've matured a bit and don't have to push to the absolute limit each and every time just to prove I'm worth something, but the reality is, I'm just getting old. Still, it's nice to know I can do this kind of thing once in a while. I may not be as sprightly or determined as in the past, but at least I can still do it. I generally need a nap in the afternoon, and am out like a light by 8:30 at night after a long day, but overall I feel pretty good, despite being a bit drained today.

Later in the afternoon, as I near Athabasca Falls and the temperature peaks as one of the last truly warm afternoons of the season begins to wane, a voice suddenly punctures the quiet.

"I love it here."

The voice is startling and foreign, completely out of place in this wide and silent valley, and I almost do a double take. The voice is mine, of course, as I have not seen another soul, or even a car, in at least 20 minutes, but it is still a surprise because I had no intention of speaking. The words just kind of spilled out as I pedalled along, lost in thought. I quickly glance over my shoulder to make sure nobody has heard me, and then realize that this is extremely unlikely, before finally coming to the conclusion that I don't care if anybody did. Because the views up and down the valley are magnificent, I end up swerving across the road to a convenient guardrail on which to lean my bike, and pull over abruptly before shouting at the top of my lungs: "I FUCKING LOVE IT HERE!"

The words reverberate through the entire valley, projected by the light breeze out along the route I've covered over the last few weeks. But it's only me that hears – which, when you think about the nature of the journey, is as it should be.

• • •

About half as big as Banff and a third the size of Canmore, Jasper Townsite sits in a broad valley near the point where the Athabasca River begins to veer north and then east before spilling out onto the prairies, and the town marks the end of my voyage. Riding casually through my first urban landscape since Banff, down Connaught Avenue and then back in a loop along Patricia Street, I still have time before the afternoon light begins to die away to try and absorb the atmosphere of the little town. Coming to an area of development after an absence is refreshing, as even mountains and trees can become tedious company after a while, and in the warm glow Jasper is truly charming. All the required amenities are here, yet it lacks the same hustle and bustle often found in the mountain towns farther south. After finally deciding on a hotel, I can't help but wonder, is this the Canmore of my early Rocky Mountain hopes and wishes and dreams? It could very well be.

Checking into the Whistlers Inn right in the heart of things is not an experience in extravagance; the lodging is basic in the early Holiday Inn and Motel 6 style but is still luxurious compared to my tent. The hallways are bright and liberally decorated with framed Norman Rockwell prints, and my room is clean and spacious, if a little noisy due to the pub located one floor below. On

TV, the baseball playoffs have just started, and I fire off 50 push-ups and 50 sit-ups to match the 50 kilometres pedalled after lunch, just for symmetry.

After a shower (a thoroughly disappointing experience in the absence of a shower cap), I end up at the Whistle Stop Pub downstairs and order up pint and a shot of Jägermeister to celebrate. The Whistle Stop is what I would call a locals' watering hole, a place that's a little rough around the edges, in both decor and clientele. A place where you can get a cheap pint of beer and a burger served in a red plastic basket with a wax paper liner. It's somewhere to go after a game of shinny out on the pond, a kick around in the park or a long bike ride through the mountains, and the after-work happy-hour crowd is in full decompression mode.

Taking up my place at the end of the bar, I realize I don't know what day it is but suspect it's getting close to the weekend because the pub is busy for six o'clock, and it's a good kind of busy. All around me there's a liveliness that's enough to provide atmosphere but not so much as to be considered loud or obnoxious. It's comforting, familiar and jovial, and I recognize it from another part of my life.

After a second round at the bar, it's time for a walk and some dinner, and I am determined to find a hole-in-the-wall pizza joint I vaguely remember from a visit here years ago. Connaught is lined on one side by shops and businesses and on the other by the Canadian National railway station and yard. It's not a complicated cityscape, yet I manage the impossible: I get lost. Taking a left instead of a right out front of Whistlers, I pass Jasper's Central Park and a number of business interests and a pub before coming to a pizza joint that I fear could be my beloved North

Face Pizza, but in a newer, snazzier, much bigger and re-branded form. Inside, the smell of fresh pizza pies is intoxicating, but this clearly isn't the 20-seat takeaway joint I was looking for, so I quickly scurry back out on the street in a state of thorough confusion, a state surely heightened by fatigue and alcohol.

Retracing my steps, I pass by Whistlers once again and quite naturally miss North Face completely, only to end up at the Jasper Brewing Company, a microbrewery established in 2005. If you want to make a bundle in a small mountain town, start a little microbrewery – it's all the rage. And JBC is doing brisk business. Put together in a slick modern style, with slate floors, a granite bar top and flat screen TVs everywhere, the place is sharp and stylish. The atmosphere can only be described as pleasant, congenial and welcoming, and I have to admit it's nice to be back in this environment, for the moment at least, with all the familiar sights and sounds and smells.

Now, it could be said I'm a beer lover, but I don't love the intricate subtleties or overpowering tastes common with many craft beers. The often bland major brewery offerings are not exactly my thing either (I prefer something in between the two extremes), but there is no doubt the subtleties of the microbrew are lost on me. I simply don't have the palate for it. You might as well send me to Napa to sample varietals; it's going to be a waste of time. Eventually I decide on an in-house brewed honey-wheat concoction, a seat at the bar and a menu.

Not quite ready for proper interaction but not wanting to go back outside again for a third search for my pizza place, I settle for a little eavesdropping and learn the bartender is stretched thin, working a regular job with Parks plus this bar gig a couple of nights a week to make ends meet. One of the servers is also a part-time gymnastics coach. Buddy sitting down at the end is moving on soon, maybe to Banff, maybe to the big city, he doesn't exactly say, and it seems that in some ways things aren't significantly different here than in Canmore. Soon enough, three Edmonton businessmen sit down on the last stools at the bar, crowding me and the good tunes playing in the background with their physical presence and loud talking. As it turns out, one of them is the world's authority on beer, at least in his mind, and I'm just tired enough, just tipsy enough and just happy enough to give this guy a deserved slap, so I move over to a recently vacated booth by the windows.

Outside, the world drifts by. A few tourists wander the sidewalk in the gloom of nightfall, and the occasional car drives by along Connaught. Out in the rail yard, double-stacked cargo containers are the order of the day. ZIM, China Shipping, Capital, COSCO and Maersk, among many other lesser players in the international shipping game, are being shunted and jostled and pushed around before continuing the journey inland from the CN terminal in Prince Rupert. It seems a strange place for so much industrious activity, and it will be a few days still before I learn from my shuttle driver back to Canmore that this northern route gets cargo from China to Chicago two days faster than deliveries through Vancouver or Seattle do. After so much protected wilderness, the whole scene is off-putting. Here, the economy charges endlessly onward just outside the window, whether I like it or not, and much like a glacier it is also a living, breathing thing in its own way. The major difference is, it insists on moving at a pace that kills.

Turning my attentions back inside, I'd love to share

these observations with someone, but one of the things I've learned over the years is no one at the bar you end up at after a trip gives a rat's ass about what you just did. The completion of a journey, no matter how epic, is only a celebration for those involved, and even that success is fleeting. When you travel alone, the anticlimax is even more pronounced because there are no travel buddies – or in the case of a major expedition, teammates – to share the memories with. You have to be careful who you talk to right off the road or trail, because everyone else has been travelling a different path, caught up in their own lives and their own struggles, and rightfully so. If you're not careful, you might end up sounding like a businessman from Edmonton, awfully loud with nothing interesting to say.

But that doesn't mean the adventure is not worth celebrating, so I order up another beer from my bartender the Parks employee, keep my big mouth shut and break out my notebook for some quality time. Admittedly, I didn't set the world on fire with my pace today, but it was the longest single day of the trip, and it capped off a perfectly respectable 194 mountain kilometres in the last two days. Success often depends on how you measure it. I didn't get hit by a car or eaten by a bear. I didn't fall off a mountain or get buried in an avalanche or rock slide. I made it to Jasper in one piece and finished my trip over budget but on schedule, and no one cares.

That's perfectly okay though, because I care.

PART FOUR

EPILOGUE

18.

A WINTER WONDERLAND

No one can convince me we aren't gluttons for our doom,
But I tried to make this place my place,
And I asked for Providence to smile upon me with his sweet face.
—Emily Saliers (Indigo Girls)

Make voyages! Attempt them! There's nothing else.
—Tennessee Williams

When the crusty chunk of snow, roughly the size of a paperback book, blew off the top of Lawrence's boot and was ripped from the side of Mount Olive, I should have turned around right then and there. I was out of my element, and I knew it. The trouble is, I had already struggled through the psychological crux of the climb, and everything that happened from that moment forward was, for lack of a better description, really fucking cool. From the adrenaline-charged perspective I was working off, it's easy to see how people get in trouble in the mountains.

This particular attempt on Mount Olive occurred six months after I finished my bike ride in Jasper, and Lawrence and I were trying to create a more consistent habit of getting out into the mountains on the weekends. We were already higher in the Rockies than I had ever been before in winter without the mechanical aid of a chairlift, and conditions were bordering on abysmal. The wind was blowing sideways, and the intermittent snow felt more like pellets than flakes. The ambient temperature on the lower, leeward side of the ridge was reasonable, and had the sun been able to burn through the stubborn cloud cover, I'm sure it would have been above zero, but the wind was doing double duty up high. The gale was carrying miniature BBs intent on punching holes in anything daring to stand in their path, and in its excitement was trying very hard to freeze exposed flesh. Had I not been with an experienced climber, I would have come to my senses at the col – and possibly lower down than that – but as we traversed along the wind-stripped upper summit ridge, it looked a good bet we were going to make the top for my first winter ascent.

Perseverance pays off, I thought, as a surge of energy pulsed through my tired body and the chunk of snow from Lawrence's boot flipped over a fantastically sculpted cornice hanging over the oblivion to our left, before dropping thousands of metres into the unseen valley below. Fifteen minutes earlier, the summit had seemed out of the question, at least from my perspective. *Too steep, too far and too windy* kept running through my mind, but Lawrence just kept on climbing, so I followed.

"Are you all right?" he asked, standing on a wide flat ledge a few metres above me. I was boot-kicking up a snow slope as steep as any pitch I'd found the courage to scale in dry summer conditions and was trying to yank the long end of my ice axe out of the gigantic snowdrift glued to the sheltered side of the ridge. I wasn't in trouble but wasn't exactly all right either.

"I'm not going to lie to you," I said. "I'm freaking out a little bit."

"It's the wind," He said calmly. "Distorts perception and makes everything seem harder."

He was referring, of course, to the surprising effect wind has on the human body. The way it batters without remorse or conscience, the way it attacks with an unrelenting drive that is inhuman. A stiff wind slaps, bullies, prods and harasses without surcease. A good gust strips a man of the tiny cocoon of personal air that surrounds him, leaving the him vulnerable and exposed, even if he's well-dressed. Sure, his mind will try to convince him it's no big deal, just a little wind, but because the affront is so vague and so persistently subtle, a man will scarcely realize he's under attack after the first few minutes of being out in the elements. After a quarter-hour there are only two choices: abandon the effort, or ignore and endure.

A fist, by comparison, is a concentrated assault. Even a verbal onslaught has a measure of directionality, but the wind seems to come at you from everywhere as it hits you all over. It quietly chips away at your sanity, making you crazy even as you become habituated to its presence, forgetting it's there. I am familiar with the experience from years of bicycle touring, and most cyclists I know will choose big hills, heavy rain and bad roads over a day of obnoxious headwinds. In the effort of travelling this far, I had forgotten we were being beaten up much of the way.

"Good point," I said with sudden calm as I reached the comparative comfort of the wide platform. "Just give me a second to pull myself together."

Our trip to Mount Olive had started out in fine form. The plan was to retrace our steps from October up to the Bow Hut, only on skis this time. Once there, we were going to overnight at the hut, climb onto the Wapta Icefield in the morning, bag a peak and bomb back down to the car in time to make it home for dinner. It had been a bad year for avalanches, due to an early freeze followed closely by heaps of snow and a repeating cycle of freeze and thaw, but in the previous few weeks conditions had finally stabilized and spring was taking hold all across the Rockies. The short-term forecast was good.

With the promising weather window ahead, we clicked into our skis on the beach at the edge of Bow Lake in front of Num-Ti-Jah Lodge at 10:15 a.m. and headed directly west, leaving a group of gawking Japanese tourists in our wake. Though the temperature in Canmore was approaching 15 degrees Celsius and there was no snow left on the ground, Bow Lake, 1000 metres higher up, was still frozen over and covered in snow. The shortcut across the lake eliminates at least a kilometre from the journey, and with good coverage all the way, we reached the hut in just over three hours, Lawrence leading with a quiet efficiency while I dragged my ass noticeably in the last hour. After we stowed our gear and had some lunch, we set out for Bow Glacier to practise some rope work.

That's about when the wind started.

It began imperceptibly at first, a slight rattle in a window frame during lunch, a bit of sound building at the edges of the hut where only a boiling kettle could be heard a moment before – that sort of thing – but anyone with any experience with mountain weather will tell you change isn't just possible, it's practically guaranteed. By the time we reached the terminus of the glacier, the wind was a monster, pouring down off the Wapta Icefield like a raging river, and visibility varied between 20 and 200 metres. The glacier was there, buried in the clouds that enveloped us, but even when the sky cleared enough to see much of anything, the upper reaches still blended seamlessly into the tempest, creating a visually impenetrable wall of off-white and grey that was broken only where the exposed rock on St. Nicholas Peak occasionally loomed high above and to our left.

Resigned to the situation, we had a laugh about what a nice day it had turned into and put our backs to the wind to practise knots and prusiks while reviewing the procedures for safe glacier travel. I'm sure we were both quietly hoping the weather would clear by the next morning, in time for our excursion onto the glacier proper, but at the same time there was a perverse thrill in refusing to succumb to nature's wrath. I could see it in Lawrence's eyes and read it in his expression. We were outside and had made the effort to get to the foot of a river of ice that has existed for tens of thousands of years. We weren't going in until we were damn good and ready! Besides, happy hour was fast approaching with its warm fire, brie cheese and crackers and small bottle of Glenfiddich tucked in one of the backpacks – a reality that tempered any discomfort we may have been feeling.

Overnight, the wind made every effort to tear the hut from its moorings. It would blow past with a steady anger that created a menacing hum around the edges of our resilient shelter, then lull with palpable frustration at not being able to get to the bodies inside. It would then gather up again and slam the side of the building with a force that could wake even a man wearing earplugs. I didn't sleep well. But by morning the wind abated somewhat and a "sucker hole" – as in, "C'mon, suckers, I dare ya to try" – settled in. We quietly made breakfast and prepared to step out into the last gasp of winter.

"You ready for this?" Lawrence asked as he secured some equipment in his pack and pulled his cold-weather gear on for the final time of the season.

"Sure," I replied with a little more nonchalance than I was feeling. "What the hell."

Climbing up the glacier took a bit of effort, aided by a handful of carefully planned switchbacks, but the snow was wind-hammered, and our skis only penetrated the surface, where flat elliptical drifts had accumulated. Our skins were gripping nicely. With no sign of crevasses and only a repetitive slog to worry about, my mind eventually went away from freezing to death on the stubborn remains of the last ice age and began to drift in the designs carved by what must have been a winter's worth of hard weather. Sastrugi pockets – parallel wavelike ridges common in polar regions – dominated the scene, remarkably symmetrical and, if not exactly beautiful, then certainly intriguing.

They brought to mind sand formations I remember from a dive trip to the Great Barrier Reef off Australia back in 1988. It was an overnight trip out of Townsville, North Queensland, and one of the options available in the package was a night dive. Impossibly coloured fish and spectacular coral formations are expected on a visit to that great wonder of the world, and the early dives of the day certainly didn't disappoint. (It had also been a thrill to hang off at 25 metres on the outer portion of a reef on a separate trip out of Cairns, with a wall of marine diversity to one side and the endless expanse of blue that is the Pacific Ocean on the other.)

But drifting on a lazy current ten metres below the surface near John Brewer Reef, in the dark, just before midnight, was easily the most exhilarating experience during my visit Down Under. To the best of my memory (I was 20 at the time and more intent on chasing girls and drinking beer in a foreign land than paying proper attention to anything resembling a life experience), there were six or seven of us out paddling around the ocean that night. I do remember we were bunched together like a school of herring, all slipping and sliding in a vain attempt to maintain position at the centre of the school and away from possible predators. The adrenaline-charged highlight came when the dive master switched off the final of our three lamps and we were plunged into complete and utter darkness. After a few moments of unrestrained panic, a whole undersea world of bioluminescent animals – small floating jellyfish-like blobs and tiny glowing plankton – presented itself, and my pulse slowed to a more reasonable 780 beats per minute. We drifted on the light current for awhile, captivated by the strange creatures suspended all around, and when the dive master flipped the light back on a few minutes later and my breathing returned to something that approximated normal, the sandy bottom became strangely comforting, an anchor to reality.

The exact pattern on the bottom escapes me now (the girls, the booze, you know), but in the previous weeks I had seen dry, soft sand beaches above the tide line, hard-packed wet sand at the water's edge and an assortment of formations below the surface, carved by the whims of the tides and the currents. At that moment, in the dead of night 70 kilometres off the Australian coast, the sand brought me back to earth after an experience that was otherworldly, and now, 20 years later and 2500 metres up in the Canadian Rockies, I was seeing another variation of the same process that created those patterns, with wind and snow replacing water and sand with a remarkable and subtle elegance. Nature is an artist and can truly be a wonder when you take the time to go and have a look.

Crossing the southeastern edge of the Wapta proved

relatively easy, a more gradual slope with only a few centimetres of penetration on the surface snow. Mount Gordon was the original goal, but its location at the far western edge of the icefield convinced Lawrence to alter the plan. Gordon was out there somewhere, but we couldn't see it, and a previous party had placed a series of wands all the way to the Olive/St. Nicholas col, so if the whiteout conditions that persisted at the north and west ends of the glacier did eventually consume us, we would still have a general direction to follow on the ski out. Lawrence took a compass reading just to be sure, and then – suddenly, it seemed – we were battling the full brunt of the wind and clomping along the summit ridge, picking our way through patches of verglas deposited intermittently on the rocks beneath our feet and kicking up the occasional crusty chunk where our path crossed an ankle-deep bank of snow, all the while revelling in what amounted to a mountaineer's version of a beautiful day.

• • •

At the time of this writing, it's been four and a half years since I came down from Mount Olive with Lawrence and five years since I packed my bike up in a cardboard box in Jasper and took the Brewster shuttle back to Canmore. Often, there's a letdown after a big trip is completed because it's hard to suddenly stop moving. Then, as time passes and life's little details take over once again, the lessons you learned fade and hard-earned realizations drift to the back of one's consciousness. After a time, it can almost feel like you never went, and the experience becomes just another one of those things that you've done; a set of fading snapshots in a scrapbook you rarely open anymore. Empirical knowledge may never be forgotten, but it can easily get tucked away in the dusty corners of the inattentive or distracted mind.

True to form, my Rocky Mountain escape followed that pattern, but I'm trying very hard to retain the spirit of it all. Going back to work, reacquainting myself with friends, telling stories about the adventures, and easing back into a daily routine were all part of being assimilated back into society. It's a normal adjustment, and is even desirable after spending time sleeping outside on the ground, but there is also a part of my psyche that doesn't want to let go of the freedom and growth active travel always seems to inspire. When you push yourself in the direction of that little voice inside that craves adventure, it is impossible not to expand your being. A good voyage is psychologically and physically demanding if you're doing it right, but is also energizing and intoxicating and life-affirming and is the reason so many people from so many cultures in so many eras have set out toward an unknown horizon.

Reluctantly, I now admit that coming home is also a necessary part of the process. I can't live out there on the road indefinitely, and – my idealistic and hopelessly romantic tendencies aside – I am not entirely sure I would want to. Batteries need to be recharged, and a little missing makes the hunger grow again, but I have to make sure I don't lose sight of the fact that coming home is also a small death. There are rules and expectations and responsibilities here that are necessary for modern living but have nothing to do with being alive, and even as the mind convinces us it's okay to settle in, the soul knows the truth. It's not. Not really. The human animal always needs something to aspire to, somewhere to go and something to do. The urge was likely written directly on our DNA when our earliest ancestors hunted and gathered as part of their everyday existence, but I believe it is also still imprinted somewhere on the modern spirit, and a workaday urban routine will never fill that need for long, at least not as far as I can tell.

If I concede I'm never going to completely "fit in" around here, I do feel a bit better. Canmore really is beautiful, and in the years that have passed since I stormed out in a huff, there have been some subtle changes. Changes that have come, in large part, as a result of the collapse of the global economy, but that I hope will persist as the pendulum swings back toward centre again. Real estate prices have tanked, and there are a few more empty storefronts on Main Street these days, but I would argue there is also a friendlier feel to the place. Some shops have come while others have changed ownership, and others still have simply caved in on themselves. For example, my little piece of local Chinese architecture on Main Street has now been reborn – it was stripped of its pagoda and painted pale beige, and a long-standing rumour of a forthcoming Brazilian BBQ has finally come true. Following in the footsteps of Marra's Grocery (now a high-end furniture shop), the old SAAN department store has also undergone a major facelift but remains largely empty. The Quarry Bistro is now a Calgary-based franchise coffee bar.

The second-hand bookstore on Main Street is also gone now, a victim of the massive flooding that struck Alberta in 2013, one of those one-in-a-hundred-year events that appear to be happening with notable frequency around the globe. Canmore was hit hard in the neighbourhoods of Cougar Creek and Teepee Town, among others, and we were very lucky the Bow River never breached its banks – a catastrophe that was averted by a foot or two, from what I hear.

Over beers at the Canmore Hotel one afternoon, I asked my friend Bob Sandford if we should be more worried about the subtle changes occurring here at the edge of our beloved wilderness. The lively weather, the uncertainty of survival for a number of species that rely on large, intact ecosystems, and the melting glaciers must all indicate a transformation in the foundation of this place. The answer was given without hesitation.

"We are in middle of a slow-motion emergency."

Bob is a policy maker with a job that requires he be familiar with the science behind the rhetoric surrounding many issues related to the environment. He has forgotten more about climate systems than I will probably ever manage to learn, but even I can understand that rising temperatures around the globe are now helping to create a meandering jet stream capable of producing unusual weather events, both warm and cold, in places that haven't seen such things in years, or even generations. Add five degrees Celsius to the air temperature (a near certainty in the coming decades), and suddenly there is 30 to 40 per cent more water vapour in that air, which would make these unusual events an even bigger threat, because more rain is likely to fall during any given downpour. The Bow will surely spill its banks in that case.

While it is true that we've only bumped the temperature up by about one degree Celsius in my lifetime, these storms point to an important threshold that may be coming sooner than expected. The climate models used to try and predict the coming changes in weather and temperature use years like 2030, 2050 and 2100 as important benchmarks, but key indicators like bigger storms, and the massive recession of the world's glaciers and sea ice, suggest that the process is speeding up. Admittedly, the hard science can be difficult for the average person to absorb and harder still to apply to everyday life, but we can't escape the fact that the glaciers in the Rocky Mountains are melting fast, and the weather around here is likely to get a little wilder. It is a cause for worry.

As I walk down Main Street with a bad hangover the day after my tête-à-tête with Bob, my town appears immune for the moment to the coming onslaught. The weather has been positively unremarkable since June, and it's business as usual for a collection of souls intent on rebuilding after a difficult economic period. There's no question people here are either struggling or cautiously recovering, and most are a little less cocky than they were in the glory days of 2006 and 2007, when it seemed like this town was made of money. A lot of the more obnoxious "big shots" have either skipped town or are keeping a low profile, and after suffering through a "market correction," tourism is beginning to come around to pre-recession levels, the month after the flood notwithstanding.

Small-business owners (including my bosses, incidentally) will probably want to string me up for saying this, but I'm concerned about this shift back toward hyperactive prosperity. I admit I'm happier when it's a little quieter around here, because it makes me feel like this might be a place worth investing some time and effort into after all. I mean, really, who wants to build a community worth being proud of, only to be overrun by strangers? It doesn't make sense. I contend it's impossible to make a meaningful connection to a place if you don't even have time to slow down and take a breath, let alone smell the roses.

But even if we collectively fail to figure out that money isn't everything and that unlimited growth is an impossible goal, I've still got options. When I reach my "humanity limit," I can simply go out for a bike ride, or make the effort to go climb something. I'll be less inclined to slap a tourist or yell at one of my regular customers for being an ignoramus if I keep those more socially acceptable options open. Turns out I'm not prone to violence or burdened with an excessively anti-social personality, I just get a little ticked off sometimes, and with the luxury of time and a more balanced outlook, I can sit back and appreciate my little journey through the mountains all those years ago for what it really was: a few steps on the road to sanity.

Because let's face it: riding, walking and camping beats getting up and going to work any day of the week, and riding, walking and checking into a hotel is even better. These kinds of wandering outdoor adventures are also good fodder for stories and have inspired future adventures. Granted, I didn't stay out for as long as I imagined, cover as many miles as planned, or climb as many peaks as I had set out to, but I did manage 565 kilometres on the bike and another 75 on foot. Not a world-beating distance, but respectable at least, and achieved without stepping into a motorized vehicle until I boarded the shuttle in Jasper to return to Canmore.

Still, a restless soul is never satisfied, so the question nags at me: Did the experience change my life, as in my more desperate moments I hoped it would? Probably not. There were no overpowering epiphanies, and I didn't escape to another way of life, never to return. All those potent and compelling reasons to travel aside, the truth is that breaking camp in freezing temperatures sucks, and sometimes the miles out on the road are boring, tiresome, hard on the body and lonely. Worrying about bad drivers and bear encounters and what I was going to do for work once winter hit was no fun either. Wander that path out to the horizon long enough, and eventually you will want to come back to the comforts and habits of home. Then, perhaps predictably, it isn't long before "where to go next" becomes a preoccupying force.

In *A Walk in the Woods*, Bill Bryson summarizes the never-ending internal quarrel that active travel can inspire. After leaving the northern end of the Appalachian Trail earlier than planned, he was happy for the experience, yet conflicted by the decision to stop. "I was weary of the trail, but still strangely in its thrall; found the endless slog tedious but irresistible; grew tired of the boundless woods but admired their boundlessness; enjoyed the escape from civilization and ached for its comforts."

Turns out I have the same contradictory feelings here in the Canadian Rockies. I often ignore the rugged side of this beautiful country I live in, only to be lured back outside and challenged anew. I'm forced to admit I like sitting like a lump at home in my crappy old armchair, watching reruns of *Law & Order* and *Californication* and *Dexter*, with Jocey over on the couch or sitting nearby working on her laptop, our three cats lying about. It appears I'm also fond of two or three or six pints of beer with the boys down at the Rose & Crown after soccer practice on a Tuesday or Thursday evening in the summertime.

But eventually all that comfort and familiarity wears off and I yearn to be out in the wilder world, where I might get snowed on while pedalling up a high mountain pass, only to be denied a view I've already seen before on a different trip to exactly the same location. Or, in good weather, to see something alarmingly similar to something I've seen elsewhere in my travels. Mountains are, after all, just like people, nearly identical the world over, yet strangely compelling in their quirks and differences. Add a little weather and a fading slant of light, and even the same mountain is never the exactly the same twice.

One year almost to the day after clambering to the top of Mount Olive, Lawrence, Frank and I took another stab at Mount Gordon. Predictably, the Wapta tried to beat us back with a squall midway across the ice sheet, but as we neared the summit, the weather cleared and the wind died and the temperature soared as we spent an hour at the top that could not have been more perfect. We were standing on the spot where Norman Collie, Peter Sarbach, Charles Fay and Arthur Michael made their first ascent in 1896, turned and gazed to the northwest, and abruptly abandoned plans for Mount Assiniboine in favour of the largely unexplored wilderness that lay before them. A decision that would prompt two more trips to the region, lead to the discovery of the Columbia Icefield and further perpetuate the myth of the ever-elusive Mount Hooker and Mount Brown.

At the summit of Mount Gordon 114 years after that first ascent, I found it hard to imagine how they picked any specific bearing to inspire further exploration. It all looked good to me. At 3153 metres, Gordon is hardly a giant compared to Columbia (3747 metres) or Assiniboine (3618 metres) or Robson (3954 metres), but its position on the Continental Divide allows a stunning 360-degree view. There are countless craggy peaks stretching out in every direction, and a sense that here, at least, the world is both lasting and new. While I may never climb any of the Rockies' more coveted peaks, or visit all the remote valleys that constitute the true wilderness of these increasingly popular parks, that doesn't mean I am not inspired to one day try. Two decades after I first laid eyes on the Canadian Rockies, there is something here I am duty-bound to find, and it occurs to me that in this searching I'm just another restless soul set adrift in paradise.

In this rugged landscape, I am forever lost and found.

THE END

ACKNOWLEDGMENTS

Writing a book is a solitary endeavour like no other. The audience is some distance away, in both time and space, and once they are finally able to hold a hard copy of your thoughts and efforts in their hands, the inevitable tears, frustrations and triumphs of putting pen to paper are finally in the past. Writer and reader experience the same project in different universes.

Getting that book to print, however, relies on a lot of other people to make it happen. That's why writers go to great lengths to try and thank anyone and everyone who spent even ten minutes in contact with their idea, as I will do here. It is a given that I will forget someone (perhaps lots of people), and for that I am deeply sorry.

Thanks must go out to one of my early readers, Devin Nielson, who saw a rough and not altogether coherent early version of the first three chapters and was kind enough to say, "Hey, I get it. I totally get it. We're coming from the same place, that's for sure." At least that's how I choose to remember the conversation – we might have been drinking beer at the time.

I also have to thank Marcie Januska, Stacey Fraser and my brother Jesse, who all suffered through early versions of other projects that have yet to see the light of day. That was back when I was living in Calgary and still trying to figure out what it meant to be a writer, and the content was probably worse than what Devin had to plow through. Melanie Jones must also be thanked for the same suffering.

Playwright Eugene Stickland was always good for a humorous story about the perils of life spent with a pen in hand, but peppered in with the laughs was some truly sage advice. Come to think of it, the entire Calgary theatre community was an early muse as I served them drinks at the Auburn Saloon and listened to their stories about making a living in the arts.

Here in Canmore, Mike Reed, Jay Gingrich and Mike Gerlach gave very helpful feedback and encouragement. Martin van den Akker, Frank Vermeulen, Lawrence White and Neil Orchard, in addition to being fun guys to go skiing or hiking with, all took an interest in the idea and made me feel like it was worth doing. Rob and Megan Anderson gave me a job whenever I needed one and tolerated my absences when I didn't. Not a single person I ever worked with in the bar industry (or most of my regular customers, for that matter) ever thought it was crazy or stupid to try and do something outside the meat grinder that is service. Thank you all for putting up with my ranting and raving.

Jennifer Groundwater edited an early version of my manuscript, and Rob Alexander was incredibly helpful with later versions. During a short stint as a freelancer, I watched real writers and photographers at work, and the staff at the *Rocky Mountain Outlook* has been an inspiration. Don Gorman at Rocky Mountain Books had a well of patience for this novice writer that at times appeared bottomless, and Peter Norman helped clean up the last of my sloppy behaviour at the page. Bob Sandford cannot be thanked enough for all he does for writers, photographers and artists in the Bow Valley.

And finally my mother, Dena, and my stepfather, Brian, must be thanked for dragging me kicking and screaming to the out-of-doors as a teenager, where I developed an appreciation for the natural world. Brothers Jesse and Scott were often there and are fun travelling companions to this day, when we can find the time. And of course there's my partner, Jocey. No one understands the trials and tribulations of the creative mind quite like another creative person. I'm sure just about anyone else would have smothered me in my sleep by now. She is without a doubt one of the good ones.

I hope you enjoyed the book, wherever and whenever you are.

RECOMMENDED READING

Auld, Jerry. *Hooker & Brown*. Brindle & Glass, 2009.

Alexander, Rob. *The History of Canmore*. Summerthought, 2010.

Bryson, Bill. *A Short History of Nearly Everything*. Anchor Canada, 2004.

Bryson, Bill. *Neither Here Nor There: Travels in Europe*. Morrow, 1992.

Bryson, Bill. *A Walk in the Woods*. Doubleday Canada, 1998.

Byrne, David. *Bicycle Diaries*. Viking Penguin, 2009.

Cahill, Tim. *Hold the Enlightenment*. Vintage Departures, 2003.

Gailus, Jeff. *The Grizzly Manifesto*. Rocky Mountain Books, 2010.

Jenkins, Mark. *The Hard Way*. Simon & Schuster, 2002.

Kane, Alan. *Scrambles in the Canadian Rockies*. Rocky Mountain Books, 2006.

Kerr, Michael. *When Do You Let the Animals Out?* Fifth House, 1998.

Lakusta, Ernie. *Canmore & Kananaskis History Explorer*. Altitude, 2002.

Marty, Sid. *Switchbacks*. McClelland & Stewart, 2001.

Matthiessen, Peter. *The Snow Leopard*. Penguin Classics, 1987.

Patton, Brian. *Parkways of the Canadian Rockies*. Summerthought, 2008.

Pole, Graeme. *Canadian Rockies*. Altitude, 1997.

Sandford, Robert William. *Cold Matters*. Rocky Mountain Books, 2012.

Sandford, Robert William. *Ecology & Wonder*. Athabasca University Press, 2010.

Sandford, Robert William. *The Weekender Effect*. Rocky Mountain Books, 2008.

Sandford, Robert William. *Water, Weather and the Mountain West*. Rocky Mountain Books, 2007.

Shaughnessy, Susan. *Walking on Alligators*. HarperSanFrancisco, 1993.

Snow, John. *These Mountains Are Our Sacred Places: The Story of the Stoney People*. Fifth House, 2005.